浙江省普通高校"十三五"新形态教材

U0598228

国际贸易系列教材

DOCUMENTS PRACTICE FOR FOREIGN TRADE

新编外贸单证实训教程

朱春兰　佘雪锋 ◎主　编

翁旭青　李瀚曦 ◎副主编

ZHEJIANG UNIVERSITY PRESS
浙江大学出版社

图书在版编目(CIP)数据

新编外贸单证实训教程 / 朱春兰,佘雪锋主编. —
杭州:浙江大学出版社,2020.12(2024.1重印)
ISBN 978-7-308-19427-3

Ⅰ.①新… Ⅱ.①…朱 ②佘… Ⅲ.①进出口贸易—
原始凭证—高等职业教育—教材 Ⅳ.①F740.44

中国版本图书馆 CIP 数据核字(2019)第 167072 号

新编外贸单证实训教程

朱春兰　佘雪锋　主编

策划编辑	李　晨
责任编辑	李　晨
责任校对	董齐琪　虞雪芬
封面设计	春天书装
出版发行	浙江大学出版社
	(杭州市天目山路 148 号　邮政编码 310007)
	(网址:http://www.zjupress.com)
排　　版	杭州林智广告有限公司
印　　刷	杭州钱江彩色印务有限公司
开　　本	787mm×1092mm　1/16
印　　张	14.5
字　　数	370 千
版 印 次	2020 年 12 月第 1 版　2024 年 1 月第 2 次印刷
书　　号	ISBN 978-7-308-19427-3
定　　价	45.00 元

前　言

　　外贸单证工作是外贸从业人员必须掌握的基础性工作，外贸单证员是外贸企业开展业务的基础人才，因此外贸单证员的培养至关重要。基于这一现实需要，我们联合了具有丰富教学经验的一线骨干教师和具有多年外贸单证工作经验的企业人士共同编写了本教材。

　　本教材在编写过程中注重知识的时效性，采用最新版本的规章、制度、规定等。本教材的合同、单据、信用证等都来自外贸企业，但涉及的原交易当事人、交易内容、单位编号等关键信息均已虚化。所述内容如不慎与真实生活中的人物、组织或事件雷同，纯属巧合。

　　本教材以职业能力培养为目标，强调对各种外贸单证操作能力的训练，通过实训，达到巩固、强化的目的。本教材分单项实训和综合实训两个模块。单项实训模块设有十个项目，即信用证条款分析、信用证审核与修改、商业发票填制、装箱单填制、保险单据填制、原产地证书填制、运输单据填制、商业汇票填制、其他常用结汇单据填制、开证申请书填制。综合实训模块设有七个项目，即信用证方式 FOB 下出口单据填制、信用证方式 CFR 下出口单据填制、信用证方式 CIF 下出口单据填制、信用证方式 FOB 下结汇单据填制、信用证方式 CIF 下结汇单据填制、信用证方式下出口单据审核、信用证方式下进口单据填制。单项实训模块的每个项目按"实训目标、实训指导、实训任务"的体例编写，综合实训模块的每个项目按"实训目标、实训任务"的体例编写。其中，每个"实训任务"都配有相应的空白单据供学生使用。

　　本教材由浙江经贸职业技术学院朱春兰、台州职业技术学院佘雪锋任主编，浙江经贸职业技术学院翁旭青、李瀚曦任副主编，浙江凯喜雅股份有限公司单证科李韶辉对教材进行了审定。此外，参加本教材编写和视频制作的还有吴玮、冯芳、罗俊勤、施秦等。

　　本教材是浙江省省级精品课程和浙江省省级精品在线开放课程的配套教材，也是浙江省普通高校"十三五"新形态教材。 本教材可作为高职高专国际贸易、国际商务、商务英语、应用英语等相关专业的教学用书，也可作为外贸单证员的培训教材，还可供经贸类管理人员和从业人员参阅。

本教材在编写和出版过程中得到了有关外贸公司领导及专家的大力支持和帮助，他们为本教材提供了大量外贸单证材料，在此表示衷心的感谢！编者还参阅和引用了国内外有关论著、网站的资料和观点，书中未一一列出，在此一并向有关作者表示诚挚的谢意！

由于编者学识水平和能力有限，教材中仍可能存在错误之处，敬请广大读者批评指正，以便再版时予以修正、完善。

编　者
2020 年 7 月

目　录
CONTENTS

单项实训

项目一　信用证条款分析

实训目标

能够分析信用证条款。

信用证种
类的辨别

实训指导

一、对信用证本身的说明

信用证主要有信用证号码(L/C No.)、开证日期和地点(date of issue and place)、有效期和有效地点(expiry date and place)、交单期(presentation period)、信用证种类(types of L/C)、信用证当事人、信用证金额和币种(L/C amount and currency)、费用条款(details of charges)等内容。

1. 信用证号码

信用证号码,即开证行对信用证的编号,一般以 L/C No.或 Our Ref. No.注明。

2. 开证日期和地点

开证日期和地点,即开证行开立信用证的日期和地点。

3. 有效期和有效地点

有效期,又称到期日,指交单付款、承兑或议付的最后期限。未规定有效期/到期日的信用证是无效的。凡过了有效期/到期日提交的单据,银行有权拒收。

有效地点,又称到期地点,在我国的出口业务中,原则上应争取在我国到期,以便我方在交付货物后能及时办理议付,要求付款或承兑。

4. 交单期

交单期是指向银行提交单据要求付款、承兑或议付的特定期限。信用证未规定交单期,按惯例单据在运输单据签发日后 21 天内提交,但不得迟于信用证的有效期。信用证规定的交单期距装运期过近,如运输单据签发日后 2 天或 3 天交单,则应要求开证人修改信用证推迟交单期限,以保证能在装运货物后如期向银行交单。

5. 信用证种类

信用证根据不同的角度可分为不同的种类。

（1）根据开证行对开出的信用证所负的责任不同，信用证可分为不可撤销信用证（irrevocable L/C）和可撤销信用证（revocable L/C）。

不可撤销信用证是指信用证一经开出，在有效期内，非经信用证各当事人（即开证行、保兑行和受益人）的同意，不得修改或撤销的信用证。

可撤销信用证是指信用证开立后，在付款、承兑或议付前，不必事先通知或征得受益人同意就有权随时撤销或修改的信用证。

UCP500 规定：信用证应明确注明是可撤销的或是不可撤销的。如无此注明，应视为不可撤销的。UCP600 规定：信用证都是不可撤销的，无可撤销信用证的说法。

（2）根据受益人对信用证权利可否转让，信用证可分为可转让信用证（transferable L/C）和不可转让信用证（untransferable L/C）。

可转让信用证是指受益人有权将信用证的全部或部分金额转让给第三者（即第二受益人）使用的信用证。可转让信用证只能转让一次。

不可转让信用证是指受益人不能将信用证权利转让给第三者的信用证。

凡可转让信用证，必须注明"可转让"字样，如未注明，则被视为不可转让信用证。不可转让信用证只限受益人本人使用。

（3）根据是否有另一家银行对信用证加以保兑，信用证可分为保兑信用证（confirmed L/C）和不保兑信用证（unconfirmed L/C）。

保兑信用证是指开证行开出的信用证由另一家银行加以保兑，即另一家银行保证对符合信用证条款规定的单据履行付款义务的信用证。

不保兑信用证是指未经另一家银行加以保兑的信用证。

凡使用保兑信用证的，应在信用证上注明保兑行加保的文句。

（4）根据信用证使用方法（付款方法/兑付方式）不同，信用证可分为付款信用证（payment L/C）、承兑信用证（acceptance L/C）和议付信用证（negotiation L/C）。

凡指定某一银行付款的信用证，称为付款信用证。此种信用证一般不要求受益人开具汇票，而仅凭受益人提供的单据付款。付款信用证根据付款时间不同，可分为即期付款信用证和远期付款信用证。

凡指定某一银行承兑的信用证，称为承兑信用证。采用此种信用证时，指定银行应承兑受益人向其开具的远期汇票，并于汇票到期日履行付款义务。

议付信用证是指允许受益人向某一指定银行或任何银行交单议付的信用证。通常在单证相符条件下，银行扣取垫付利息和手续费后，即付给受益人。议付信用证可分为自由议付信用证和限制议付信用证。前者任何银行均可办理，后者则由指定银行办理。

信用证中应标明是即期付款、延期付款、承兑或议付,即:

credit available with... by...   □by payment at sight 即期付款

□by deferred payment at 延期付款

□by acceptance of drafts at 承兑

□by negotiation 议付

(5) 根据付款时间不同,信用证可分为即期信用证(sight L/C)和远期信用证(usance L/C)。

即期信用证是开证行或付款行收到符合信用证条款的汇票或单据,立即履行付款责任的信用证。由于即期信用证可使受益人通过银行付款或议付及时取得货款,因而在国际贸易结算中被广泛使用。

远期信用证是开证行或付款行收到远期汇票或单据后,在规定的一定期限内付款的信用证。其主要作用是便利进口商资金融通。银行承兑信用证和延期付款信用证都属远期信用证。

付款时间规定方法大致有:

①at sight(见票即付);

②at... days after sight(见票后若干天付款);

③at... days after date of B/L(提单日后若干天付款);

④at... days after date of draft(汇票日后若干天付款)。

如采用第一种规定方法,即为即期信用证;如采用后三种即为远期信用证。

(6) 根据结算过程中有无货运单据,信用证可分为跟单信用证(documentary credit)和光票信用证(clean credit)。

跟单信用证是指开证行凭跟单汇票或单纯凭单据付款的信用证。所谓"跟单",大多是指代表货物所有权或证明货物已装运的运输单据、商业发票、保险单、商检证书、海关发票、产地证书、装箱单等。

光票信用证是指开证行仅凭受益人开具的汇票或简单收据而无须附带单据付款的信用证。光票信用证在贸易货款的结算上使用不广,它主要用于贸易总公司与各地分公司间的货款清偿及贸易从属费用和非贸易费用的结算。

6. 信用证当事人

信用证当事人主要有开证行(opening bank/issuing bank)、开证申请人/开证人(applicant/opener)、受益人(beneficiary)、通知行(advising bank/notifying bank)、议付行(negotiating bank)等。

开证行是指接受开证申请人的委托,开立信用证的银行。它承担保证付款的责任。开证行一般是进口商所在地银行。

开证申请人又称开证人,是指向银行申请开立信用证的人,一般为进口商,即买卖合同的买方。

受益人是指信用证上所指定的有权使用该证的人,一般为出口商,即买卖合同的卖方。

通知行是指接受开证行的委托,将信用证转交给出口商的银行。通知行一般为出口商所在地银行,它只需鉴别信用证的表面真实性,无须承担其他义务。

议付行是指愿意买入或贴现受益人交来的跟单汇票和单据的银行。议付行可以是信用证条款中指定的银行,也可以是非指定的银行,这由信用证的条款来规定。

7. 信用证金额和币种

信用证金额是开证行所承担的付款责任的最高数额。有的信用证视交易需要会规定一定比例的上下浮动幅度。在 SWIFT(全球银行间金融电讯协会)电文中,数字不使用分格号,小数点用逗号","来表示。

8. 费用条款

费用条款中的银行费用一般包括通知费、保兑费、承兑费、议付费、修改费等。我国的习惯做法是出口地的银行费用由出口方负担,进口地的银行费用由进口方负担。

二、对汇票的说明

对汇票的说明主要包括出票人(drawer)、付款人/受票人(payer/drawee)、汇票金额(draft amount)、汇票期限(tenor)、出票条款(drawn clause)等内容。不需汇票的信用证没有此项内容。

三、对装运的说明

对装运的说明主要包括装运港(port of loading/loading in charge)、目的港(port of discharge/for transportation to)、装运期(latest date of shipment)、分批装运(partial shipment)和转运(transshipment)等内容。

四、对货物的说明

对货物的说明主要包括货物名称和规格(description and specification)、数量(quantity)、单价(unit price)、总值(total amount)、包装(packing)等内容。

五、对单据的要求

对单据的要求主要包括应提交单据名称、份数和具体要求。

常见单据有商业发票(commercial invoice)、提单(bill of lading)、保险单(insurance policy)、原产地证书(certificate of origin)、检验证书(inspection certificate)、受益人证明(beneficiary's certificate)、装船通知(shipping advice)、装箱单(packing list)等。

常见单据份数的英文表述为 in duplicate(triplicate, quadruplicate, quintuplicate, sextutplicate, septuplicate, octuplicate, nonuplicate, decuplicate),即一式两份(三、四、五、六、七、八、九、十份)。

对于正本单据和副本单据的要求,根据 UCP600 的规定:信用证中规定的各种单据必须至少提供一份正本。如果信用证要求提交副本单据,则提交正本单据或副本单据均可。如果信用证使用诸如"一式两份"(in duplicate)、"两张"(in two fold)、"两份"(in two copies)等术语要求提交多份单据,则可以提交至少一份正本,其余份数以副本来满足。但单据本身另有相反指示者除外。

六、特殊条款

特殊条款主要指根据进口国政治经济贸易情况的变化或每一笔具体交易的需要而做出的特别规定。

七、其他内容

1. 给议付行/付款行/承兑行的指示(instructions to negotiating bank/paying bank/accepting bank)

给议付行/付款行/承兑行的指示一般包括偿付方式、寄单方式和议付金额背书条款等内容。如:

You are authorized to reimburse yourself for the amount of your negotiation by drawing as per arrangement on our account with United Bank Limited, London. 兹授权你行索偿你行议付金额,按约定办法请向伦敦联合银行我账户内支取。

2. 开证行保证付款条款

常见的条款有:

We hereby undertake to honour all drafts drawn in accordance with terms of this credit.凡按本信用证所列条款开具并提示的汇票,我行保证承兑。

We hereby engage with drawers and/or bona fide holders that draft(s) drawn and negotiated on presentation and that draft(s) accepted within the terms of this credit will be duly honoured at maturity.我行向对出票人及/或善意持有人保证,凡按本信用证条款开具及议付的汇票一经提交即予承兑;凡依本信用证条款承兑的汇票,到期即予照付。

We hereby engage with drawers, endorsers and bona fide holders of drafts drawn under and in compliance with the terms of this credit that such drafts shall be duly honoured on the presentation and delivery of documents as specified.我行向根据本信用证并符合本信用证所开立的汇票的出票人、背书人及善意持票人保证,一旦提交规定的有关单据,汇票将被支付。

3. 适用惯例

在信用证里一般要明确该信用证所适用的国际惯例,作为买卖双方遵守的原则和依据。完整的适用惯例条款规定为:

This credit is subject to the *Uniform Customs and Practice for Documentary*

Credits(2007 Revision) International Chamber of Commerce Publication No.600.**本证根据国际商会 2007 年修订本第 600 号出版物《跟单信用证统一惯例》办理。**

⊙ 实训任务

✎**任务一：** 仔细阅读下列信用证，指出信用证种类并填写信用证分析单。

LETTER OF CREDIT

RECEIVED FROM：TDOMCATTMTL

            TORONTO-DOMINION BANK，THE MONTREAL

DESTINATION：ABOCCNBJA110

            AGRICULTURAL BANK OF CHINA，HANGZHOU(ZHEJIANG BRANCH)

MESSAGE TYPE：700 **ISSUE OF A DOCUMENTARY CREDIT**

DATE：MARCH 19，2020

SEQUENCE OF TOTAL　27：1/1

FORM OF DOCUMENTARY CREDIT　40A：IRREVOCABLE

DOCUMENTARY CREDIT NUMBER　20：1518843

DATE OF ISSUE　31C：20200318

DATE OF EXPIRY,PLACE OF EXPIRY　31D：20200430 AT NEGOTIATION BANK

APPLICANT　50：RAPASPORT INC.

         9400 ST. LAURENT BLVD. SUITE 100 MONTREAL，QUEBEC

BENEFICIARY　59：JJJ IMPORT AND EXPORT COMPANY

         NO.2 XUEYUAN ROAD，HANGZHOU，CHINA

CURRENCY CODE,AMOUNT　32B：USD 25,328.80

PERCENTAGE CREDIT AMOUNT TOLERANCE　39A：05/15

AVAILABLE WITH... BY...　41D：ANY BANK IN CHINA BY NEGOTIATION

DRAFTS AT...　42C：45 DAYS AFTER SIGHT

DRAWEE　42D：OURSELVES

PARTIAL SHIPMENTS　43P：ALLOWED

TRANSSHIPMENT　43T：ALLOWED

LOADING ON BOARD/DISPATCH/TAKING IN CHARGE　44A：CHINESE PORT

FOR TRANSPORTATION TO...　44B：MONTREAL，CANADA

DESCRIPTION OF GOODS AND/OR SERVICES　45A：

    CHILDREN'S ENSEMBLES

COVERD BY

P.O.NOS. 11517，11518，11519，11520 AND 11521

TO BE SHIPPED NOT LATER THAN APRIL 10，2020

P.O.NOS. 11522 AND 11523

TO BE SHIPPED NOT LATER THAN APRIL 15，2020

CIF MONTREAL

DOCUMENTS REQUIRED　46A：

　　+SIGNED COMMERCIAL INVOICE IN DUPLICATE.

　　+CANADA CUSTOMS INVOICE OF DEPARTMENT OF NATIONAL REVENUE/ CUSTOMS AND EXCISE IN DUPLICATE.

　　+PACKING LIST IN DUPLICATE SHOWING SIZE AND COLOR ASSORTMENT AS PER P.O.

　　+ OCEAN TRANSPORT DOCUMENT CONSIGNED TO ORDER OF THE TORONTO DINUBUIB BANK MARKED FREIGHT COLLECT SHOWING CREDIT NUMBER NOTIFY APPLICANT.

　　+ INSURANCE POLICY ISSUED TO THE APPLICANT，COVERING ALL RISKS AND WAR RISK AS PER CIC OF PICC DATED 19810101 FOR 110% OF THE INVOICE VALUE， MARKED PREMIUM PAID， SHOWING CLAIM PAYABLE AT MONTREAL.

　　+BENEFICIARY'S CERTIFICATE STATING THAT PRODUCTION SAMPLES 1 PIECE OF EACH COLOR IN ASSORTED SIZES HAVE BEEN COURIERED TO RAPASPORT INC AT TIME OF ACTUAL SHIPMENT AND STATING THAT ORIGINAL EXPORT LICENCE/CERTIFICATE AND COPIES OF CANADA CUSTOMS INVOICE HAVE BEEN SENT BY COURIER TO RAPASPORT INC NOT LATER THAN 10 DAYS AFTER DATE OF SHIPMENT.

ADDITIONAL CONDITIONS　47A：

　　+ UPON RECEIPT OF YOUR DOCUMENTS IN GOOD ORDER，WE WILL REMIT THE PROCEEDS TO THE ACCOUNT DESIGNATED BY NEGOTIATION.

CHARGE　71B：

　　ALL BANKING COMMISSIONS AND CHARGES， INCLUDING REIMBURSEMENT CHARGES AND POSTAGE OUTSIDE CANADA ARE FOR ACCOUNT OF BENEFICIARY.

PERIOD FOR PRESENTATION　48：

　　DOCUMENTS MUST BE PRESENTED WITHIN 15 DAYS AFTER THE DATE

OF SHIPMENT BUT WITHIN CREDIT VALIDITY.

CONFIRMATION INSTRUCTIONS：49：WITHOUT

INSTRUCS TO PAYING/ACCEPTING/NEGOTIATING BANK　78：

　　＋THE AMOUNT OF EACH NEGOTIATION（DRAFT）MUST BE ENDORSED ON THE REVERSE OF THIS CREDIT BY THE NEGOTIATING BANK.

　　＋ALL DOCUMENTS MUST BE FORWARDED DIRECTLY BY COURIER SERVICE IN ONE LOT TO TORONTO-DOMINION BANK L/C IMPORT DEPT. 500 ST. JACQUES，10TH FLOOR，MONTREAL，QUEBEC H3C 3B7.

　　＋IF DOCUMENTS ARE PRESENTED WITH DISRCREPANCIES，A DISCREPANCY FEE OF USD 60.00 OR EQUIVALENT SHOUL（WILL）BE DEDUCTED FROM THE REIMBURSMENT CLAIM（THE PROCEEDS）.THIS FEE SHOULD BE CHARGED TO THE BENEFICIARY.

"ADVISE THROUGH" BANK　57D：

　　PLS ADVISE THRU YR HANGZHOU BRANCH INT'L DEPT.

SENDER TO RECEIVER INFORMATION　72：

　　THIS CREDIT IS SUBJECT TO I.C.C. PUBLIC. NO. 600（2007 REVISION）.

　　　　　　　　　　　　　　　　　　　　　　——THE END

　　1. 指出信用证种类

　　（1）从可否撤销角度：

　　（2）从可否转让角度：

　　（3）从付款时间角度：

　　（4）从兑付方式角度：

　　（5）从是否保兑角度：

　　（6）从是否随附货运单据角度：

2. 填写信用证分析单

信用证分析单

(1)编号：								
(2)本证　年　月　日收到								
开证行(3)				开证日(4)				
申请人(5)				受益人(6)				
信用证金额(7)				信用证号码(8)				
汇票付款人(9)				汇票期限(10)				
可否转运(11)				可否分批(12)				
装运期限(13)		信用证有效期(14)			到期地点(15)			
运输标志(16)				交单日(17)				
单据名称	提单(18)	发票(19)	装箱单(20)	保险单(21)	检验证(22)			
银行								
客户								
提单或承运单据	抬头(23)							
	通知(24)							
	注意事项							
保险	险别(25)							
	加成(26)							
其他注意事项：								

任务二： 仔细阅读下列信用证，指出信用证种类并填写信用证分析单。

LETTER OF CREDIT

FROM UCO BANK，KOWLOON，HONG KONG

DATE OF ISSUE：20190924

TEST：FOR USD 5，174.40 TESTED DATE 20190924

WE OPEN IRREVOCABLE CREDIT NO.KHL36227 FOR USD 5，174.40

SAY USD FIVE THOUSAND ONE HUNDRED AND SEVENTY FOUR AND CENTS FORTY ONLY

FAVOURING：NINGBO NINGHAI FOREIGN ECONOMIC AND TRADING CORPO RATION，
   FOREIGN ECONOMIC AND TRADING BUILDING，HUANCHENGROAD，
   NINGHAI，ZHEJIANG，CHINA

ACCOUNTEE：WIN INTERNATIONAL(H.K.)LTD，KOWLOON，HONG KONG

MERCHANDISE COVERING：

   MINI FLASH LIGHT

   COLOR：WHITE 30，000 PCS BLACK 18，000 PCS

   (PACKING：EACH PC IN AN INDIVIDUAL BOX)

   CIF HONG KONG

SHIPMENT FROM NINGBO TO HONG KONG

SHIPMENT DATE NOT LATER THAN 20191007

NEGOTIATION DATE NOT LATER THAN 20191021

PARTIAL SHIPMENTS BEING PROHIBITED

TRANSSHIPMENT BEING PROHIBITED

   CREDIT IS AVAILABLE BY DRAFTS AT SIGHT WITHOUT RECOURSE FOR FULL INVOICE VALUE ACCOMPANIED BY THE FOLLOWING DOCUMENTS：

   ＋FULL SET OF CLEAN SHIPPED OR ON BOARD OCEAN BILLS OF LADING SIGNED BY MASTER OR S.S. AGENTS MARKED FREIGHT PREPAID TO SHIPPERS ORDER ENDORSED IN BLANK. BILLS OF LADING TO SHOW BENEFICIARY AS SHIPPER AND TO NOTIFY WIN INTERNATIONAL （HK）LTD RM 10，4/F H.K.IND. CENTRE BLK C，489-491 CASTLE PEAK RD；LAI CHI KOK，KOWLOON.TEL：7429183 (FORWARDING AGENTS RECEIPTS NOT ACCEPTABLE.) EVIDENCING SHIPMENT OF GOODS AS DESCRIBED ABOVE.

   ＋DRAFT MUST BE MARKED DRAWN UNDER UCO BANK，KOWLOON CREDIT NO KHL-36227.

+ SIGNED DETAILED INVOICE IN TRIPLICATE CERTIFYING GOODS ARE OF CHINESE ORIGIN.

SPECIAL INSTRUCTIONS AND ADDITIONAL DOCUMENTS REQUIRED:

+ THE NEGOTIATING BANK SHOULD SEND THE DOCUMENTS TO US BY AIRMAIL IN TWO LOTS AND INCIDENTAL CHARGES SUCH AS STAMPS, POSTAGE, COMMISSION ETC. OF THE NEGOTIATING BANK SHOULD BE RECOVERED FROM DRAWERS.

+ NEGOTIATIONS UNDER THIS CREDIT ARE UNRESTRICTED.

+ DOCUMENTS MUST BE PRESENTED FOR NEGOTIATION WITHIN 15 DAYS AFTER THE DATE OF ISSUANCE OF BILL OF LADING BUT WITHIN THE VALIDITY OF THIS CREDIT .

+ USD 50.00 FOR EACH PRESENTATION FOR DISCREPANT DOCUMENTS IF ACCEPTED WILL BE DEDUCTED FROM THE PROCEEDS.

+ ALL BANK ING CHARGES OUTSIDE HONG KONG INCLUDING L/C ADVISING AND AMENDMENT CHARGES ARE ON ACCOUNT OF BENEFICIARY.

+ CERTIFICATE OF ORIGIN ISSUED BY CHINA C/O REQUIRED.

+ HOUSE BILL OF LADING IS ACCEPTABLE.

+ MARINE AND WAR RISK INSURANCE POLICIES OR CERTIFICATES IN DUPLICATE (BROKERS CERTIFICATES NOT ACCEPTABLE) IN CURRENCY OF THE CREDIT IN NEGOTIABLE FORM COVERING THE FULL INVOICE AMOUNT PLUS A MARGIN OF NOT LESS THAN 10 PCT, W. A. INCLUDING CUSTOMARY INSTITUTE WAREHOUSE TO WAREHOUSE CLAUSE WAR RISK IS TO BE COVERED IN CONFORMITY WITH CURRENT INSTITUTE WAR CLAUSES CLAIMS TO BE PAYABLE AT PORT OF DESTINATION IN THE CURRENCY OF THE DRAFT.

REIMBURSEMENT INSTRUCTIONS:

+ UPON RECEIPT OF THE DOCUMENTS BY US TOGETHER WITH THE CERTIFICATE OF NEGOTIATION, WE SHALL REIMBURSE THE NEGOTIATING BANK BY REMITTING TELEGRAPHICALLY THE AMOUNT OF THE DRAWING TO THEIR NAMED CORRESPONDENTS OR ACCORDING TO THEIR INSTRUCTIONS AFTER DEDUCTING OUT TELES CHARGES.

WE HEREBY ENGAGE WITH THE DRAWERS, ENDORSERS AND BONA-FIDE HOLDERS OF DRAFTS DRAWN UNDER AND IN COMPLIANCE WITH THE TERMS OF THE CREDIT THAT SUCH DRAFTS SHALL BE DULY

HONOURED ON DUE PRESENTATION AND DELIVERY OF DOCUMENTS AS SPECIFIED ABOVE EXCEPT AS OTHERWISE EXPRESSLY STATED.

THIS TELEX IS AN OPERATIVE INSTRUMENT AND NO MAIL CONFIRMATION TO FOLLOW.

THIS DOCUMENTARY CREDIT IS SUBJECT TO THE UNIFORM CUSTOMS AND PRACTICE FOR DOCUMENTARY CREDIT REV. 2007，ICC PUBLIC. 600.

1. 指出信用证种类

（1）从可否撤销角度：

（2）从可否转让角度：

（3）从付款时间角度：

（4）从兑付方式角度：

（5）从是否保兑角度：

（6）从是否随附货运单据角度：

2. 填写信用证分析单

信用证分析单

(1) 编号：									
(2) 本证　　年　　月　　日收到									
开证行(3)				开证日(4)					
申请人(5)				受益人(6)					
信用证金额(7)				信用证号码(8)					
汇票付款人(9)				汇票期限(10)					
可否转运(11)				可否分批(12)					
装运期限(13)		信用证有效期(14)				到期地点(15)			
运输标志(16)				交单日(17)					
单据名称	提单(18)	发票(19)	装箱单(20)	保险单(21)	检验证(22)				
银行									
客户									
提单或承运单据	抬头(23)								
	通知(24)								
	注意事项								
保险	险别(25)								
	加成(26)								
其他注意事项：									

🔗任务三

子任务一：浙江凯喜雅股份有限公司收到了由中国银行浙江省分行发出的信用证。仔细阅读信用证，并找出下列内容。

1. 信用证的种类
2. 信用证号码
3. 开证日期
4. 信用证的有效期、有效地点
5. 开证申请人
6. 受益人
7. 付款行
8. 开证行
9. 通知行
10. 信用证金额及币种
11. 分批装运、转运
12. 装运港（地）、目的港（地）
13. 最迟装运期
14. 货名及规格
15. 货物数量
16. 价格术语
17. 海运提单种类
18. 交单期限
19. 信用证要求的单据
20. 信用证特别条款

2019APR30 13：47：51   LOGICAL TERMINAL H020

MT S700 **ISSUE OF A DOCUMENTARY CREDIT**   PAGE 00001

                                                    FUNC MSG700

                                                    UMR 40501961

MSGACK   DWS765I AUTH OK，KEY DIGEST，BKCHCNBJ BOTKJPJT RECORD

BASIC HEADER   F 01 BKCHCNBJA910 1751 951800

APPLICATION HEADER   0 7001447 180430 BOTKJPJTAOSA 1569 057082 180430 1347 N

                        ＊ BANK OF TOKYO-MITSUBISHI UFJ，LTD

```
                          * THE OSAKA
USER HEADER            SERVICE CODE        103：
                      BANK. PRIORITY       113：
                      MSG USER REF.        108：
                      INFO. FROM CI        115：
```

SEQUENCE OF TOTAL   *27：1/1

FORM OF DOC. CREDIT   *40A：IRREVOCABLE

DOC. CREDIT NUMBER   *20：S-441-2000029

DATE OF ISSUE   31C：20190430

APPLICABLE RULES   *40E：UCP LATEST VERSION

EXPIRY   *31D：DATE 20190730   PLACE IN BENEFICIARIES' COUNTRY

APPLICANT   *50：HOEI SEN-I CO. LTD

　　　　　　172 MOTOKITAKOJI-CHO，IMADEGAWA

　　　　　　OMIYA NISHIIRU，KAMIGYO-KU，KYOTO

BENEFICIARY   *59：ZHEJIANG CATHAYA INTERNATIONAL CO. LTD

　　　　　　117 TIYU CHANG ROAD，HANGZHOU，CHINA

AMOUNT   *32B：CURRENCY USD AMOUNT 30,000.00

POS./NEG.TOL.(%)   39A：10/10

AVAILABLE WITH/BY   *41D：ANY BANK

　　　　　　　　　BY NEGOTIATION

DRAFTS AT...   42C：AT SIGHT

　　　　　IN DUPLICATE

　　　　　INDICATING THIS L/C NUMBER

DRAWEE   42D：ISSUING BANK

PARTIAL SHIPMENTS   43P：ALLOWED

TRANSSHIPMENT   43T：PROHIBITED

PORT OF LOADING   44E：SHANGHAI, CHINA

PORT OF DISCHARGE   44F：OSAKA, JAPAN

LATEST DATE OF SHIP.   44C：20190709

DESCRIPT. OF GOODS   45A：SILK KNITTED GARMENTS

　　　　　FOB SHANGHAI

DOCUMENTS REQUIRED   46A：

　+SIGNED COMMERCIAL INVOICES IN 3 ORIGINALS.

+FULL SET LESS ONE ORIGINAL OF CLEAN ON BOARD OCEAN BILLS OF LADING MADE OUT TO ORDER OF SHIPPER AND BLANK ENDORSED MARKED FREIGHT COLLECT NOTIFY APPLICANT .

+ BENEFICIARY'S CERTIFICATE STATING THAT ONE SET OF ORIGINAL DOCUMENTS INCLUDING 1/3 ORIGINAL B/L HAVE BEEN SENT DIRECTLY TO THE APPLICANT.

ADDITIONAL COND. 47A：

+INSURANCE IS TO BE EFFECTED BY BUYER.

DETAILS OF CHARGES 71B：

+ ALL BANKING CHARGES OUTSIDE JAPAN ARE FOR ACCOUNT OF BENEFICIARY.

PRESENTATION PERIOD 48：

+DOCUMENTS MUST BE PRESENTED WITHIN 21 DAYS AFTER THE DATE OF SHIPMENT，BUT WITHIN THE VALIDITY OF THE CREDIT.

CONFIRMATION 49：WITHOUT

INSTRUCTIONS 78：

+REIMBURSEMENT BY TELECOMMUNICATION IS PROHIBITED.

+ THIS CREDIT IS AVAILABLE ON SIGHT BASIS. ALL DOCUMENTS MUST BE SENT TO US, I.E. THE BANK OF TOKYO-MITSUBISHI UFJ，LTD GLOBAL SERVICE CENTRE 1-1 KAWARAMACHI 2-CHOME，CHUO-KU，OSAKA 541-0048 JAPAN IN ONE LOT BY COURIER SERVICE. IN REIMBURSEMENT WE SHALL REMIT PROCEEDS ACCORDING TO YOUR INSTRUCTIONS.

+A DISCREPANCY FEE OF USD 45.00 WILL BE DEDUCTED FROM THE PROCEEDS IF DOCUMENTS CONTAINING DISCREPANCIES ARE PRESENTED TO US UNDER THIS CREDIT.

TRAILER   ORDER IS ＜MAC：＞＜PAC：＞＜ENC：＞＜CHK：＞
                           ＜TNG：＞＜PDE：＞
                           MAC：8EC9ADEA
                           CHK：E57C9DA0353D

子任务二：浙江凯喜雅股份有限公司对信用证进行了认真审核,发现一些不能接受而需要修改的条款,于是向买方提出改证的要求。过后,浙江凯喜雅股份有限公司收到由中国银行浙江省分行发出的信用证的修改。仔细阅读信用证的修改,比较与原证的区别,并填写信用证分析单。

2019JUL17 12：47：51   LOGICAL TERMINAL H020

MT S707   AMENDMENT TO A DOCUMENTARY CREDIT   PAGE 00001

                                               FUNC MSG700

                                               UMR 41710126

MSGACK   DWS765I AUTH OK，KEY DIGEST，BKCHCNBJ BOTKJPJT RECORD

BASIC HEADER   F 01 BKCHCNBJA910 1778 261570

APPLICATION HEADER   0 707 1328 180717 BOTKJPJTAOSA 1584 815346 180717 1228 N

                        ＊ BANK OF TOKYO-MITSUBISHI UFJ，LTD

                        ＊ THE OSAKA

USER HEADER   SERVICE CODE   103：

                        BANK. PRIORITY   113：

                        MSG USER REF.   108：

                        INFO. FROM CI   115：

SENDER'S REF.   ＊20：S-441-2000029

RECEIVER'S REF.   ＊21：NON REF

DATE OF ISSUE   31C：20190430

DATE OF AMENDMENT   30 ：20190717

NUMBER OF AMENDMENT   26E：01

APPLICABLE RULES   ＊40E：UCP LATEST VERSION

BENEFICIARY   ＊59：ZHEJIANG CATHAYA INTERNATIONAL CO. LTD

                  117 TIYU CHANG ROAD，HANGZHOU，CHINA

NEW DATE OF EXPIRY   31E：20191015

INCREASE DOC. CREDIT   32B：CURRENCY USD AMOUNT 23,000.00

NEW AMOUNT   34B：CURRENCY USD AMOUNT 53,000.00

POS./NEG.TOL.(%)   39A：10/10

LATEST DATE OF SHIP.   44C：20190924

＊＊REPEATABLE SEQUENCE 001＊＊＊＊＊＊＊＊＊＊＊＊OCCURRENCE 00001

TRAILER   ORDER IS＜MAC：＞＜PAC：＞＜ENC：＞＜CHK：＞

                        ＜TNG：＞＜PDE：＞

                        MAC：F02FD807

                        CHK：B81919F459DB

信用证分析单

(1) 编号：				
(2) 本证 年 月 日收到				

开证行(3)		开证日(4)		
申请人(5)		受益人(6)		
信用证金额(7)		信用证号码(8)		
汇票付款人(9)		汇票期限(10)		
可否转运(11)		可否分批(12)		
装运期限(13)		信用证有效期(14)		到期地点(15)	
运输标志(16)		交单日(17)		

单据名称	提单(18)	发票(19)	装箱单(20)	保险单(21)	检验证(22)			
银行								
客户								

提单或承运单据	抬头(23)		
	通知(24)		
	注意事项		
保险	险别(25)		
	加成(26)		

其他注意事项：

任务四： 仔细阅读信用证，并找出下列内容。

1. 信用证的种类

2. 信用证号码

3. 开证日期

4. 信用证的有效期、有效地点

5. 开证申请人

6. 受益人

7. 付款行

8. 开证行

9. 通知行

10. 信用证金额及币种

11. 分批装运、转运

12. 装运港（地）、目的港（地）

13. 最迟装运期

14. 货名及规格

15. 货物数量

16. 价格术语

17. 海运提单种类

18. 交单期限

19. 信用证要求的单据

20. 信用证特别条款

LETTER OF CREDIT

DATE：18 DEC 2019   SWIFT MESSAGE-MT700

STANDARD CHARTERED BANK（HONG KONG）LTD

15TH FLOOR，STANDARD CHARTERED TOWER，

NO. 388 KWUN TONG ROAD，KWUN TONG，HONG KONG

{1：F01NWBKGB2LXXXX0000000000}{2：1700SCBLHKHHXXXXN1005}{4：

SEQUENCE OF TOTAL   27：1/1

FORM OF DOCUMENTARY CREDIT   40A：IRREVOCABLE

DOCUMENTARY CREDIT NUMBER   20：TFPCYF922786

DATE OF ISSUE   31C：20191218

APPLICABLE RULES 40E：UCP LATEST VERSION

DATE AND PLACE OF EXPIRY 31D：20200320 CHINA

APPLICANT 50：NOBLECONTROL LTD, T/A FIGURE CLOTHING,

NO. 25-31 CHEETHAM HILL ROAD, MANCHESTER M4 4FY

BENEFICIARY 59：HANGZHOU DALI GARMENT COMPANY

NO. 37 HUANGTANG ROAD, HANGZHOU, CHINA 311100

AMOUNT 32B：CURRENCY CODE，AMOUNT USD 80,350.00

AVAILABLE WITH... BY... 41D：ANY BANK IN CHINA BY NEGOTIATION

DRAFTS AT... 42C：AT SIGHT

DRAWEE 42D：THE ROYAL BANK OF SCOTLAND PLC HONG KONG

PARTIAL SHIPMENTS 43P：ALLOWED

TRANSSHIPMENT 43T：ALLOWED

PORT OF LOADING/AIRPORT OF DEPARTURE 44E：SHANGHAI PORT

PORT OF DISCHARGE/AIRPORT OF DESTINATION 44F：ANYU.K. PORT

LATEST DATE OF SHIPMENT 44C：20200228

DESCRIPTION OF GOODS AND/OR SERVICES 45A：

COVERING：LADIES GARMENTS

STYLES LL4936/FIG21

TOTAL VALUE OF GOODS USD 80,350.00

SHIPPING TERMS：FOB SHANGHAI

DOCUMENTS REQUIRED 46A：

+1）INVOICE IN 3 COPIES EACH INDIVIDUALLY SIGNED.

+2）FULL SET OF CLEAN ON "BOARD OCEAN" MARINE BILLS OF LADING ISSUED TO ORDER AND BLANK ENDORSED AND EVIDENCING FREIGHT COLLECT AND NOTIFY PARTY—NOBLECONTROL LTD, T/A FIGURE CLOTHING, NO. 25-31 CHEETHAM HILL ROAD, MANCHESTER M4 4FY.

+3）COPY PACKING LIST.

+4）COPY CERTIFICATE OF ORIGIN.

+5）COPY CERTIFICATE OF ORIGIN GSP FORM "A".

+6）BENEFICIARY'S CERTIFICATE CONFIRMING THAT THE FOLLOWING DOCUMENTS HAVE BEEN SENT BY REGISTERED COURIER (COPY OF COURIER RECEIPT TO BE ATTACHED) AT SENDERS RISK TO THE L/C APPLICANT (ALL DOCUMENTS TO BE ORIGINAL).

A. INVOICE IN TRIPLICATE EACH INDIVIDUALLY SIGNED.

B. PACKING LIST.

C. CERTIFICATE OF ORIGIN GSP FORM "A".

D. CERTIFICATE OF ORIGIN.

＋7）BENEFICIARY'S CERTIFICAIE CONFIRMING PRODUCTION SAMPLES COVERING ALL STYLES, COLOURS AND SIZES ON ORDER HAVE BEEN SENT TO L/C APPLICANT FOR THE APPROVAL BY ANUJ VIJ.

＋8）INSPECTION REPORT PURPORTED TO BE ISSUED AND SIGNED BY ANUJ VIJ APPROVING THE PRODUCTION SAMPLES AND CONFIRMING THAT THE GOODS CAN BE DESPATCHED.

ADDITIONAL CONDITIONS 47A：

＋WE UNDERSTAND THAT THE INSURANCE IS BEING CARED FOR BY THE APPLICANT.

＋A DOCUMENT HANDLING FEE OF USD 40.00 OR EQUIVALENT AND A REIMBURSEMENT FEE OF USD 60.00 OR EQUIVALENT ARE TO BE PAID ON ALL DRAWINGS.

＋A DISCREPANCY FEE OF USD 65.00 OR EQUIVALENT AND ANY RELATED CABLE CHARGES FOR DISCREPANT DOCS ARE FOR BENEFICIARYS ACCOUNT.

＋ALL DOCUMENTS CALLED FOR UNDER THIS L/C OTHER THAN THOSE WHICH BY ITS TERMS ARE PERMITTED TO BE COPIES MUST BE ISSUED CLEARLY MARKED ORIGINAL ON THEIR FACE.

＋ALL DOCUMENTS AND DRAFTS MUST BE SENT IN ONE LOT BY COURIER THROUGH YOUR BANKERS TO 7TH FLOOR, STANDARD CHARTERED TOWER, NO. 388 KWUN TONG ROAD, KWUN TONG, HONG KONG ATTN THE ROYAL BANK OF SCOTLAND PLC HONG KONG, L/C PROCESSING CENTRE.

＋ANY COMMUNICATION CAN BE SENT BY FAX 852 23771823, TELEX 77923 SCHNKHX OR SWIFT SCBLHKHH WITH REQUEST TO RELAY MESSAGE TO THE ROYAL BANK OF SCOTLAND PLC HONG KONG, L/C PROCESSING CENTRE.

＋THE NUMBER AND DATE OF THE CREDIT AND NAME OF OUR BANK MUST BE QUOTED ON ALL DRAFTS REQUIRED.

＋ALL BANKING CHARGES INCLUDING OPENING COMMISSION OF USD 340.42 AND EXAMINATION COMMISSION CALCULATED AT 0.125 PER CENT PER PRESENTATION (MINIMUN USD 75) ARE FOR THE BENEFICIARYS ACCOUNT.

CHARGE 71B:

ALL BANKING CHARGES ARE FOR ACCOUNT OF BENEFICIARY.

PERIOD FOR PRESENTATION 48: 21 DAYS AFTER SHIPMENT DATE

CONFIRMATION INSTRUCTIONS 49: WITHOUT

INSTRUCTIONS TO PAYING/ACCEPTING/NEGOTIATING BANK 78:

+THIS L/C IS ISSUED BY THE ROYAL BANK OF SCOTLAND PLC HONG KONG WHICH UNDERTAKE TO HONOUR DRAFTS ACCOMPANIED BY DOCUMENTS IF PRESENTED IN CONFORMITY WITH CREDIT TERMS.

"ADVISE THROUGH" BANK 57D: SHANGHAI PUDONG DEVELOPMENT BANK
YUHANG, HANGZHOU, CHINA

SENDER TO RECEIVER INFORMATION 72: PRIV/RBOS
ORIGINATING IBC CITY

✎任务五：杭州纺织品贸易有限公司收到了号码为 108217060139 的信用证。 要求：仔细阅读信用证，分析信用证各条款内容，填写信用证分析单。

17/03/19-07：12：19　　　MCNS-2209-000099　　　132

-----------------------Instance Type and Transmission -----------------------

Original Received from SWIFT

Priority　　　　　　：Normal

Message Output Reference：1838 190316AXISCNSHAXXX1506067963

Correspondent Input Reference：1638 190316ALARBDDHA0828133624609

------------------------ Message Header-----------------------------------

Swift Output：FIN 700 Issue of a Documentary Credit

Sender：ALARBDDH082

　　　　　AL-ARAFAH ISLAMI BANK LTD

　　　　　（UTTARA BRANCH）

　　　　　DHAKA BD

Receiver：AXISCNSHAXXX

　　　　　AXIS BANK LIMITED SHANGHAI BRANCH

SHANGHAI CN

----------------------------- Message Text--------------------------------

27：SEQUENCE OF TOTAL

　　1/1

40A：FORM OF DOCUMENTARY CREDIT

　　　IRREVOCABLE

20：DOCUMENTARY CREDIT NUMBER

　　　108217060139

31C：DATE OF ISSUE

　　　20190316

40E：APPLICABLE RULES

　　　UCP LATEST VERSION

31D：DATE AND PLACE OF EXPIRY

　　　20190410 CHINA

51A：APPLICANT BANK-FI BIC

　　　ALARBDDH082

　　　AL-ARAFAH ISLAMI BANK LTD

（UTTARA BRANCH）

DHAKA BD

50：APPLICANT

MAZIM FASHION LTD

211,219 SATAISH，TONGI

GAZIPUR，BANGLADESH

59：BENEFICIARY

HANGZHOU TEXTILE TRADING CO. LTD

NO. 37 ZHONGHE ZHONG ROAD，HANGHZHOU，CHINA

TNT-0086-57186929

FAX：0086-57186925

32B：CURRENCY CODE，AMOUNT

USD 16,085.40

39B：MAXIMUM CREDIT AMOUNT

NOT EXCEEDING

41D：AVAILABLE WITH... BY... NAME & ADDR

ANY BANK IN HONGKONG BY NEGOTIATION

42C：DRAFTS AT...

120 DAYS FROM THE DATE OF NEGOTIATION

42A：DRAWEE-FI BIC

ALARBDDH082

AL-ARAFAH ISLAMI BANK LTD

（UTTARA BRANCH）

DHAKA BD

43P：PARTIAL SHIPMENTS

ALLOWED

43T：TRANSSHIPMENT

ALLOWED

44E：PORT OF LOADING/AIRPORT OF DEPARTURE

ANY SEAPORT OF CHINA

44F：PORT OF DISCHARGE/AIRPORT OF DESTINATION

CHITTAGONG SEAPORT，BANGLADESH

44C：LATEST DATE OF SHIPMENT

20190330

45A：DESCRIPTION OF GOODS AND/OR SERVICES

FABRICS FOR 100 PERCENT EXPORT ORIENTED READYMADE GARMENTS INDUSTRIES CERTIFYING DESCRIPTION，QUALITY，QUANTITY AS PER BENEFICIARY'S PROFORMA INVOICE NO. J-011C/GILCO/17 DTD 2019-02-15 SUBMITTED AT OUR COUNTER. CFR CHITTAGONG，BANGLADESH.

46A：DOCUMENTS REQUIRED

（1）MANUALLY SIGNED INVOICE IN 8 FOLDS CERTIFYING MERCHANDISE TO BE OF CHINA ORIGIN BEING IMPORTED AGAINST LCA NO.73820 IRC NO.BA-0173443，ERC NO. RA-0084323 APPLICANTS BIN：18051011412 BANKS BIN：19011031524 ISSUED UNDER BACK TO BACK CREDIT FACILITIES AND BONDED WARE HOUSE LICENCE，SYSTEM AND EXPORT L/C NO.00014728 DTD 2019-03-08 AND H.S. CODE NO.6001.92.00.

（2）DETAILED PACKING LIST IN SIX FOLDS.

（3）FULL SET OF CLEAN "SHIPPED ON BOARD"（DULLY AUTHENTICATED）OCEAN BILL OF LADING OF A REGULAR LINER VESSEL DRAWN OR ENDORSED TO THE OREDR OF AL-ARAFAH ISLAMI BANK LTD，UTTARA MODEL TOWN BRANCH，HOUSE-13，ROAD-14/A，SECTOR-4，DHAKA-1230，BANGLADESH，TEL：8959228 SHOWING "FREIGHT PREPAID" MARKED NOTIFY APPLICANT AND US GIVING FULL NAME AND ADDRESS.

（4）CERTIFICATE OF ORIGIN ISSUED BY CHAMBER OF COMMERCE OR ANY OTHER SIMILAR ORGANISATIONS.

（5）ALL SHIPMENTS UNDER THIS CREDIT MUST BE ADVISED SEPARATLEY BY THE BENEFICIARY IMMEDIATELY AFTER SHIPMENT DIRECTLY TO M/S CRYSTAL INSURANCE COMPANY LTD.CORPORATE OFFICE，(BOOTH)DR TOWER (14TH FLOOR)，65/2/2，BOX CULVERT ROAD，PURANA PALTAN，DHAKA-1000 BANGLADESH，FAX NO.：88-02-9567205，APPLICANT AND US MENTIONING INSURANCE COVER NOTE NO.CICL/CO(BOOTH)/MC-0024/03/2019 DATED：2019-03-16 AND ABOVE MENTIONED L/C NUMBER COPY OF SUCH ADVICE MUST ACCOMPANY THE ORIGINAL DOCUMENT.

（6）ONE SET OF NON-NEGOTIABLE SHIPPING DOCUMENTS INCLUDING DETAILED PACKING LIST UNDER THIS L/C MUST BE DESPATCHED TO THE

APPLICANT BY THE BENEFICIARY THROUGH MAIL/FAX WITHIN 5 (FIVE) DAYS FROM THE DATE OF SHIPMENT. MAIL/FAX CONFIRMATION RECEIPT IN THIS RESPECT SHOULD BE PRESENTED ALONG WITH ORIGINAL DOCUMENTS.

(7) PRE-SHIPMENT INSPECTION CERTIFICATE TO BE ISSUED BY THE BENEFICIARY ACCEPTABLE.

47A: ADDITIONAL CONDITIONS

(1) THIRD PARTY, SHORT FORM, BLANK BACKED, CHARTER PARTY BILL OF LADING NOT ACCEPTABLE.

(2) SHIPMENT BY ISRAELI FLAG VESSEL IS PROHIBITED. A CERTIFICATE FROM MASTER OF VESSEL/SHIPPING AGENT/AIR LINE IS REQUIRED TO THIS EFFECT.

(3) SHIPMENT PRIOR TO L/C DATE NOT ACCEPTABLE.

(4) COUNTRY OF ORIGIN MUST BE MENTIONED ON PACKING/CARTON/ CASE/ROLL AS THE CASE MAY BE FOR CUSTOM CLEARANCE.

(5) L/C NO. AND EXPORT S/C NO. AND DATE MUST BE MENTIONED IN ALL DOCUMENTS.

(6) IF DOCS. PRESENTED WITH DISCREPANCIES WILL DEDUCT USD 50.00 FOR EACH SET OF DISCREPANT DOCS. PRESENTED TO US AT THE TIME OF PAYMENT.

(7) NEGOTIATING BANK SCHEDULE MUST CERTIFY THAT ALL CHARGES AND COMMISSION DUE TO ADVISING BANK HAVE ALREADY BEEN PAID BY THE BENEFICIARY.

(8) ALL CHARGES OF ADVISING BANK INCLUDING ANY AMENDMENTS/ CONFIRMATION ETC. SHALL BE RECOVERED FROM THE BENEFICIARY AT THE TIME OF RELEASING ORIGINAL L/C AMENDMENT.

(9) CONSTRUCTION OF FABRICS SHOULD BE MENTIONED ON EACH ROLL FACE BY PRINTING TO COMPLY WITH THE M. M. ACT OF BANGLADESH CUSTOMS AND EACH ROLL OF FABRIC MUST NOT BE LESS THAN 20 DAYS AND A CERTIFICATE TO THIS EFFECT MUST ACCOMPANY THE ORIGINAL DOCS.

(10) COMMERCIAL INVOICE MUST SHOW THE GOODS'S FOB VALUE, FREIGHT CHARGES, INSURANCE, COMMISSION AND OTHER CHARGES(IF ANY) SEPARATELY.

(11) THE NEGOTIATING BANK MUST SUBMIT A CREDIT REPORT AS TO THE FINANCIAL MEANS, STANDING REPUTATION AND CREDIT WORTHINESS

OF THE BENEFICIARY AND A CERTIFICATE OF WHICH MUST ACCOMANY THE ORIGINAL DOCUMENTS.

71B：CHARGES

ALL BANKING CHARGES OUTSIDE BANGLADESH INCLUDING REIMBURSEMENT CHARGES ARE ON BENEFICIARY'S ACCOUNT.

48：PERIOD FOR PRESENTATION

15 DAYS FROM SHIPMENT DATE BUT WITHIN THE VALIDITY OF THE CREDIT.

49：CONFIRMATION INSTRUCTIONS

WITHOUT

78：INSTRUCTIONS TO PAYG/ACCPTG/NEGOTG BANK

＋UPON RECEIPT OF THE DOCTS. COMPLYING STRICTLY WITH THE CREDIT TERMS WE SHALL EFFECT PAYMENT AS PER INSTRUCTION OF NEGOTIATING BANK/COLLECTING BANK ON MATURITY.

＋DOCS. WITH DISCREPANCY MUST NOT BE NEGOTIATED EVEN AGAINST GUARANTEE OR UNDER RESERVED WITHOUT OUR PRIOR APPROVAL.

57A："ADVISE THROUGH" BANK-FI BIC

CIBKCNBJ310

CHINA CITIC BANK

（HANGZHOU BRANCH）

HANGZHOU CNINA

72：SENDER TO RECEIVER INFORMATION

THE UNIFORM CUSTOMS AND PRACTICE FOR DOCUMENTARY CREDIT. 2007 REVISION，ICC PUBLICATION

NO.600（UCP）PLS ADVISE THE L/C TO THE BENEFICIARY UNDER INTIMATION TO US.

————————————— Message Trailer —————————————

CHK：7619A4033C97

PKI SIGNATURE：MAC-EQUIVALENT

信用证分析单

(1) 编号：
(2) 本证　　年　　月　　日收到

开证行(3)		开证日(4)	
申请人(5)		受益人(6)	
信用证金额(7)		信用证号码(8)	
汇票付款人(9)		汇票期限(10)	
可否转运(11)		可否分批(12)	

装运期限(13)		信用证有效期(14)		到期地点(15)	
运输标志(16)			交单日(17)		

单据名称	提单(18)	发票(19)	装箱单(20)	保险单(21)	检验证(22)			
银行								
客户								

提单或承运单据	抬头(23)	
	通知(24)	
	注意事项	
保险	险别(25)	
	加成(26)	

其他注意事项：

项目二　信用证审核与修改

实训目标

能够根据合同和国际贸易惯例审核与修改信用证。

实训指导

一、审证负责者

信用证审核由通知行和受益人负责。通知行在收到信用证后主要负责审核开证行的背景、资信、信用证真假等内容。受益人在收到信用证后,主要根据合同和国际贸易惯例,审核信用证是否符合合同规定和业务做法。

二、出口公司审证要点之一：审核信用证是否符合合同规定

1. 货物条款的审核

信用证中关于货物的名称、质量、数量、包装等的规定必须与合同一致,如有错误,则提出相应修改。

2. 价格条件、币种、金额的审核

首先,审核信用证中的价格条件、币种与合同规定是否一致。

其次,核对信用证金额与合同是否相符。注意:(1)信用证金额可以超过合同金额,但不能低于合同金额;(2)如数量有溢短装,信用证金额应相应增减;(3)如有佣金或折扣,信用证金额不低于减除佣金或折扣后的净值;(4)如合同订明部分金额以信用证付款,余额以托收付款,那么信用证金额仅是部分的金额。

此外,信用证金额有大写和小写,应核对大、小写是否一致,避免发生纠纷。

3. 装运时间、地点、转运、分批装运的审核

装运时间、地点、转运、分批装运的审核要结合实际情况审核清楚。根据 UCP600 规定,信用证如果没有规定是否可以分批装运和转运,应理解为允许分批装运和转运。

4. 保险险别、投保金额的审核

信用证中保险条款的规定应与合同相符,保险险别、投保金额不得超出合同规定。

5. 信用证种类的审核

信用证种类的规定应与合同相符。

6. 汇票的付款期限审核

汇票的付款期限原则上应与合同规定一致,但也可接受更有利于我方融资的付款期限。

7. 受益人、开证人名称和地址的审核

审核信用证上的受益人、开证人的名称和地址是否正确。在填制单据时,受益人名称不正确或照抄信用证上写错了的买方公司名称和地址,都会给今后的收汇带来不便。

三、出口公司审证要点之二: 审核信用证是否符合业务做法

1. 信用证是否有限制生效的条款

按惯例,信用证在送到受益人时即生效,但有些信用证中会有不合理的限制性或保留条款。如信用证规定"若开证行不给予开证通知,信用证是无效的(This credit is non-operative unless the opening bank gives further advice.)";又如信用证规定"信用证要获得有关当局的进口许可证后方生效(This credit is operative only after the buyer obtains the import license.)"或"等收到货物的样品并以函电确认后方能生效(This credit is operative until the sample of the goods is received and confirmed by letter and telegram.)"等类似条款,这些在审证时都要注意。

2. 信用证是否有到期日(有效期)、到期地点

信用证中必须有到期日,没有规定到期日的信用证为无效信用证。为掌握交单时间以保证安全收汇,在出口业务中我国应争取到期地点在中国境内。

3. 到期日和装运期关系是否合理

信用证的到期日一般应比装运期迟一定的合理时间(通常是 15 天),以便在装运后有足够的时间办理制单结汇。如果最后装运期和到期日为同一天,这称为"双到期",在这种情况下,应在信用证到期日前提早几天将货物装运,以便留出足够时间来制单交单。如果到期日比装运期早,这是属于不合理的,需要修改。

4. 汇票付款人是否合理

信用证是银行信用,开证行或付款行承担第一性付款责任,所以汇票付款人应是开证行或其指定的付款行。

5. 银行费用规定是否合理

银行费用一般包括通知费、保兑费、承兑费、议付费、修改费等。我国的习惯做法是出口地的银行费用由出口方负担,进口地的银行费用由进口方负担。

6. 单据种类是否与交易条件相符

如空运方式下要求提供海运提单,FOB 术语下要求提供保险单,CIF 术语下漏列保险单,这些都是不合理的。

7. 提单运费规定是否与成交条件矛盾

CFR 、CIF 术语下,提单运费规定应为 freight prepaid/paid;FOB 术语下,提单运费规定应为 freight to collect。

8. 运输工具限制是否过严

如果信用证对船龄、船籍、船公司或港口等有限制条款,则要考虑能否办到。

9. 信用证中的单据条款是否合理

特别要注意一些软条款,如商业发票经买方复签生效,正本提单全部或部分直接寄交客户,要求由开证行或开证行指定的人在检验证书上签字,要求提供一些需要特别机构认证的单据,等等。

10. 交单期是否合理

交单期不能太短,一般运输单据签发后 7 天内交单可视为较短。信用证未规定交单期,按惯例是在运输单据签发日后 21 天内,但必须在信用证有效期内交单。

⏱ 实训任务

✎**任务一:** 根据出口合同对信用证进行审核,指出信用证存在的问题并提出具体的改证要求。

(一)销售确认书

销售确认书

SALES CONFIRMATION

NO. LT09060

DATE:AUG.10,2019

THE SELLER:AAA IMPORT AND EXPORT CO.　　THE BUYER:BBB TRADING CO.

　　　　　　NO. 222 JIANGUO ROAD　　　　　　　　　　P.O. BOX 203

　　　　　　DALIAN,CHINA　　　　　　　　　　　　GDANSK,POLAND

下列签字双方同意按以下条款达成交易:

The undersigned seller and buyer have agreed to close the following transactions according to the terms and conditions stipulated below:

品名与规格 COMMODITY AND SPECIFICATION	数量 QUANTITY	单价 UNIT PRICE	金额 AMOUNT
LADIES SKIRTS			CIF GDANSK
65% POLYESTER 35% COTTON			
STYLE NO.A101	200 DOZ	USD 60/DOZ	USD 12,000.00
STYLE NO.A102	400 DOZ	USD 84/DOZ	USD 33,600.00
	TOTAL:600 DOZ		USD 45,600.00
ORDER NO. HMW0901			

总值 <u>TOTAL VALUE</u>：U.S. DOLLARS FORTY FIVE THOUSAND SIX HUNDRED ONLY.

装运口岸 <u>PORT OF LOADING</u>：DALIAN

目的地 <u>DESTINATION</u>：GDANSK

转运 <u>TRANSSHIPMENT</u>：ALLOWED

分批装运 <u>PARTIAL SHIPMENTS</u>：ALLOWED

装运期限 <u>TIME OF SHIPMENT</u>：DECEMBER，2019

保险 <u>INSURANCE</u>：BE EFFECTED BY THE SELLERS FOR 110％ INVOICE VALUE COVERING F.P.A. RISKS OF PICC CLAUSE

付款方式 <u>PAYMENT</u>：BY TRANSFERABLE CONFIRMED L/C PAYABLE 60 DAYS AFTER B/L DATE，REACHING THE SELLERS 45 DAYS BEFORE THE SHIPMENT

一般条款 GENERAL TERMS：

(1) 合理差异：质地、重量、尺寸、花形、颜色均允许有合理差异,对合理范围内差异提出的索赔,概不受理。

Reasonable tolerance in quality，weight，measurements，designs and colors is allowed，for which no claims will be entertained.

(2) 卖方免责：买方对下列各点所造成的后果承担全部责任。

①使用买方指定包装、花形图案等；

②不及时提供生产所需的商品规格或其他细则；

③不按时开信用证；

④信用证条款与售货确认书不符合而不及时修改。

The buyers are to assume full responsibilities for any consequences arising from：

①the use of packing，designs or pattern made of order；

②late submission of specifications or any other details necessary for the execution of this sales confirmation；

③late establishment of L/C；

④late amendment to L/C inconsistent with the previsions of this sales confirmation.

买方（THE BUYER）   卖方（THE SELLER）

BBB TRADING CO.   AAA IMPORT AND EXPORT CO.

David King   Wang Daji

请在本合同签字后寄回一份。

Please sign，and return one copy.

（二）信用证

LETTER OF CREDIT

FORM OF DOC. CREDIT　　　　＊40A：IRREVOCABLE

DOC. CREDIT NUMBER　　　　＊20：70/1/5822

DATE OF ISSUE　　　　　　　＊31：20191007

EXPIRY　　　　　　　　　　＊31D：DATE 20200115 PLACE POLAND

ISSUING BANK　　　　　　　＊51D：SUN BANK，

　　　　　　　　　　　　　　　　P.O.BOX 201 GDANSK，POLAND

APPLICANT　　　　　　　　　＊50：BBB TRADING CO.

　　　　　　　　　　　　　　　　P.O. BOX 303，GDANSK，POLAND

BENEFICIARY　　　　　　　　＊59：AAA EXPORT AND IMPORT CO.

　　　　　　　　　　　　　　　　NO. 222 JIANGUO ROAD，DALIAN，CHINA

AMOUNT　　　　　　　　　　＊32B：CURRENCY HKD AMOUNT 45,600.00

AVAILABLE WITH/ BY　　　　＊41A：BANK OF CHINA，DALIAN BRANCH BY

　　　　　　　　　　　　　　　　DEFERRD PAYMENT

DEFERRED PAYM. DET.　　　　＊42P：60 DAYS AFTER SIGHT

PARTIAL SHIPMENTS　　　　　＊43P：NOT ALLOWED

TRANSSHIPMENT　　　　　　　＊43T：ALLOWED

LOADING IN CHARGE　　　　　＊44A：SHANGHAI

FOR TRANSPORT TO　　　　　＊44B：GDANSK

LATEST DATE OF SHIPMENT　＊44：20191131

DESCRIPT OF GOODS　　　　　＊45A：

　　LADIES SHIRTS

　　65％ POLYESTER 35％ COTTON

　　STYLE NO. 101　200 DOZ @ USD 60/PC

　　STYLE NO. 102　400 DOZ @USD 84/PC

　　ALL OTHER DETAILS OF GOODS ARE AS PER CONTRACT NO. LT 09060
DATED AUG. 10，2019

　　DELIVERY TERMS：CIF GDANSK(INCOTERMS 2010)

DOCUMENTS REQUIRED　　　　＊46A：

　　(1) COMMERCIAL INVOICE MANUALLY SIGNED IN 2 ORIGINALS PLUS 1
COPY MADE OUT TO DDD TRADING CO.，P.O.BOX 211，GDANSK，POLAND.

　　(2) FULL SET(2/3) OF ORIGINAL CLEAN ON BOARD BILL OF LADING PLUS

3/3 NON NEGOTIABLE COPIES, MADE OUT TO ORDER OF ISSUING BANK AND BLANK ENDORSED, NOTIFY THE APPLICANT, MARKED FREIGHT COLLECT, MENTIONING GROSS WEIGHT AND NET WEIGHT.

（3）ASSORTMENT LIST IN 2 ORIGINALS PLUS 1 COPY.

（4）CERTIFICATE OF ORIGIN IN 1 ORIGINAL PLUS 2 COPIES SIGNED BY CCPIT.

（5）MARINE INSURANCE POLICY IN THE CURRENCY OF THE CREDIT ENDORSED IN BLANK FOR CIF VALUE PLUS 30 PCT MARGIN COVERING ALL RISKS OF PICC CLAUSES INDICATING CLAIMS PAYABLE IN POLAND.

（6）BENEFICIARY'S CERTIFICATE STATED THAT 1/3 SET OF ORIGINAL BILL OF LADING HAS BEEN AIRMAILED DIRECTLY TO APPLICANT WITHIN 48 HOURS AFTER SHIPMENT.

ADDITIONAL COND.　＊47A：

＋ ALL DOCS. MUST BE ISSUED IN ENGLISH.

＋ SHIPMENTS MUST BE EFFECTED BY FCL.

＋ B/L MUST SHOWING SHIPPING MARKS：BBB，S/C LT09060，GDAND，C/NO.

＋ ALL DOCS. MUST NOT SHOW THIS L/C NO. 70/1/5822.

＋ FOR DOCS. WHICH DO NOT COMPLY WITH L/C TERMS AND CONDITIONS, WE SHALL DEDUCT FROM THE PROCEEDS A CHARGE OF EUR 50.00 PAYABLE IN USD EQUIVALENT PLUS ANY INCCURED SWIFT CHARGES IN CONNECTION WITH.

＋THIS CREDIT IS NON-OPERATIVE UNLESS THE NAME OF CARRYING VESSEL HAS BEEN APPROVED BY APPLICANT AND TO BE ADVISED BY L/C ISSUING BANK IN FORM OF AN L/C ADMENDMENT TO BENEFICIARY.

DETAILS OF CHARGES　＊71B：

＋ALL BANKING COMM/CHRGS OUTSIDE POLAND ARE ON BENEFICIARY'S ACCOUNT.

PERIOD FOR PRESENTATION　＊48：

＋15 DAYS AFTER B/L DATE，BUT WITHIN THE VALIDITY OF THE CREDIT.

CONFIRMATION　＊49：WITHOUT

INSTRUCTIONS　＊78：WE SHALL REIMBURSE AS PER YOUR INSTRUCTIONS.

SENT TO REC. INFO　＊72：CREDIT SUBJECT TO ICC PUBL. 600/2007 REV.

✎**任务二：** 根据下述合同内容审核信用证，指出不符之处，并提出修改意见。

（一）销售合同

SHANGHAI ANDYS TRADING CO. LTD

SALES CONTRACT

THE SELLER：

SHANGHAI ANDYS TRADING CO. LTD　　　NO. AD18007

NO. 126 WENHUA ROAD, SHANGHAI,CHINA　DATE：MAR. 16，2019

　　　　　　　　　　　　　　　　　　SIGNED AT：SHANGHAI，CHINA

THE BUYER：

HAZZE AB HOLDING

BOX 1237，S-111 21 HUDDINGE，SWEDEN

　　This contract is made by and between the Seller and Buyer，whereby the Seller agrees to sell and the Buyer agrees to buy the under-mentioned commodity subject to the terms and conditions as stipulated below：

Commodity & Specification	Quantity	Unit Price	Amount
Gas Detectors ART NO.BX616 ART NO.BX319	50 pcs 50 pcs	USD 380.00/pc USD 170.00/pc	FOB SHANGHAI USD 19,000.00 USD 8,500.00
Total	100 pcs		USD 27,500.00
Total Amount： SAY U.S. DOLLARS TWENTY SEVEN THOUSAND AND FIVE HUNDRED ONLY				

PACKING： In Carton.

SHIPPING MARKS： HAZZE/AD2019007/STOCKHOLM, SWEDEN/NOS.1- UP

TIME OF SHIPMENT： During July，2019.

PLACE OF LOADING AND DESTINATION： From Shanghai，China to Stockholm，Sweden with partial shipment and transshipment are allowed.

INSURANCE： To be effected by the Buyer.

TERMS OF PAYMENT： By irrevocable confirmed L/C at sight which should be issued before May 31，2019，valid for negotiation in China for further 15 days after time of shipment.

INSPECTION： In the factory.

　　This contract is made in two original copies and becomes valid after signature，one

35

copy to be held by each party.

THE SELLER   **THE BUYER**

SHANGHAI ANDYS TRADING CO. LTD   HAZZE AB HOLDING

Ardyn   Hazze

（二）信用证

MT 700   ISSUE OF A DOCUMENTARY CREDIT

SENDER   SWEDBANK

RECEIVER   BANK OF CHINA, SHANGHAI, CHINA

SEQUENCE OF TOTAL   27：1 / 1

FORM OF DOC. CREDIT   40A：IRREVOCABLE

DOC. CREDIT NUMBER   20：BCN1008675

DATE OF ISSUE   31C：20190612

APPLICABLE RULES   40E：UCP LATEST VERSION

DATE AND PLACE OF EXPIRY   31D：DATE 20190630 PLACE IN SWEDEN

APPLICANT   50：HAZZE ABC HOLDING

    BOX 1237，S-111 21 HUDDINGE，SWEDEN

BENEFICIARY   59：SHANGHAI ANDY TRADING CO. LTD

    NO. 126 WENHUA ROAD，SHANGHAI，CHINA

AMOUNT   32B：CURRENCY EUR AMOUNT 27,000.00

AVAILABLE WITH/BY   41D：ANY BANK IN CHINA，BY NEGOTIATION

DRAFTS AT...   42C：30 DAYS AFTER SIGHT

DRAWEE   42A：HAZZE AB HOLDING

PARTIAL SHIPMENTS   44P：NOT ALLOWED

TRANSSHIPMENT   44T：NOT ALLOWED

PORT OF LOADING   44E：TIANJIN，CHINA

PORT OF DISCHARGE   44F：STOCKHOLM，SWEDEN

LATEST DATE OF SHIPMENT   44C：20190615

DESCRIPTION OF GOODS   45A：

 1,000 PCS OF GAS DETECTORS AS PER S/C NO. AD13007

 CIF STOCKHOLM

 PACKED IN CARTONS

DOCUMENTS REQUIRED   46A：

+ COMMERCIAL INVOICE SIGNED MANUALLY IN TRIPLICATE.

+ PACKING LIST IN TRIPLICATE.

+ CERTIFICATE OF CHINESE ORIGIN CERTIFIED BY CHAMBER OF COMMERCE.

+ INSURANCE POLICY/CERTIFICATE IN DUPLICATE ENDORSED IN BLANK FOR 110% INVOICE VALUE，COVERING ALL RISKS AND WAR RISK OF CIC OF PICC (1/1/1981).

+ FULL SET OF CLEAN ON BOARD OCEAN BILLS OF LADING MADE OUT TO ORDER MARKED FREIGHT PREPAID AND NOTIFY APPLICANT.

ADDITIONAL CONDITION 47A：

+ ALL PRESENTATIONS CONTAINING DISCREPANCIES WILL ATTRACT A DISCREPANCY FEE OF USD 50.00. THIS CHARGE WILL BE DEDUCTED FROM THE BILL AMOUNT WHETHER OR NOT WE ELECT TO CONSULT THE APPLICANT FOR A WAIVER.

CHARGES 71B：

+ALL CHARGES AND COMMISSIONS ARE FOR ACCOUNT OF BENEFICIARY.

CONFIRMATION INSTRUCTION 49：WITHOUT

🔗任务三： 根据出口合同对信用证进行审核，指出信用证存在的问题并提出具体的改证要求。

（一）销售合同

SALES CONTRACT

NO. ST05-016

DATE：AUGUST 08，2019

PLACE：NANJING, CHINA

BUYER：JAD & SONS PAPERS COMPANY

　　　NO. 203 LODIA HOTEL OFFICE 1546，

　　　DONG-GU BUSAN，REPUBLIC OF KOREA

SELLER：BLUESKY INTERNATIONAL TRADE COMPANY LIMITED

　　　NO. 529 QIJIANG ROAD，HEDONG DISTRICT，

　　　TIANJIN，CHINA

THIS CONTRACT IS MADE BY THE SELLER；WHEREBY THE BUYERS AGREE TO BUY AND THE SELLER AGREE TO SELL THE UNDER-MENTIONED COMMODITY ACCORDING TO THE TERMS AND CONDITIONS STIPULATED BELOW：

(1) COMMIDITY：UNBLEACHED KRAFT LINERBOARD

　　UNIT PRICE：USD 390.00/PER METRIC TON，CFR BUSAN

　　TOTAL QUANTITY：100 METRIC TONS，±10％ ARE ALLOWED

　　PAYMENT TERM：BY IRREVOCABLE CONFIRMED L/C AT 90 DAYS

　　　　AFTER B/L DATE

(2) TOTAL VALUE：USD 39,000.00 (SAY U.S. DOLLARS THIRTY NINE THOUSAND ONLY. ＊＊＊10％ MORE OR LESS ALLOWED)

(3) PACKING：TO BE PACKED IN STRONG WOODEN CASE(S)，SUITABLE FOR LONGDISTANCE OCEAN TRANSPORTATION

(4) SHIPPING MARK：THE SELLER SHALL MARK EACH PACKAGE WITH FADELESS PAINT THE PACKAGE NUMBER，GROSS WEIGHT，MEASUREMENT AND THE WORDINGS："KEEP AWAY FROM MOISTURE" "HANDLE WITH CARE"，ETC. AND THE SHIPPING MARK：ST05-016 BUSAN REPUBLIC OF KOREA

(5) TIME OF SHIPMENT：ON OR BEFORE OCTOBER 31，2019

(6) PORT OF SHIPMENT：MAIN PORTS OF CHINA

(7) PORT OF DESTINATION：BUSAN，REPUBLIC OF KOREA

(8) INSURANCE：TO BE COVERED BY THE BUYER AFTER SHIPMENT. (FOB TERM)

(9) DOCUMENT：

　＋SIGNED INVOICE INDICATING L/C NO. AND CONTRACT NO.

　＋ FULL SET (3/3) OF CLEAN ON BOARD OCEAN BILL OF LADING MARKED "FREIGHT TO COLLECT"/"FREIGHT PREPAID" MADE OUT TO ORDER BLANK ENDORSED NOTIFYING THE APPLICANT.

　＋ PACKING LIST/WEIGHT LIST INDICATING QUANTITY/GROSS AND NET WEIGHT.

　＋ CERTIFICATE OF ORIGIN.

　＋ NO SOLID WOOD PACKING CERTIFICATE ISSUED BY MANUFACTURER.

(10) OTHER CONDITIONS REQD. IN L/C：

　＋ ALL BANKING CHARGES OUTSIDE THE OPENING BANK ARE FOR BENEFICIARY'S A/C.

　＋ DO NOT MENTION ANY SHIPPING MARKS IN YOUR L/C.

　＋ PARTIAL AND TRANSSHIPMENT ALLOWED.

(11) REMARKS：THE LAST DATE OF L/C OPENING：20 AUGUST，2019

（二）信用证

BANK OF KOREA LIMITED，BUSAN

SEQUENCE OF TOTAL　＊27：1/1

FORM OF DOC. CREDIT　＊40 A：IRREVOCABLE

DOC. CREDIT NUMBER　＊20：S100-108085

DATE OF ISSUE　＊31C：20190825

EXPIRY　＊31 D：DATE 20191001 PLACE APPLICANTS COUNTRY

APPLICANT　＊50：JAD & SONS PAPERS COMPANY

　　　　　　　203 LODIA HOTEL OFFICE 1564，DONG-GU，BUSAN，RERUBLIC

　　　　　　　OF KOREA

BENEFICIARY　＊59：BLUESKY COMPANY LIMITED

　　　　　　　NO. 529，QIJIANG ROAD，HEDONG DISTRICT，TIANJIN，CHINA

AMOUNT　＊32 B：CURRENCY HKD AMOUNT 39,000.00

AVAILABLE WITH/ BY　＊41 D：ANY BANK IN CHINA BY NEGOTIATION

DRAFTS AT...　＊42C：DRAFTS AT 90 DAYS AFTER SIGHT FOR FULL

　　　　　　　INVOICE COST

DRAWEE　＊42 A：BANK OF KOREA LIMITED，BUSAN

PARTIAL SHIPMENTS　＊43P：ALLOWED

TRANSSHIPMENT　＊43T：NOT ALLOWED

LOADING ON BOARD　＊44A：SHANGHAI，CHINA

FOR TRANSPORTATION TO　＊44B：BUSAN，REPUBLIC OF KOREA

LATEST DATE OF SHIPMENT　＊44C：20191031

DESCRIPTION OF GOODS　＊45A：

　　＋ COMMODITY：UNBLEACHED KRAFT LINERBOARD

　　U/P：USD 390.00/MT TOTAL：100MT±10％ ARE ALLOWED

　　PRICE TERM：CIF BUSAN

　　COUNTRY OF ORIGIN：P.R.CHINA

　　PACKING：STANDARD EXPORT PACKING

　　SHIPPING MARK：ST05-016

　　　　　　　BUSAN REPUBLIC OF KOREA

DOCUMENTS REQUIRED　＊46A：

　　（1）COMMERCIAL INVOICE IN 3 COPIES INDICATING LC NO. CONTRACT

NO. ST05-018.

(2) FULL SET (3/3) OF CLEAN ON BOARD OCEAN BILL OF LADING MADE OUT TO ORDER AND BLANK ENDORSED, MARKED FREIGHT TO COLLECT, NOTIFYING THE APPLICANT.

(3) PACKING LIST/WEIGHT LIST IN 3 COPIES INDICATING QUANTITY/ GROSS AND NET WEIGHTS.

(4) CERTIFICATE OF ORIGIN IN 3 COPIES.

ADDITIONAL COND.   * 47B:

+ALL DOCUMENTS ARE TO BE PRESENTED TO US IN ONE LOT BY COURIER/SPEED POST.

DETAILS OF CHARGES   * 71B:

+ALL BANKING CHARGES ARE FOR ACCOUNT OF BENEFICIARY.

PERIOD FOR PRESENTATION   * 48:

+DOCUMENTS TO BE PRESENTED WITHIN 2 DAYS AFTER THE DATE OF SHIPMENT BUT WITHIN THE VALIDITY OF THE CREDIT.

CONFIRMATION   * 49: WITHOUT

INSTRUCTIONS   * 78:

+WE HEREBY UNDERTAKE THAT DRAFTS DRAWN UNDER AND IN COMPLY WITH THE TERMS AND CONDITIONS OF THIS CREDIT WILL BE PAID MATURITY.

SEND. TO REC. INFO.   * 72:/ SUBJECT UCP 2007 ICC PUBLICATION 600.

✎任务四：将信用证内前后矛盾、我方不宜接受的条款指出来，并提出具体的改证要求。

DOCUMENTARY CREDIT NO. 8169/26598

ISSUING：KOREA EXCHANGE BANK, SEOUL

APPLICANT：G AND Y TRADING CO. LTD

        RM 908PHOENIX BLDG.702-23, YUKSAM-DONG KANGNAM-KU,

        SEOUL, REPUBLIC OF KOREA

ADVISING：BANK OF CHINA TIANJIN

BENEFICIARY：TIANJIN SUNSHINE INTERNATIONAL TRADING CO. LTD

        HUASHENG BLDG., NO. 85 LIUWEI RD.,

        HEDONG DISTRICT, TIANJIN, CHINA

AMOUNT：USD 33,264.00

SAY US DOLLARS THIRTY THREE THOUSAND TWO HUNDRED SIXTY ONLY

DATE OF ISSUE：APR. 2，2019

EXPIRY：MAY 15，2019 IN REPUBLIC OF KOREA

WE HEREBY ISSUE IN YOUR FAVOR THIS IRREVOCABLE DOCUMENTARY CREDIT WHICH IS AVAILABLE BY NEGOTIATION OF YOUR DRAFT AT SIGHT DRAWN ON BENEFICIARY BEARING THE CLAUSE："DRAWN UNDER DOCUMENTARY CREDIT NO. 8169/26589 DATED APR. 5，2019 OF KOREA EXCHANGE BANK SEOUL" ACCOMPANIED BY THE FOLLOWING DOCUMENTS：

＋SIGNED COMMERCIAL INVOICE IN TRIPLICATE SHOWING FOB，FREIGHT AND INSURANCE COSTS SEPARATELY.

＋PACKING LIST IN TRIPLICATE.

＋FULL SET OF CLEAN ON BOARD AIRWAY BILLS OF LADING MADE OUT TO ORDER MARKED FREIGHT PREPAID AND NOTIFY APPLICANT.

＋FORM A CERTIFICATE OF ORIGIN.

＋INSURANCE POLICY/CERTIFICATE IN DUPLICATE ENDORSED IN BLANK FOR 150 PCT OF THE INVOICE VALUE WITH CLAIMS PAYABLE IN REPUBLIC OF KOREA IN THE CURRENCY OF DRAFT，COVERING THE INSTITUTE CARGO CLAUSE ALL RISKS.

＋CERTIFICATE OF SHIPPING CO. INDICATING THAT THE CARRYING STEAMER IS A NEW VESSEL NOT EXCESS OF TEN YEARS OLD.

DESCRIPTION OF GOODS：

＋COUNTRT OF ORIGIN：CHINA

＋65 PCT POLYESTER 35 PCT COMBED COTTON BLENDED WOVEN FABRIC 45 * 45 110 * 76 47″ IN GREY

P/LENGTH：90PCT 117-121 YDS 10PCT 40 YDS UP

WEIGHT：ABOUT 110GR/YD

100,000YDS IN TWO SHIPMENTS AT CFR BUSAN USD 0.5/YD

SHIPMENT：

FROM TIANJIN TO TOKYO BY STEAMER NOT LATER THAN MAY 20，2019 AND MUST REACH THE PORT OF DESTINATION ON OR BEFORE THE END OF MAY 2019.

PARTIAL SHIPMENTS & TRANSSHIPMENT：PROHIBITED

SPECIAL CONDITIONS：

＋ALL BANKING CHARGES INCLUDING REIMBURSING CHARGE ARE

FOR ACCOUNT OF BENEFICIARY.

　　+ SHIPPER MUST FAX ADVISE BUYER SHIPMENT PARTICULARS IMMEDIATELY AFTER SHIPMENT.

　　+ ONE COPY OF SIGNED COMMERCIAL INVOICE AND NON-NEGOTIABLE B/L TO BE AIRMAILED IN ADVANCE TO BUYER.

　　+ NO HOOKS USED.

　　+ DOCUMENTS MUST BE PRESENTED WITHIN 2 DAYS AFTER SHIPPING DATE SHOW ON B/L，BUT WITHIN THE VALIDITY OF THE L/C.

　　+ THE DOCUMENTS BENEFICIARY PRESENT SHOULD INCLUDE AN INSPECTION CERTIFICATE SIGNED BY APPLICANT OR ITS AGENT.

INSTRUCTIONS TO THE NEGOTIATING BANK：

　　+ T/T REIMBURSEMENT NOT ALLOWED.

　　+ THE DISCREPANCY FEE OF USD 60.00 (OR EQUIVALENT) SHOULD BE DEDUCTED FROM YOUR REIMBURSEMENT CLAIM TO THE REIMBURSING BANK OR WILL BE DEDUCTED FROM PROCEEDS BY US IF DOCUMENTS ARE PRESENTED WITH DISCREPANCY.

　　+ ALL DOCS MUST BE DESPATCHED TO US IN ONE LOT.

✎任务五： 根据销售合同对信用证进行审核，指出信用证存在的问题并提出具体的改证要求。

（一）销售合同

销售合同
SALES CONTRACT

Sellers：SHANGHAI TOOL IMPORT & EXPORT CO. LTD　　　Contract No.：RT05342

Address：NO. 31 GANXIANG ROAD, SHANGHAI, CHINA

Tel：021-65756156 Fax：021-65756155　　　　　　　　Date：Mar. 20，2019

Buyers：MAMUT ENTERPRISE SAV

Address：TARRAGONA75-3ER, BARCELONA, SPAIN　　　Signed at：SHANGHAI

Tel：024-4536-2453　Fax：024-4536-2452

　　THIS CONTACT IS MADE BY AND BETWEEN THE SELLERS AND BUYERS，WHEREBY THE SELLERS AGREE TO SELL AND THE BUYERS AGREE TO BUY THE UNDERMENTIONED GOODS SUBJECT TO THE TERMS AND CONDITIONS AS STIPULATED BELOW：

(1) 货号、品名及规格	(2) 数量	(3) 单价	(4) 金额
NAME OF COMMODITY AND SPECIFICATIONS	QUANTITY	UNIT PRICE	AMOUNT
HAND TOOLS 1）9PC EXTRA LONG HEX KEY SET 2）8PC DOUBLE OFFSET RING SPANNER 3）12PC DOUBLE OFFSET RING SPANNER 4）12PC COMBINATION SPANNER 5）10PC COMBINATION SPANNER AS PER PROFORM INVOICE NO20180329 DATED MARCH 10，2018	1,200 SETS 1,200 SETS 800 SETS 1,200 SETS 1,000 SETS	FOB USD 1.76 USD 3.10 USD 7.50 USD 3.55 USD 5.80	SHANGHAI USD 2,112.00 USD 3,720.00 USD 6,000.00 USD 4,260.00 USD 5,800.00
TOTAL	5,400 SETS		USD 21,892.00

（5）PACKING：8PC DOUBLE OFFSET RING SPANNER，PACKED IN 1 PLASTIC CARTON OF 16 SET EACH；9PC EXTRA LONG HEX KEY SET，12PC COMBINATION SPANNER，10PC COMBINATION SPANNER，PACKED IN 1 PLASTIC CARTON OF 10 SETS EACH；12PC DOUBLE OFFSET RING SPANNER，PACKED IN 1 PLASTIC CARTON OF 8 SETS EACH.

PACKED IN THREE 40′ CONTAINER.

（6）DELIVERY FROM：SHANGHAI，CHINA TO BARCELONA，SPAIN

（7）SHIPPING MARKS：M.E

BARCELONA

C/NO.1-UP

（8）TIME OF SHIPMENT：LATEST DATE OF SHIPMENT MAY.10,2019

（9）PARTIAL SHIPMENTS：ALLOWED

（10）TRANSSHIPMENT：ALLOWED

（11）TERMS OF PAYMENT：

＋BY 100％ CONFIRMED IRREVOCABLE LETTER OF CREDIT TO BE AVAILABLE AT SIGHT.

＋DRAFT TO BE OPENED BY THE SELLERS.

＋L/C MUST MENTION THIS CONTRACT NUMBER.

＋L/C ADVISED BY BANK OF CHINA SHANGHAI BRANCH.

＋ALL BANKING CHARGES OUTSIDE CHINA（THE MAINLAND OF CHINA）ARE FOR ACCOUNT OF DRAWEE.

（12）ARBITRATION：

ANY DISPUTE ARISING FROM THE EXECUTION OF OR IN CONNECTION

WITH THIS CONTRACT SHALL BE SETTLED AMICABLY THROUGH NEGOTIATION. IN CASE NO SETTLEMENT CAN BE REACHED THROUGH NEGOTIATION, THE CASE SHALL THEN BE SUBMITTED TO CHINA INTERNATIONAL ECONOMIC & TRADE ARBITRATION COMMISSION IN SHANGHAI (OR IN BEIJING) FOR ARBITRATION IN ACCORDANCE WITH ITS ARBITRATION RULES. THE ARBITRATION AWARD IS FINAL AND BINDING UPON BOTH PARTIES. THE FEE FOR ARBITRATION SHALL BE BORNE BY LOSING PARTY UNLESS OTHERWISE AWARDED.

The Seller: The Buyer:

SHANGHAI TOOL IMPORT & EXPORT CO. LTD   MAMUT ENTERPRISE SAV

Lili   Jhon

（二）信用证

DOCUMENTARY CREDIT

SEQUENCE OF TOTAL   *27: 1/1

FORM OF DOC. CREDIT   *40A: REVOCABLE

DOC. CREDIT NUMBER   *20: 31173

DATE OF ISSUE   31C: 20190401

DATE AND PLACE OF EXPIRY   *31D: DATE 20190531 PLACE SPAIN

APPLICANT   *50: MAMUT ENTERPRISE SAV

TARRAGONA 75-3ER

ISSUING BANK   52A: CREDIT ANDORRA

ANDORRA LA VELLA, ANDORRA

BENEFICIARY   *59: SHANGHAI TOOL EXPORT & IMPORT CO. LTD

NO. 31 GANXIANG ROAD, SHANGHAI, CHINA

AMOUNT   *32 B: CURRENCY EUR AMOUNT 21,892.00

AVAILABLE WITH/ BY   *41 D: ANY BANK IN CHINA BY NEGOTIATION

DRAFTS AT...   42 C: AT 30 DAYS AFTER SIGHT

DRAWEE   42 A: CREDIT ANDORRA

ANDORRA LA VELLA, ANDORRA

PARTIAL SHIPMENTS   43P: NOT ALLOWED

TRANSSHIPMENT   43T: NOT ALLOWED

LOADING ON BOARD   44A: SHANGHAI

FOR TRANSPORTATION TO   44B：BARCELONA（SPAIN）

LATEST DATE OF SHIPMENT   44C：20190510

DESCRIPTION OF GOODS   45A：

　　HAND TOOLS AS PER PROFORMA INVOICE NO. 20180339

　　DATED MAR.10，2019 FOB BARCELONA

DOCUMENTS REQUIRED   46A：

　　+SIGNED COMMERCIAL INVOICE，1 ORGINAL AND 4 COPIES.

　　+PACKING LIST，1 ORGINAL AND 4 COPIES.

　　+CERTIFICATE OF ORIGINAL GSP CHINA FORM A，ISSUED BY THE CHAMBER OF COMMERCE OR OTHER AUTHORITY DULY ENTITLED FOR THIS PURPOSE.

　　+FULL SET OF B/L（2 ORIGINALS AND 5 COPIES）CLEAN ON BOARD，MARKED "FREIGHT PREPAID"，CONSIGNED TO：MAMUT ENTERPRISESAV，TARRAGONA75-3ER BARCELONA，SPAIN，TEL ＋376 823 323 FAX ＋376 860 914-860807，NOTIFY：BLUE WATER SHIPPING ESPANA，ER 2NA，A，08003 BARCELONA（SPAIN）TEL 34 93 295 4848，FAX 34 93 268 16 81.

　　+ INSURANCE POLICY OR CERTIFICATE ENDORSED IN BLANK FOR 110％ OF CIF VALUE，COVERING WPA RISK AND WAR RISK AS PER CIC.

CHARGES   71B：

　　ALL BANKING CHARGES OUTSIDE SPAIN ARE FOR ACCOUNT OF BENEFICIARY.

PERIOD FOR PRESENTATION   48：

　　DOCUMENTS MUST BE PRESENTED WITHIN 15 DAYS AFTER THE DATE OF SHIPMENT BUT WITHIN THE VALIDITY OF THE CREDIT.

项目三　商业发票填制

能够根据有关资料填制商业发票。

☐**实训指导**

商业发票的
填制

商业发票无统一的格式,由出口商自行设计,其各栏目的内容填制如下。

1. 出票人名称和地址

发票出票人,通常是出口商或信用证的受益人。出票人名称和地址描述必须醒目、正确。由于发票出票人名称和地址是相对固定的,因此出口企业在印刷空白发票时一般就印上这些内容,或将这些内容编入电脑程序一并打印。

2. 发票名称

发票上应标有"Commercial Invoice"或"Invoice"的字样。一般在出口业务中使用的、由出口方出具的发票都是商业发票,所以并不要求一定标出"Commercial(商业)"的字样,但信用证要求标明的除外。发票名称中不能有"Provisional Invoice(临时发票)"或"Pro Forma Invoice(形式发票)"等字样出现。

3. 发票抬头人(to)

汇付或托收方式下,发票抬头人一般为合同的买方,填写合同买方的名称和地址。信用证方式下,如果信用证上有指定抬头人,则按信用证规定填制;如果信用证没有指定,则根据 UCP600 第 18 条 a 款的规定,必须做成以申请人的名称为抬头。填写发票抬头人时,抬头的名称和地址一般分行打印。

4. 发票号码(invoice No.)

发票号码由出口公司根据公司的实际情况自行编制,一般采用顺序号,便于查对。

5. 发票日期(invoice date)

发票的签发日期是所有单据中最早的。根据 UCP600 的规定,如果信用证没有特殊规定,银行可以接受签发日期早于开证日的发票。

6. 信用证号码(L/C No.)

信用证号码参照信用证填制。如信用证无特殊规定或没有开证行授权,两个或两个以上信用证项下的货物不能合并在同一份发票内反映,所以一份发票内只能注明一个信用证号码。如不使用信用证方式,此栏空白或删掉。

7. 合同号码(S/C No.)

填合同号码。一笔交易有几份合同的号码,都应打在发票上。如信用证上列明的合同号码与实际不符且来不及修改,发票上合同号应与信用证上列明的一致。不过,可在错误的合同号码后面注明"正确的合同号码应为……"。当合同名称不是"Contract",而是"Confirmation""Order""Purchase Order"等时,应将本栏目的名称修改后,再填写该合同号码。

8. 支付方式(terms of payment)

填写该笔业务的付款方式。如 L/C、T/T、D/P、D/A 等。

9. 起运港(地)和目的港(地)(from...to...)

填写货物实际的起运港(地)、目的港(地)。起运港(地)和目的港(地)均应明确具体,不能笼统。如果货物需经转运,应把转运港的名称表示出来。

10. 唛头(shipping marks)

信用证有指定唛头的,按照信用证规定制唛;如无指定,可参考合同;如合同也无指定,出口商可自行设计唛头,也可打上 N/M(no mark)。

注意:

(1) 唛头设计一般以简明、易于识别为原则。唛头内容包括收货人名称的缩写、参考号码(合同号、发票号等)、目的港、件号等几个部分。

(2) 如信用证规定的唛头含有"QTY,G.W."等,但没有"仅限于(restricted to...)"等类似字样,则唛头可以按文字要求加注实际内容,如"QTY 100 SET,G.W.1,000 KGS"。

(3) 如信用证规定的唛头要用英文表示图形,例如"in diamond"或"in triangle"等,则唛头应将菱形或三角形等具体图形表示出来。

(4) 如信用证规定的唛头含有 NO.1-UP,则 UP 要由最大包装件数替代。

11. 货物描述(description of goods)

货物描述包括名称、质量、包装、参见合同等内容,这部分与数量、单价、金额组成发票的中心内容。UCP600 第 18 条 c 款规定:商业发票中货物、服务或履约行为的描述应该与信用证中的描述一致。可见,商业发票对货物的描述必须符合信用证中的描述;而在所有其他单据中,货物的描述可使用统称,但不能与信用证中货物的描述有抵触。发票中的货物描述必须与信用证规定的一致,这并不要求如同镜子反射那样一致,信用证中货物描述中的数量、单价、金额、装运等内容应填写在与发票对应的栏目中。

12. 数量(quantity)

商品数量的计量单位同单价中的计量单位要保持一致。

13. 单价(unit price)

单价由四个部分组成:计价货币、单位数额、计量单位和贸易术语。如果信用证中写明了贸易术语的来源,则发票必须表明相同的来源。如信用证条款规定,CIF Singapore INCOTERMS 2010,那么 CIF Singapore 和 CIF Singapore INCOTERMS 都不符合信用证的要求,只有 CIF Singapore INCOTERMS 2010 符合信用证的要求。

14. 金额(amount)

金额应为数量和单价的乘积。

注意:

(1)发票总金额一般不应超过信用证金额。

(2)凡"约""大概""大约"或类似的词语用于信用证数量、金额时,应理解为有关数量、金额可有不超过 10% 的增减幅度。

(3)金额必须准确计算,正确缮打,并认真复核,特别要注意小数点的位置是否正确,金额和数量的横乘、竖加是否有矛盾。

(4)总金额一般要有大、小写,大、小写金额应一致。大写金额的货币名称一般打在数额前,货币名称应用全称,金额之后还应加"only"表示"整",也可在货币名称前加"say"表示"计"。如:USD 100.20 大写金额可表述为"(say) United States dollars one hundred and cents twenty only"。其中"0.20"有以下几种写法:①cents twenty;②20%;③20/100。

(5)价格中含有佣金、折扣时,在填制发票总金额一栏时应注意以下三点。①信用证有扣除条款,则应扣除相应折扣、佣金。如,信用证规定"5% commission to be deducted from invoice value",则在制发票时应扣除相应的佣金。②信用证没有扣除条款,但信用证的总金额已扣除,则仍要扣除折扣、佣金。如信用证规定"金额为 USD 950.00,共 100 PCS,单价为 USD 10.00 per PC CIF C5 London",则在制发票时也应扣除相应的佣金。③信用证没有扣除条款,信用证的总金额未扣除,则不要扣除折扣、佣金。

15. 其他说明

按信用证要求,加注特别说明。如,按信用证要求注明货物是中国原产的;按信用证要求证明所列内容真实无误;按信用证要求标出各种费用金额,如运费、保险费和 FOB 金额等;按信用证要求加注特定号码,如进口证号、配额许可证号码等;出口澳大利亚享受 GSP 待遇,往往要求加注"发展中国家声明"等。这些内容一般打在发票商品栏以下的空白处。

16. 出票人名称及签名(name of beneficiary and signature)

商业发票由出口商或信用证中规定的受益人出具。如果信用证没有规定,用于对外收汇的商业发票不需要签署(但用于报关、退税等国内管理环节的发票必须签署)。当信用证要求"signed commercial invoice...",发票需要签署。若来证要求"manually signed",则必须手签。

⏱ 实训任务

✎**任务一：** 根据下列资料填制商业发票。

（一）信用证资料

ISSUING BANK：NATIONAL COMMERCIAL BANK，JEDDAH

ADVISING BANK：BANK OF CHINA，ZHEJIANG BRANCH

DATE OF ISSUE：JAN.3，2019

L/C NO.：DC668839

L/C AMOUNT：USD 29,040.00

APPLICANT：JEDDAH XYZ FOOD COMPANY，JEDDAH

BENEFICIARY：HANGZHOU ABC FOOD COMPANY，HANGZHOU

PARTIAL SHIPMENTS：NOT ALLOWED

MERCHANDISE：

ABOUT 48,000 CANS OF MEILING BRAND CANNED ORANGE JAM，

250 GRAM/CAN,12 CANS IN A CARTON

UNIT PRICE：USD 0.55/CAN CIFC5 JEDDAH

COUNTRY OF ORIGIN：P.R.CHINA

DOCUMENTS REQUIRED：

＋MANUALLY SIGNED COMMERCIAL INVOICES IN 3 COPIES DATED THE SAME DATE AS THAT OF L/C ISSUANCE DATE INDICATING COUNTRY OF ORIGIN OF THE GOODS AND CERTIFIED TO BE TRUE AND CORRECT, INDICATING CONTRACT NO. SUM356/2019 AND L/C NO.

...

ADDITIONAL CONDITIONS：

＋ALL DOCUMENTS MUST INDICATE SHIPPING MARKS AS JAM IN DIAMOND JEDDAH.

＋ALL DOCUMENTS INCLUDING INVOICE MUST BE IN NAME OF JEDDAH XYZ FOOD COMPANY，JEDDAH.

＋5％ COMMISSION TO BE DEDUCTED FROM INVOICE VALUE .

＋ INVOICE SHOULD SHOW FOB VALUE，FREIGHT CHARGES AND INSURANCE PREMIUM SEPARATELY.

（二）其他资料

INVOICE NO.：ABC123/2019

受益人有权签字人：吴一帆

出仓单显示：50,000 CANS OF MEILING BRAND CANNED ORANGE JAM

提单显示：货物从宁波运往吉达

船名：LINDA V.123

海运运费：USD 154.00

保险费：USD 28.00

HANGZHOU ABC FOOD COMPANY

NO. 35 QIAOSI ROAD，HANGZHOU，ZHEJIANG，CHINA

COMMERCIAL INVOICE		
(1) SELLER	(3) INVOICE NO.	(4) INVOICE DATE
(2) BUYER	(5) L/C NO.	(6) S/C NO.
(7) TRANSPORT DETAILS FROM TO PARTIAL SHIPMENTS TRANSSHIPMENT BY	(8) TERMS OF PAYMENT	

(9) MARKS	(10) DESCRIPTION OF GOODS	(11) QUANTITY	(12) UNIT PRICE	(13) AMOUNT

(14)TOTAL AMOUNT IN WORDS

(15) ISSUED BY
SIGNATURE

任务二： 根据下列资料填制商业发票。

L/C NO. 291-11-6222531 DATED APRIL 2ND, 2019

DATE AND PLACE OF EXPIRY：OCT.15, 2019 IN COUNTRY OF BENEFICIARY

APPLICANT：WOODLAND LIMITED

　　　　　　NO. 450 CASTLE PEAK ROAD, KLN., HONG KONG, CHINA

BENEFICIARY：ZHEJIANG ANIMAL BY-PRODUCTS IMP. & EXP. CORPORATION

　　　　　　NO. 76 WULIN ROAD, HANGZHOU, CHINA

L/C AMOUNT：USD 16,663.00

LOADING IN CHARGE：SHANGHAI PORT, CHINA

FOR TRANSPORTATION TO：HONG KONG, CHINA

LATEST DATE OF SHIP.：20190930

DESCRIPTION OF GOODS：42,500 PIECES OF STUFFED TOY AS PER
　　　　　　SALES CONTRACT
　　　　　　18ZA16IA0019 DATED 20190313

STYLE NO.	QUANTITY	UNIT PRICE
ZEAPEL01	7,000 PCS	USD 0.345/PC
ZEAPEL02	500 PCS	USD 0.65/PC
ZEAPEL03	5,000 PCS	USD 1.10/PC
ZEAPEL04	30,000 PCS	USD 0.31/PC

CIF C5 HONG KONG AS PER INCOTERMS 2010

DOCUMENTS REQUIRED：

　　+COMMERCIAL INVOICE IN 1 ORIGINAL AND 3 COPIES LESS THAN 5％ COMMISSION AND HANDSIGNED BY BENEFICIARY.

　　...

ADDITIONAL COND.：

　　+PACKING IN CARTONS OF 50 PCS EACH.

　　+CARTONS TO BE MARKED WITH：Z.J.A.B/HONGKONG/C/NO.1-UP

　　提示：填制时请注意佣金的处理及签字方式。

ZHEJIANG ANIMAL BY-PRODUCTS IMP. & EXP. CORPORATION

NO. 76 WULIN ROAD，HANGZHOU，CHINA

COMMERCIAL　INVOICE

TO：				NO.	
				DATE	
				L/C NO.	
				S/C NO.	
FROM		TO			
MARKS & NOS.	DESCRIPTION OF GOODS		QUANTITY	UNIT PRICE	AMOUNT

任务三： 根据下列资料填制商业发票。

DC NO.：DC TST188986

EXPIRY：APR. 15，2019

APPLICANT：LEON INC.

        1200 NEW YORK DRIVE

        PASADENA，CA.91108

BENEFICIARY：ZHEJIANG TEXTILES IMP. & EXP. CORPORATION

        NO. 165 ZHONGHE ZHONG RD.，HANGZHOU, CHINA

L/C AMOUNT：USD 124,390.00

LOADING ON BOARD/DESPATCH FROM：NINGBO PORT，CHINA

FOR TRANSPORTATION TO：NEW YORK

LATEST DATE OF SHIP.：MAR. 31，2019

COVERING：

    LADIES' 80％ VISCOSE 12％ NYLON 8％ ELASTANE KNITTED CARDIGAN

    P.O.NO. 6199，10900 PCS AT USD 4.60 PER PC

    P.O.NO. 6200，19800 PCS AT USD 3.75 PER PC

    TOTAL 307,00 PCS，USD 124,390.00

    SALES CONTRACT NO.18PA0010

DELIVERY TERMS：CIF NEW YORK

PACKING：PLASTIC，CARTON WITH MARK

        6199/6200/18PA0010/NEW YORK

DOCUMENTS REQUIRED：

    +SIGNED COMMERCIAL INVOICE IN 4-FOLD.

    ...

SPECIAL INSTRUCTIONS：

    +ALL DOCUMENTS INCLUDING INVOICE MUST BE IN NAME OF ALANT
CORPORATION，111 AVENUE OF THE NEW YORK，NY 10036 U.S.A.

    + INVOICE MUST INDICATE THE FOLLOWING：

        1)OCEAN FREIGHT，INSURANCE COST AND FOB VALUE

        2)EACH ITEM IS LABELLED "MADE IN CHINA"

        3)GOODS SHIPPED IN ONE 40 FOOT FCL

    备注：OCEAN FREIGHT 和 INSURANCE COST 分别按 USD 3,000.00 和 USD
124.39 计。

ZHEJIANG TEXTILES IMP. & EXP. CORPORATION

NO. 165 ZHONGHE ZHONG RD.，HANGZHOU，CHINA

COMMERCIAL INVOICE

TO：				NO.	
				DATE	
				L/C NO.	
				S/C NO.	
FROM		TO			
MARKS & NOS.	DESCRIPTION OF GOODS		QUANTITY	UNIT PRICE	AMOUNT

任务四： 根据以下资料，审核并修改已填制的商业发票，在已填制的 17 个栏目中，即标号（1）—（17）中找出若干处填制错误，并说明原因。

（一）信用证资料

THE ROYAL BANK OF CANADA

CABLE ADDRESS：ROYAL BANK

PLACE & DATE OF ISSUE：CANADA APR. 20，2019

OPEN TYPE：CABLE

ADVISING BANK：BANK OF CHINA，SHANGHAI BRANCH

CREDIT NUMBER：LC0501-FTC

EXPIRY：DATE JUN. 22，2019 FOR NEGOTIATION IN CHINA

APPLICANT：MAURICIO DEPORTS INTERNATIONAL S.A.

NO. 890 FINCH STREET，TORONTO，CANADA

BENEFICIARY：ZHEJIANG SUMING IMPORT AND EXPORT CO. LTD

RM1900 JUXING BLDG，NO.807 JIAOGONG ROAD，

HANGZHOU 310012，CHINA

AMOUNT：CURENCY USD AMOUNT 17,250.00

DRAFTS AT：15 DAYS AFTER SIGHT FOR FULL INVOICE VALUE

PARTIAL SHIPMENTS：ALLOWED

TRANSSHIPMENT：ALLOWED

PORT OF LOADING：SHANGHAI，CHINA

FOR TRANSPORTATION TO：TORONTO，CANADA

LATEST DATE OF SHIPMENT：JUN. 15，2019

DESCRIPTION OF GOODS：VALVE SEAT INSERT

W77T6　　1050 PCS @USD 5.00/PC

W88T9　　2000 PCS@USD 6.00/PC

AS PER SALES CONTRACT NO. ZJ2018-HZ08 DATED MAR. 31，2019 CIF TORONTO

DOCUMENTS REQUIRED：

＋ ORIGINAL SIGNED COMMERCIAL INVOICE IN TRIPLICATE AND SHOULD BEAR THE FOLLOWING CLAUSE："WE HEREBY CERTIFY THAT THE CONTENTS OF INVOICE HEREIN ARE TRUE AND CORRECT."

...

（二）装箱资料

NOS. AND KINDS OF PACKAGES：61 WOODEN CASES

GROSS WEIGHT/VOLUME：8,000 KGS/12 CBM

（三）已填制的商业发票

浙江山名进出口公司（1）

ZHEJIANG SUMING IMPORT AND EXPORT CO. LTD

RM1900 JUXING BLDG，NO. 807 JIAOGONG ROAD，

HANGZHOU 310012，CHINA

COMMERCIAL INVOICE（2）

TO：（3） MAURICIO DEPORTS INTERNATIONAL S.A. 890 FINCH，STREET，TORONTO，CANADA	NO.：（4）ZS35789
	DATE：（5）JUN. 23，2019
	S/C NO.：（6）ZJ2001-HZ08
	L/C NO.：（7）

FROM：SHANGHAI,CHINA   TO：TORONTO,CANADA（8）

MARKS & NOS. （9）	DESCRIPTION OF GOODS （10）	QUANTITY （11）	UNIT PRICE （12）	AMOUNT （13）
M.D. TORONTO NO.1-61	VALVE SEAT INSERT	3,050 PCS	CIF TORONTO USD 5.00/PC USD 6.00/PC	USD 17,250.00
		3,050 PCS		USD 17,250.00

TOTAL AMOUNT：SAY U.S. DOLLARS SEVENTEEN THOUSAND TWO HUNDRED
 AND FIFTY ONLY （14）

PACKING IN 61 WOODEN CASES （15）

（16）

E.&O.E.

浙江山名进出口公司（17）

ZHEJIANG SUMING IMPORT AND EXPORT CO. LTD

项目四　装箱单填制

实训目标

能够根据有关资料填制装箱单。

实训指导

装箱单(重量单/尺码单)无统一的格式,其各栏目的内容填制如下。

1. 单据名称

单据名称,应符合信用证规定。如信用证要求提供重量单,则名称应为 weight list;如信用证要求提供尺码单,则名称应为 measurement list。

2. 抬头

除非信用证特别要求,银行可接受装箱单表面无抬头(即无开证申请人名称和地址)的表示。

3. 号码

即装箱单号码,一般填发票号码。

4. 日期

即装箱单填制日期,一般与发票日期相同。如信用证未作规定,也可不注明出单日。

5. 唛头

填写唛头,且须与发票、信用证及实物印刷完全一致;如无唛头,填 N/M。

6. 货物描述

货物描述包括名称、质量、包装等内容。

包装包括:包装规模、包装材料、包装方式、颜色与尺寸搭配等。

装箱单中标明的货物应为发票中所描述的货物,但也可以用与其他单据无矛盾的统称来表示。

7. 数量

按商品的正常计量单位填。

8. 包装数

填最大包装种类和件数。

9. 净重、毛重、体积

填写商品的净重、毛重、体积。净重和毛重以千克为单位,保留整数。商品的体积,以立方米为单位,保留三位小数。

10. 其他说明

按信用证的要求,加注一些其他的说明。

11. 签署

如果信用证没有规定装箱单签名时,可以不盖章签名。盖章签名时,填出口公司名称及法定代表名称。

⏱ 实训任务

🔗 **任务一: 根据以下资料填制装箱单。**

1. 客户名称地址:AL. BALOUSHI TRADING EST JEDDAH,P.O. BOX 31248,JEDDAH 21497,KINGDOM OF SAUDI ARABIA

2. 付款方式:20% T/T BEFORE SHIPMENT AND 80% D/P AT SIGHT

3. 装运信息:指定 APL 承运,装运期:不迟于 20190429,起运港:NINGBO,目的港:JEDDAH

4. 价格条款:CFR JEDDAH

5. 唛头:ROYAL/19AR225031/JEDDAH/ C/N:1-UP

6. 货物描述:

P.P INJECTION CASES 14″/22″/27″/31″ 230SET@ USD 42.00/SET USD 9,660.00

P.P INJECTION CASES 14″/19″/27″/31″ 230SET@ USD 41.00/SET USD 9,430.00

(中文品名:注塑箱四件套)

7. 装箱资料:

箱号	货号	包装	件数(件)	毛重(KGS)	净重(KGS)	体积(CBM)
1-230	ZL0322+BC05	CTNS	230	18.5/4255	16.5/3795	34
231-460	ZL0319+BC01	CTNS	230	18.5/4255	16.5/3795	34

8. 合同号:19AR225031,签订日期:2019 年 3 月 30 日

9. 商业发票号:AC19AR031

10. 商业发票日期:2019 年 4 月 23 日

11. 出口商名称及地址:JIANGNAN LIGHT INDUSTRIAL PRODUCTS CORPORATION,NO.188 EAST ZHONGSHAN ROAD,NINGBO,CHINA

江南轻工业品公司

JIANGNAN LIGHT INDUSTRIAL PRODUCTS CORPORATION

NO.188 EAST ZHONGSHAN ROAD，NINGBO，CHINA

PACKING   LIST

(1) SELLER	(3) INVOICE NO.	(4) INVOICE DATE
	(5) FROM	(6) TO
	(7) TOTAL PACKAGES (IN WORDS)	
(2) BUYER	(8) MARKS & NOS.	

(9) C/NOS.	(10) NOS. & KINDS OF PKGS	(11) ITEM	(12) QTY.	(13) G.W.	(14) N.W.	(15) MEAS.
(16)						

(17) ISSUED BY：

(18) SIGNATURE：

✎**任务二： 根据以下资料填制装箱单。**

1. 出口商公司名称及地址：SHANGHAI JINHAI IMP. & EXP. CORP. LTD,720 DONGFENG ROAD, SHANGHAI, CHINA

2. 进口商公司名称及地址：ANTAK DEVELOPMENT LTD, STUTTGART STIR. 5, D-84618, SCHORNDORF, GERMANY

3. 支付方式：20% T/T BEFORE SHIPMENT AND 80% L/C AT 30 DAYS AFTER SIGHT

4. 装运条款：FROM SHANGHAI TO HAMBURG NOT LATER THAN SEP. 30，2019

5. 价格条款：CFR HAMBURG

6. 货物描述：MEN'S COTTON WOVEN SHIRTS

货号/规格	装运数量及单位	单价	毛重/净重(件)	尺码
1094L	700 DOZ	USD 27.4/DOZ	33 KGS/31 KGS	68 CM * 46 CM * 45 CM
286G	800 DOZ	USD 39.6/DOZ	45 KGS/43 KGS	72 CM * 47 CM * 49 CM
666	160 DOZ	USD 34.0/DOZ	33 KGS/31 KGS	68 CM * 46 CM * 45 CM

包装情况：一件一塑料袋装,6件一牛皮纸包,8打或10打一外箱

尺码搭配：1094L   M   L   XL

                           3   3   4＝10 打/箱

           286G   L   XL

                           1.5   3   3.5＝8 打/箱

           666   M   L   XL

                           1.5   3.5   3＝8 打/箱

7. 唛头：由卖方决定(要求使用标准化唛头)

8. 信用证号：123456,开证日期：AUG.18，2019,开证行：BANK OF CHINA, HAMBURG BRANCH

9. 通知行：BANK OF CHINA, SHANGHAI

10. 船名：HONGHE V. 188

11. 提单日期：SEP. 20，2019

12. 合同号：19SHGM3178B。签订日期：AUG. 2，2019

13. 商业发票号：SHGM70561

14. 运费：USD 160.00

15. 所需单据：

+ PACKING LIST IN 1 ORIGINAL PLUS 5 COPIES INDICATING THIS L/C NUMBER，ALL OF WHICH MUST BE MANUALLY SIGNED

......

SHANGHAI JINHAI IMP. & EXP. CO. LTD
NO. 720 DONGFENG ROAD，SHANGHAI，CHINA
PACKING   LIST

TO：		NO.：
		DATE：
SHIPPING MARKS：		S/C NO.：
		L/C NO.：
C/NOS. NOS. & KINDS OF PKGS ITEM QTY. G.W. N.W. MEAS.		

任务三：根据以下资料填制装箱单。

（一）销售确认书

销售确认书
SALES CONFIRMATION

卖方(Sellers)：

ZHEJIANG FOREIGN TRADE IMP.AND EXP. CORPORATION

267 TIANHE ROAD，HANGZHOU，CHINA

买方(Buyers)：

A.B.C. TRADING CO. LTD, HONG KONG

NO. 312 SOUTH BRIDGE STREET，HONG KONG

Contract No.：	AB44001
Date：	FEB.12，2019
Signed at：	HANGZHOU

兹经买卖双方同意按下列条款成交：

The undersigned sellers and buyers have agreed to close the following transactions according to the terms and conditions stipulated below：

货号 Art. No.	品名及规格 Description	数量 Quantity	单价 Unit Price	金额 AMOUNT
	AIR CONDITIONER(HUALING BRAND)			FOB C2 NINGBO
ART NO. P97811 KF-23GW		500 PCS @ HKD 200.00		HKD 100,000.00
ART NO. P97801 KF-25GW		500 PCS @ HKD 250.00		HKD 125,000.00
		1,000 PCS		HKD 225,000.00

数量及总值均得有　　　　％的增减，由卖方决定。

With　5　％ more or less both in amount and quantity allowed at the sellers' option.

总值

Total Value：HKD 225,000.00(H. K. DOLLARS TWO HUNDRED AND TWENTY FIVE THOUSAND ONLY)

包装

Packing：1 PC IN ONE CARTON

装运期

Time of Shipment：APR. 30，2019

装运口岸和目的地

Loading Port & Destination：FROM NINGBO TO DUBAI

保险由卖方按发票全部金额110％投保至　　　　为止的　　　　险。

Insurance：To be effected by sellers for 110％ of full invoice value covering　　　up to　　　only.

付款条件：买方须于 2019 年 3 月 10 日前将不可撤销即期信用证开到卖方，议付有效期延至上列装运期后 15 天在中国到期，该信用证中必须注明允许分运及装运。

Terms of Payment：By Irrevocable Letter of Credit to be available by sight draft to reach the sellers before MAR.10，2019 and to remain valid for negotiation in China until the 15th day after the foresaid Time of Shipment. The L/C must specify that transshipment and partial shipments are allowed.

装船标记

Shipment Mark：A.B.C./DUBAI/NOS.1-UP/MADE IN CHINA

开立信用证时请注明我成交确认书号码。

When opening L/C, please mention our S/C number.

备注

Remarks：THE CREDIT IS SUBJECT TO UCP 600 (2007 REVISION)

THE SELLER：　　　　　　　　　　　　　　　　THE BUYER：

（二）其他资料

1. 商业发票编号为 2019FT011，日期为 2019 年 3 月 12 日

2. 出仓单显示：

ART NO. P97811 510 PCS   @13.5 KGS   @11.5 KGS   0.174 CBM

ART NO. P97811 500 PCS   @14.0 KGS   @12.0 KGS   0.174 CBM

   3. PACKING LIST IN 1 ORIGINAL PLUS 5 COPIES，ALL OF WHICH MUST BE MANUALLY SIGNED

ZHEJIANG FOREIGN TRADE IMP. & EXP. CORPORATION

NO. 267 TIANHE ROAD, HANGZHOU, CHINA

PANCKING LIST

Invoice No.: _____   Date: _____

Seller: _____

_____

Buyer: _____

_____

From _____   to _____

Marks and Nos.	Description of Goods	Quantity	Package	G.W.	N.W.	Meas.

TOTAL:

SAY TOTAL:

任务四： 根据以下资料，审核并修改已填制的装箱单。

（一）信用证资料

L/C NO.：CRE557186

DATE OF ISSUE：20190510

EXPIRY：DATED 20190721 PLACE IN CHINA

APPLICANT：J.L. GROUP COMPANY LTD

        8/F，HILDER CENTRE，2 SUNG PING ST.，HUNGHOM，

        KOWLOON，HONG KONG

BENEFICIARY：CHINA TUSHU ZHEJIANG TEA IMP. AND EXP. CORP.

        NO. 310 YAN'AN ROAD，HANGZHOU，CHINA

DOCUMENTS REQUIRED：

  ＋PACKING LIST IN 3 COPIES SHOWING COLOR ASSORTMENT，SIZE BREAKDOWN，SIZE BREAKDOWN PER COLOR，GROSS WEIGHT AND NET WEIGHT.

EVIDENCING OF SHIPMENT：320 PCS LADIE'S JACKETS STYLE NO. 70016 P.O.

        NO. D42069 AT USD 30.00 PER PC

LATEST SHIPMENT DATE：20190630

SHIPPING MARKS：J.L./HONGKONG/1-UP

INVOICE NO.：TS201905

NET WEIGHT：200 KGS

GROSS WEIGHT：310 KGS

MEASUREMENT：2.300 CBM

（二）已填制的装箱单

CHINA TUSHU ZHEJIANG TEA IMP. AND EXP. CORPORATION

NO. 310 YAN AN ROAD, HANGZHOU, CHINA

PACKING LIST

TO: J. L. GROUP COMPANY LTD, 8/F, HILDER CENTRE, NO. 2 SUNG PING ST., HUNGHOM, KOWLOON, HONG KONG		NO.: TS200305		
		DATE: JUL. 5, 2019		
MARKS & NOS.	QUANTITY AND DESCRIPTION OF GOODS	NET WEIGHT	GROSS WEIGHT	MEAS.
J.L. HONG KONG 1-50	LADIE'S JACKETS STYLE NO. 70016 P.O. NO. D42069	200 KGS	310 KGS	2.300 CBM

COLOR/SIZE BREAKDOWN						
C/T NO.	COLOR	SIZE				TOTAL
		S	M	L	XL	
1-6	SAND	6				36
7-12	SAND		6			36
13-18	SAND			6		36
19-24	SAND				6	36
25	SAND	4	2			6
26	SAND		2	4		6
27	SAND				4	4
28-33	RUBY	6				36
34-39	RUBY		6			36
40-45	RUBY			6		36
46-51	RUBY				6	36
52	RUBY	4	2			6
53	RUBY		2	4		6
54	RUBY				4	4
TOTAL:		54 CTNS		320 PCS		

SIZE BREAKDOWN PER COLOR					
COLOR	S	M	L	XL	TOTAL
SAND			40		160 PCS
RUBY		40	40		160 PCS
TOTAL			80		320 PCS

CHINA TUSHU ZHEJIANG TEA IMP. AND EXP. CORP.

项目五　保险单据填制

✅ 实训目标

能够根据有关资料填制保险单据。

💼 实训指导

各家保险公司根据自身印制的保险单固定格式和投保要求,制作保险单。保险单各栏目的内容填制如下。

1. 保险公司名称(name of insurance policy)

投保人应根据信用证和合同要求去相应的保险公司办理保险单据。如来证规定:"insurance policy in duplicant by PICC",则保险单须由中国人民保险公司出具。

2. 保险单据名称(name)

此栏按照信用证和合同要求填制,如保险单、保险凭证等。如来证规定:"insurance policy in duplicant",即应出具保险单而非保险凭证(insurance certificate)。

注意:(1)保险人不一定同意出具投保回执(acknowledgement of insurance declaration),如信用证有此要求,受益人应要求对方改证;(2)不能用保险经纪人开出的暂保单代替保险单议付,银行将不予接受。

3. 发票号码(invoice No.)

填写投保货物的发票号码。

4. 保险单号码(policy No.)

填写保险公司的保险单号码。

5. 被保险人(insured)

被保险人又称保险单的抬头人,被保险人填在保险单上的"at the request of"后面,一般填出口商的名称。若信用证要求保险单做成空白抬头(to order),则在被保险人栏内填"to order";若信用证要求以特定方(如开证行或开证申请人)为被保险人,则该栏内填特定方的名称。

6. 唛头(marks & Nos.)

保险单上唛头应与发票、提单上一致,也可简单填成"as per invoice No. …"。

7. 包装及数量(quantity)

包装货物,填写最大包装件数;裸装货物,注明本身件数;煤炭、石油等散装货,则注明"in bulk",然后填写净重。有包装但以重量计价的,应把包装重量(数量)与计价重量都注上。

8. 货物名称(description of goods)

允许用统称,但不同类别的货物应注明不同类别的各自的总称。这里与提单此栏的填写一致。

9. 保险金额(amount insured)

保险金额的加成百分比应严格按信用证或合同规定掌握。如未规定,应按 CIF 或 CIP 发票价格的 110% 投保。保险金额不要小数,出现小数时采用"进一取整"的填法。所用币种应与发票一致。

10. 保险费及保险费率(premium and rate)

一般已由保险公司在保险单印刷时印上"as arranged"字样,出口公司在填写保险单时无须填写。若信用证要求具体列明此两栏,加盖校对章后可打上所需要的内容。如信用证要求"...marked premium paid",制单时应把原有的"as arranged"删掉,加盖校对章后打上"paid"字样。

11. 装载运输工具(per conveyance S.S.)

填写装载的运输工具。海运方式下填写船名,最好再加航次。如需转船,应分别填写一程船名及二程船名,中间用"/"隔开;如果第二程船名未知,则只需打上"转船"字样。铁路运输则填"by railway(train)",最好再加车号,即"by railway(train),Wagon No. ×× ×";航空运输则填"by air",邮包运输则填"by parcel post"。

12. 开航日期(slg. on or abt.)

按 B/L 中的签发日期填,还可以简单地填作"as per B/L"。

13. 起讫地点(from... to...)

起点填装运港名称,讫点填目的港名称,中途需转船的应注明中转港。如,from Ningbo to Rotterdam W/T Hong Kong。目的港与投保到达地不一致的,应注明投保到达地。如,提单上目的港为美国长滩,来证规定投保至芝加哥,则起讫地点应填"from Ningbo to Long Beach and Thence to Chicago"。

14. 承保险别(conditions)

按照信用证规定的险别投保。如信用证没有规定具体险别,则可投保最低责任险别,如 FPA 或 ICC(C)。

15. 赔款偿付地点(claim payable at)

按照信用证规定填制;若来证未规定,则填目的港。如信用证规定不止一个目的港或赔付地,则应全部照打。有些信用证规定在偿付地点后注明偿付货币名称,则应照办。

16. 日期(date)

指填写保险单的日期。保险手续要求货物离开出口仓库前办理。保险单的日期不应迟于提单签发日、货物发运日或接受监管日。

17. 签字（signature）

一般应包括保险公司名称和法人代表的签字或印章。保险单经保险公司签章后方有效。

18. 其他说明

根据信用证的要求在保险单上加注其他说明。如"所有单据注明信用证号码、开证日期和开证行名称""保险单上显示保险公司在目的地的保险代理人名称、地址、联系方法"等。

19. 份数

正本份数（number of original policy）：根据 UCP 600 规定，正本保险单必须有"正本（ORIGINAL）"字样，并显示该套保险单据正本的份数。如信用证没有特别说明保险单份数时，保险公司一般出具一套三份正本的保险单，每份正本上分别印有"第一正本（THE FIRST ORIGINAL）""第二正本（THE SECOND ORIGINAL）"及"第三正本（THE THIRD ORIGINAL）"以示区别。如信用证没有特别规定交几份正本的，则必须向银行提交全套正本。如果保险单据未注明正本份数，而信用证也没有特别规定，出口公司一般提交一套完整的保险单（一份正本、一份复本），则银行可以接受只提交一份正本的保险单据，但该保险单据必须注明是唯一正本。正本保险单可经背书转让。

⏱ 实训任务

✎**任务一：** 根据下列资料填制保险单据。

（一）信用证资料

L/C NO.DATED：6104-309-2 NOV.27，2019

ORDER ACCOUNT：... MAHARASHTRA（INDIA）

IN FAVOUR OF：ZHEJIANG CATHAYA INTERNATIONAL CO. LTD

　　　　　　　　NO. 105 TIYUCHANG ROAD，HANGZHOU，CHINA

AMOUNT：USD 60,000.00

EVIDENCING SHIPMENT OF：

　　SILK WOVEN FABRICS NOT DYED AND NOT PRINTED

　　ART. NO. 10106 7510.60M　USD 2.40/M

　　ART. NO. 10109 5056.00M　USD 3.00/M

　　ART. NO. 11206 4925.20M　USD 2.00/M

　　ART. NO. 11160 5466.20M　USD 2.65/M

CIF CHENNAI BY SEA

SHIPMENT：FROM CHINESE NINGBO PORT TO CHENNAI WITH PARTIAL

SHIPMENTS AND TRANSSHIPMENT ALLOWED

DOCUMENTS：

+INSURANCE POLICY OR CERTIFICATE IN DUPLICATE ISSUED IN AN IRREVOCABLE FORM BLANK ENDORSED COVERING THE GOODS FOR INVOICE AMOUNT PLUS 10 PERCENT AGAINST THE FOLLOWING RISKS：ALL RISKS AND WAR RISKS AS PER OCEAN MARINE CARGO CLAUSES OF THE PICC DATED 1981-01-01 AND INSURANCE POLICY OR CERTIFICATE MUST BE VALID FOR 60 DAYS AFTER THE DISCHARGE OF GOODS FROM THE VESSEL AT THE PORT OF DESTINATION CLAIMS，IF ANY，PAYABLEAT CHENNAI.

...

（二）其他资料

THE GOODS ARE PACKED IN 32 CARTONS AND THE GOODS SHIPPED FROM NINGBO BY YUETKONG-542(S.S.) ON DEC. 30，2019.

SHIPPING MARKS：KSSAR/CHENNAI/NOS.1-UP

INVOICE NO：AG(29)88012

INVOICE DATE：DEC. 21，2019

中保财产保险有限公司

THE PEOPLE'S INSURANCE (PROPERTY) COMPANY OF CHINA，LTD

发票号码	保险单号次
INVOICE NO.	POLICY NO.

海 洋 货 物 运 输 保 险 单

MARINE CARGO TRANSPORTATION INSURANCE POLICY

被保险人 Insured	

中保财产保险有限公司(以下简称本公司)根据被保险人的要求,由被保险人向本公司缴付约定的保险费,按照本保险单承担险别和背面所载条款与下列特殊条款承保下述货物运输保险,特立本保险单。

This policy of insurance witnesses that the People's Insurance (Property) Company of China, Ltd (hereinafter called "the Company"), at the request of the insured and in consideration of the agreed premium being paid to the company by the insured, undertakes to insure the undermentioned goods in transportation subject to the conditions of this policy as per the clauses printed overleaf and other special clauses attached hereon.

保险货物项目 Description of Goods	包装 Packing	单位 Unit	数量 Quantity	保险金额 Amount Insured

承保险别 Conditions	货物标记 Marks of Goods

总保险金额 Total Amount Insured	

保费 Premium		载运输工具 Per Conveyance S.S.		开航日期 Slg. on or abt.	
起运港 From			目的港 To		

所保货物,如发生本保险单项下负责赔偿的损失或事故,应立即通知本公司下述代理人查勘。如遇出险,应向本公司提交保险单正本(本保险单共有　　份正本)及有关文件。如一份正本已用于索赔,其余正本则自动失效。

In the event of loss or damage which may result in acclaim under this policy, immediate notice must be given to the Company's Agent as mentioned hereunder. Claims，if any，one of the original policy which has been issued in　original(s) together with the relevant documents shall be surrendered to the Company. If one of the original policy has been accomplished，the others to be void.

赔款偿付地点 Claim Payable at		中保财产保险有限公司浙江分公司 The People's Insurance (Property) Company of China，Ltd Zhejiang Branch
日期 Date	在 at	
地址 Address		Authorized Signature

任务二： 根据下列资料填制保险单据。

（一）信用证资料

BENEFICIARY：ZHEJIANG RONGCHANG TRADING CO. LTD

           NO.222 HONGSHENG ROAD，HANGZHOU，CHINA

APPLICANT：LUCKY VICTORY INTERNATIONAL

           STUTTGART STIR. 5，

           D-84618，SCHORNDORF，GERMANY

L/C NO.：LC06-4-1520

DATE OF ISSUE：20191118

LOADING IN CHARGE：NINGBO

FOR TRANSPORTATION TO：HAMBURG

LATEST DATE OF SHIPMENT：20200103

DOCUMENTS REQUIRED：

    +INSURANCE POLICY ISSUED TO THE APPLICANT，COVERING RISKS AS PER INSTITUTE CARGO CLAUSE（A）INCLUDING WAREHOUSE TO WAREHOUSE CLAUSE UP TO FINAL DESTINATION AT SCHORNDORF，FOR AT LEAST 110 PCT OF THE CIF VALUE，MARKED PREMIUM PAID，SHOWING CLAIM PAYABLE IN GERMANY.

    ...

（二）销售合同资料

DESCRIPTION OF GOODS：MULBERRY RAW SILK

                    40/44   4/5A

SHIPPING MARKS：LUCKY/09HM23600256/HAMBURG/NO.1-UP

PACKING：IN CARTONS OF 50 KGS EACH

QUANTITY：3,000 KGS，10% MORE OR LESS AT THE SELLER'S OPTION

UNIT PRICE：USD 41.3/KG CIF HAMBURG

（三）商业发票资料

INVOICE NO.：OC01A0120045

INVOICE DATE：NOV. 29，2019

B/L DATE：DEC. 25，2019

VESSEL：SENATOR V. 872W

SHIPMENT QUANTITY：3,200 KGS

中国人民保险公司××分公司

海洋货物运输保险单

发票号次   第一正本   保险单号次

INVOICE NO.   **THE FIRST ORIGINAL**   POLICY NO.

    中国人民保险公司(以下简称本公司)根据_____(以下简称被保险人)的要求,由被保险人向本公司缴付约定的保险费,按照本保险单承保险别和背面所载条款与下列特殊条款承保下述货物运输保险,特立本保险单。

    This policy of insurance witnesses that People's Insurance Company of China (hereinafter called "the Company") at the request of_____(hereinafter called the "Insured") and in consideration of the agreed premium being paid to the Company by the Insured, undertakes to insure the undermentioned goods in transportation subject to the conditions of this policy as per the clauses printed overleaf and other special clauses attached hereon.

标　记 Marks & Nos.	包装及数量 Quantity	保险货物项目 Description of Goods	保险金额 Amount Insured

总保险金额

Total Amount Insured _____

保费   费率   装载运输工具

Premium as Arranged   Rate as Arranged   Per Conveyance S.S. _____

开航日期   自   至

Slg. on or abt._____   From _____   To _____

承保险别:

Conditions:

    所保货物,如遇出险,本公司凭第一正本保险单及其有关证件给付赔款。所保货物,如发生本保险单项下负责赔偿的损失或事故,应立即通知本公司下述代理人查勘。

    Claims, if any, payable on surrender of the first original of the policy together with other relevant documents. In the event of accident whereby loss or damage may result in a claim under this policy immediate notice applying for survey must be given to the Company's agent as mentioned hereunder.

中国人民保险公司××分公司

The People's Insurance Co. of China

××　　Branch

赔款偿付地点

Claim Payable at_____   _____

Date_____   Authorized Signature

✎**任务三：** 根据下列资料填制保险单据。

（一）销售合同资料

DESCRIPTION OF GOODS：

CARDBOARD BOX

YL-256　　2,000 PCS　　USD 4.50/PC CIF ICD BANGALORE

YL-258　　2,500 PCS　　USD 4.00/PC CIF ICD BANGALORE

SHIPPING MARKS：CTL/BANGALORE/NOS.1-UP

PACKING：IN CARTONS OF 50 PCS EACH

INSURANCE：IS TO BE COVERED BY THE SELLERS FOR 120％ OF THE INVOICE
　　　　　　　VALUE COVERING ALL RISKS AND WAR RISK AS PER CIC.

（二）信用证资料

BENEFICIARY：ZHEJIANG UNIK CO. LTD

NO.156 YILONG ROAD，PINGHU，ZHEJIANG，CHINA

L/C NO.：LC09678

DATE OF ISSUE：20191015

LOADING IN CHARGE：SHANGHAI

FOR TRANSPORTATION TO：ICD BANGALORE

LATEST DATE OF SHIPMENT：20191130

DOCUMENTS REQUIRED：

＋INSURANCE POLICY OR CERTIFICATE ENDORSED IN BLANK FOR
110％ OF CIF VALUE，COVERING WPA RISK AND WAR RISK AS PER CIC AND
INDICATING L/C NO. AND INSURANCE CHARGES.

...

（三）其他资料

INVOICE NO.：UNIK1810

INVOICE DATE：NOV. 10，2019

B/L DATE：NOV. 29，2019

VESSEL：HYUNDAI V.526W

INSURANCE CHARGES：USD 22.00

INSURANCE AGENT：

GLADSTONE AGENCIES LIMITED

BANGALORE　OFFICE

CITY POINT（THE 3RD FLOOR）

INFANTRY ROAD BANGALORE 560001 INDIA

TEL：0091-80-2899272 FAX：0091-80-2899273

MOBILE：0091-9844021011

中国人民保险公司××分公司
海洋货物运输保险单

发票号次	第一正本	保险单号次
INVOICE NO.	**THE FIRST ORIGINAL**	POLICY NO.

中国人民保险公司(以下简称本公司)根据_____(以下简称被保险人)的要求,由被保险人向本公司缴付约定的保险费,按照本保险单承保险别和背面所载条款与下列特殊条款承保下述货物运输保险,特立本保险单。

This policy of insurance witnesses that the People's Insurance Company of China(hereinafter called "the Company") at the request of _____ (hereinafter called the "Insured") and in consideration of the agreed premium being paid to the Company by the Insured, undertakes to insure the undermentioned goods in transportation subject to the conditions of this policy as per the clauses printed overleaf and other special clauses attached hereon。

标 记 Marks & Nos.	包装及数量 Quantity	保险货物项目 Description of Goods	保险金额 Amount Insured

总保险金额
Total Amount Insured _____

保费	费率	装载运输工具
Premium as Arranged	Rate as Arranged	Per Conveyance S.S. _____

开航日期　　　　　　　　　自　　　　　　　　　　　至
Slg. on or abt._____ From_____ To_____

承保险别:
Conditions:

所保货物,如遇出险,本公司凭第一正本保险单及其他有关证件给付赔款。所保货物,如发生本保险单项下负责赔偿的损失或事故,应立即通知本公司下述代理人查勘。

Claims, if any, payable on surrender of the first original of the policy together with other relevant documents. In the event of accident whereby loss or damage may result in a claim under this policy immediate notice applying for survey must be given to the Company's agent as mentioned hereunder.

中国人民保险公司××分公司
The People's Insurance Co. of China
××　Branch

赔款偿付地点
Claim Payable at_____

Date_____　　　　　　　　　　　Authorized Signature

任务四： 根据以下资料，审核并修改已填制的保险单，在已填制的 17 个栏目，即标号（1）—（17）中找出若干处填制错误，并说明原因。

（一）商业发票、装箱单的资料

EXPORT：SHANGHAI KOCI FRAGRANCE CO. LTD

NO.559 XINLIN ROAD，XINSHEN ECONIMY AREA，

FENGXIAN DISTRICT，SHANGHAI CHINA

IMPORT：PT. MANE INDONESIA

INVOICE NO. 19-000005

L/C NO.：GDF205506

PORT OF LOADING：SHANGHAI, CHINA

PORT OF DESTINATION：JAKARTA, INDONESIA

SHIPPING MARKS：PJF

MEANS OF TRANSPORT：BY SEA

TTL N.WEIGHT：1,700 KGS

TTL G.WEIGHT：1,800 KGS

TERMS OF PRICE：CIF JAKARTA

UNIT PRICE：USD 3.7/ KGS

TOTAL AMOUNT：USD 6,290.00

NOS. & KIND OF PACKAGE：10 DRUMS

（二）信用证、提单的资料

CONDITIONS：INSURANCE POLICY COVERING MARINE TRANSPORTATION ALL

RISKS AS PER ICC（A），INCLUDING WAREHOUSE TO WAREHOUSE RISKS

INDICATING INSURANCE RATE AND PREMIUM.

船名、航次：YM NAGOYA V.11S，提单号：EURFL18N05345JAK

起运港：SHANGHAI, CHINA，卸货港：JAKARTA, INDONESIA

件数及包装：10 DRUMS，TEN（10）DRUMS ONLY

毛重：1,800 KGS

货物描述：ALLYL HEXANOATE，开船日：NOV. 20，2019

（三）合同及其他资料

保险费费率：2.5%

赔款偿付地点：JAKARTA，INDONESIA

保险经纪人：中国人民财产保险股份有限公司,徐浏

（四）已填制的保险单

PICC 中国人民财产保险股份有限公司
PICC Property and Casualty Company Limited
货物运输保险单
CARGO TRANSPORTATION INSURANCE POLICY

发票号码(1)　　　　　　　　　　　　　保险单号次
INVOICE NO. 19-000005　　　　　　　POLICY NO. PYIE20193201930000142

被保险人：(2)　SHANGHAI　KOCI　FRAGRANCE CO. LTD

　　　中国人民财产保险股份有限公司(以下简称本公司)根据被保险人的要求,由被保险人向本公司缴付约定的保险费,按照本保险单承担险别和背面所载条款与下列特别条款承保下列货物运输保险,特立本保险单。

　　　This policy of Insurance witnesses that the PICC Property and Casualty Company Ltd (hereinafter called "the Company")at the request of the Insured and in consideration of the agreed premium being paid to the Company by the Insured, undertakes to insure the undermentioned goods in transportation subject to the conditions of the policy as per the clauses printed overleaf and other special clauses attached hereon.

标　记(3) Marks & Nos.	包装及数量(4) Quantity	保险货物项目(5) Description of Goods	保险金额(6) Amount Insured
PJF	10 DRUMS	ALLYL HEXANOATE	USD 6,919.00

总保险金额(7)
Total Amount Insured　US DOLLARS SIX THOUSAND NINE HUNDRED AND NINETEEN ONLY

保费(8)　　　　　　费率(9)　　　　装载运输工具(10)
PremiumUSD 172.98　Rate 2.5%　　Per Conveyance S.S. YM NAGOYA V.11S

开航日期(13)　　　　　　　　　自(11)　　　　　　至(12)
Slg. on or abt.　NOV. 20, 2019　From　SHANGHAI　To　JAKARTA

承保险别(14)
Conditions：ALL RISKS

　　　所保货物,如发生本保险单项下负责赔偿的损失或事故,应立即通知本公司下述代理人查勘。如遇出险,应向本公司提交保正本险单(本保险单共有　2　份正本)及有关文件。如一份正本已用于索赔,其余正本则自动失效。

　　　In the event of loss or damage which may result in a claim under this policy, immediate notice must be given to the Company's agent as mentioned hereunder. Claims, if any, one of the original policy which has been issued in two original(s)together with the relevant documents shall be surrendered to the Company. If one of the original policy has been accomplished, the others to be void.

赔款偿付地点(15)
Claim Payable at　HONG KONG
日期、地点(16)
Date　NOV. 21, 2019　SHANGHAI

PICC 中国人民财产保险股份有限公司
浙江分公司国际保险营业部
PICC Property and Casualty Company Ltd
Zhejiang Branch Int'l Ins. Division
徐浏
Authorized Signature(17)

任务五： 根据以下资料，审核并修改已填制的保险单。

（一）相关资料

买方：QINGDAO ECONOMIC TRADE INT'L CO. LTD

　　　NO. 19，ZHUZHOU ROAD，QINGDAO

卖方：VICTOR MACHINERY INDUSTRY CO. LTD

　　　NO.338，BA DE STREET，SHU LIN CITY，TAIBEI

TEL/FAX：886-2-26689666/26809123

发票号：FU1011103

船名、航次：YMHORIZON V.018

装船日期：MAY 10，2019

装运港：TAIWAN MAIN PORT

目的港：QINGDAO

唛头：E.T.I

　　　QINGDAO

　　　NOS.1-UP

保险单号：PO9810101

保险单日期：MAY 8，2019

发票金额：USD 25,200.00

保险金额：按发票金额的110％投保

货物描述：ONE COMPLETE SET OF SHEET CUTTER

毛重：15,600 KGS

体积：51 CBM

包装：PACKED IN TWO WOODEN CASES

贸易术语：CIF QINGDAO

投保险别：COVERING ALL RISKS AND WAR RISK AS PER CIC.

赔付地点：QINGDAO

（二）已填制的保险单

ASIA INSURANCE
A Member of Asia Financial Group

海 洋 货 物 运 输 保 险 单
MARINE CARGO TRANSPORTATION INSURANCE POLICY

Invoice No.FU1011108	Policy No. PO9810107

Insured：QINGDAO ECONOMIC TRADE INT'L CO. LTD

亚洲保险有限公司(以下简称本公司)根据被保险人的要求,由被保险人向本公司缴付约定的保险费,按照本保险单承保险别和背面所载条款与下列特殊条款承保下述货物运输保险,特立本保险单。

This policy of Insurance witnesses that the Asia Insurance Co. Ltd (hereinafter called "the Company"), at the request of the Insured and in consideration of the agreed premium being paid to the company by the Insured, undertakes to insure the undermentioned goods in transportation subject to conditions of the policy as per the clauses printed overleaf and other special clauses attached hereon.

货物标记 Marks of Goods	包装单位 Packing Unit	保险货物项目 Description of Goods	保险金额 Amount Insured
E.T.I QINGDAO NOS.1-5	5 WOODEN CASES	ONE COMPLETE SET OF SHEET CUTTER	USD 25,200.00

总保险金额
Total Amount Insured：SAY U.S. DOLLARS TWENTY FIVE THOUSAND AND TWO HUNDRED ONLY.

保费 Premium AS ARRANGED	开航日期 Slg. on or abt. MAY 13, 2019	载运输工具 Per Conveyance S.S. YM HORIZON V. 018

承保险别
Conditions
COVERING ALL RISKS AND WAR RISK AS PER CIC DATED 01/01/1981.

起运港 Form QINGDAO To	目的港 KEELUNG

所保货物,如发生本保险单项下负责赔偿的损失或事故,应立即通知本公司下述代理人查勘。如遇出险,应向本公司提交保险单正本(本保险单共有 2 份正本)及有关文件。如一份正本已用于索赔,其余正本则自动失效。

In the event of loss or damage which may result in a claim under this policy, immediate notice must be given to the Company's agent as mentioned hereunder. Claims, if any, one of the original policy which has been issued in two original(s) together with the relevant documents shall be surrendered to the Company. If one of the original policy has been accomplished, the others to be void.

赔款偿付地点
Claim payable at   KEELUNG IN USD

日期 Date MAY 15, 2019	亚洲保险有限公司台北分公司 Asia Insurance Co. Ltd, Taibei Branch Lucy

项目六　原产地证书填制

实训目标

能够根据有关资料填制一般原产地证明书和普惠制产地证。

实训指导

一、一般原产地证明书填制说明

《中华人民共和国出口货物原产地证明书》采用 EDI 推荐标准,各栏目的技术标准执行国家技术监督局推荐标准。在证书右上角填上证书编号。此栏不得留空,否则,证书无效。一般原产地证明书各栏目的内容填制如下。

一般原产地证明书的填制

1. 出口方(exporter)

填写出口方名称、详细地址及国家(地区),此栏不得留空。出口方名称是指出口申报方名称,一般填有效合同的卖方或发票的出票人。若经其他国家或地区转口需要填写中间商时,应在出口商后面加填英文"VIA",然后再填写中间商名称、地址、国家(地区)。此栏不能直接填写境外中间商,即使信用证有此规定也不行。

2. 收货方(consignee)

填写最终收货方的名称、详细地址及国家(地区),通常是外贸合同中的买方或提单的通知人。但由于贸易的需要,信用证会规定所有单证收货人一栏留空,在这种情况下,此栏应填"to whom it may concern"或"to order",但不得留空。有中间商的同第一栏,即在收货人后面加填英文"VIA",然后再填写中间商名称、地址、国家(地区)。

3. 运输方式和路线(means of transport and route)

填写装货港、到货港及运输方式(如海运、陆运、空运)。如经转运,应注明转运地。该栏一般还要填明预计离开中国的日期,日期必须真实,不得捏造。

4. 目的国或地区(country/region of destination)

指货物最终运抵目的地国家(地区),一般应与最终收货人或最终目的港的国别(地区)一致,不能填写中间商国家名称。

5. 签证机构用栏(for certifying authority use only)

此栏为签证机构在签发后发证书、补发证书或加注其他声明时使用。证书申领单位应将此栏留空。

6. 运输标志(marks and numbers)

按照出口发票上所列唛头填写完整图案、文字标记及包装号码,不可简单地填写"按照发票(as per invoice No. …)"或者"按照提单(as per B/L No. …)"。货物无唛头,则填写"N/M"。此栏不得留空。如果唛头太多,本栏填写不下,可填写在第七、八、九栏的空白处;如还不够,可用附页填写。

7. 商品名称、包装数量及种类(description of goods;number and kind of packages)

商品名称要填写具体名称(能明确归类到 H.S.品目四位数),不得用概括性表述。如:网球拍(tennis racket),不能用运动用品(sporting goods)。

包装数量及种类要按具体单位填写,包装数量应在阿拉伯数字后加注英文表述。如:100 箱彩电,填写为"100 cartons (one hundred cartons only) of colour TV set"。如货物系散装,在商品名称后加注"IN BULK (散装)",例如:1000 公吨生铁,填写为"1,000 M/T(one thousand M/T only)pig iron in bulk"。

本栏的末行要打上表示结束的符号(＊＊＊＊＊＊),以防添加内容。信用证要求填写合同、信用证号码等内容的,可填在结束符号下的空白处。

8. 商品编码(H.S. code)

填写 H.S.编码。若同一证书包含有几种商品,则应将相应的税目号全部填写。填报 10 位商品编码时,最后两位为补充编码。此栏不得留空。

9. 数量(quantity)

此栏应以商品的正常计量单位填,如"只""件""双""台""打"等。以重量计算的则填毛重和(或)净重。

10. 发票号码及日期(number and date of invoices)

此栏分两行写,第一行为发票号码,第二行为发票日期,月份一律用英文(可用缩写)表示。

11. 出口商的声明、签字、盖章(declaration by the exporter)

出口商声明已印好,声明内容为:"下列签署人在此声明,上述货物详细情况与声明是正确的,所有货物均在中国生产,完全符合中华人民共和国原产地规则。"

此栏由出口公司填写申报地点和日期,并由已在签证机构注册的人员签字并加盖有中英文的印章。签字人员应是申请单位的法人代表或由法人代表指定的其他人员,并应保持相对稳定。申报日期不得早于发票日期(第十栏),同时不能迟于装运日期。

12. 签证机构证明、签字、盖章(certification)

签证机构证明文句也是事先印好的,内容为:"兹证明出口商声明是正确的。"所申请的证书,经签证机构审核人员审核无误后,由授权的签证人在此栏手签姓名并盖签证机构章,注明签署的时间和地点。盖章和签名不能重合。签发日期不得早于发票日期(第十栏)和申请日期(第十一栏)。

13. 其他说明

根据信用证要求加具的其他说明,如合同号、信用证号码等,可加在第七栏结束符下空白处。

二、普惠制产地证填制说明

根据 2018 年《国务院机构改革方案》，原国家质量监督检验检疫总局的出入境检验检疫管理职责和队伍划入海关总署。普惠制产地证的签证管理部门由原国家质量监督检验检疫总局变更为海关总署，签证机构中的各地出入境检验检疫机构变更为各直属海关。各直属海关于 2018 年 8 月 20 日正式启用新版证书和签证印章，8 月 20 日前原检验检疫机构签发的旧版证书仍有效。新版证书将原证书防伪印记中的 AQSIQ 改为中国海关关徽，去掉原证书左下角印刷流水号中的 AQSIQ，证书格式、内容和背页注释保持不变。印章为 42 个直属海关名称，将原印章中原直属检验检疫局中英文名称调整为对应直属海关中英文名称。

普惠制产地证各栏目的内容填制如下。

1. 出口商名称、地址、国家（goods consigned from）

此栏带有强制性，填中国境内的详细地址，包括街道名、门牌号码等。此栏不可填中间商信息。

2. 收货人名称、地址、国家（goods consigned to）

填给惠国最终收货人名称、地址、国家。如最终收货人不明确，则填发票抬头人或提单通知人，不得留空。除日本、加拿大、澳大利亚、新西兰外，如最终收货人不明确，此栏也可填"to order"或"to whom it may concern"。此栏不可填中间商名称。

3. 运输方式及路线（就所知而言）（means of transport and route）

填装货港、到货港及运输方式（如海运、陆运、空运）。如经转运，应注明转运地。该栏一般还要填明预计离开中国的日期，日期必须真实，不得捏造。

4. 供官方使用（for official use）

此栏由签证当局填写，企业申报时留空。正常情况下此栏空白。

5. 商品顺序号（item number）

填写商品顺序号。如同批出口货物有不同品种，则按不同品种分列"1""2""3"……，以此类推。单项商品，此栏填"1"。

6. 唛头及包装号（marks and numbers of packages）

按照出口发票上所列唛头填写完整，不可简单的填写，不得只写"as per invoice"或"as per B/L"。唛头不得出现在中国境外国家或地区制造的字样，也不能出现香港、澳门、台湾原产地字样。如货物无唛头，应填写 N/M（no mark）。此栏不得留空，内容多可用附页，此栏填写"see attachment"。

7. 包件数量及种类，商品名称（number and kind of packages，description of gaols）

包装数量必须同时用英文和阿拉伯数字表示，散装货物加注"in bulk"。商品名称必须具体填明，不能笼统填写"machine""garment"等。商品名称列完后，应在下一行加结束符（＊＊＊＊＊）。信用证要求填具合同、信用证号码等内容的，可填在结束符下空白处。

8. 原产地标准（origin criterion）

此栏用字最少，却是国外海关审核的核心项目。原产地标准符号的一般填法如下。

（1）完全原产品，不含任何非原产成分，出口到所有给惠国，填"P"。

（2）含有非原产成分的产品，出口到欧盟[1]、挪威、瑞士、列支敦士登、日本[2]、土耳其的，填"W"，后加四位 H.S.编码，如"W"4202。条件：①产品列入上述给惠国的"加工清单"，符合其加工条件；②产品未列入"加工清单"，但产品生产过程中使用的非原产原材料和零部件已经过实质加工，产品的 H.S.税目号不同于所有的原材料或零部件的 H.S.税目号。

（3）含有非原产成分的产品，出口到加拿大，填"F"。条件：非原产成分的价值未超过产品出厂价的 40%。

（4）含有非原产成分的产品，出口到俄罗斯、白俄罗斯、乌克兰、哈萨克斯坦，填"Y"，后加非原产成分价值占产品离岸价的百分比，如"Y"48%。条件：非原产成分的价值未超过产品离岸价的 50%。

（5）含有非原产成分的产品，销往澳大利亚、新西兰的商品，此栏留空。条件：原产成分的价值不少于该产品工厂成本价的 50%。

9. 毛重或其他数量（gross weight or other quantity）

此栏应以商品的正常计量单位填，如"只""件""双""台""打"等。以重量计算的则填毛重，只有净重的，填净重亦可，但要标上 N.W.。

10. 发票号码及日期（number and date of irvoice）

分两行写，第一行为发票号码，第二行为发票日期，月份一律用英文（可用缩写）表示。

11. 签证当局的证明（certification）

签证机构的证明事先已印好，内容为：兹证明出口商的声明是正确无误的，本批货物已有承运人运出。

此栏签证机构批注四项内容。

（1）签证当局公章：签证当局只签发正本，副本不予签字、盖章。

（2）海关签证人经审核后在此栏（正本）签名。

（3）签证日期：此栏日期不得早于发票日期（第十栏）和申报日期（第十二栏），而且应早于货物的出运日期（第三栏）。

（4）签证地点：具体的城市名。出证日期和地点由申报单位填写。

---

[1]　2015 年 1 月 1 日起，欧盟取消中国出口产品普惠制关税待遇。

[2]　2019 年 4 月 1 日起，日本不再给予中国输日货物普惠制关税待遇。

12. 出口商的声明(declaration by the exporter)

在生产国横线上填英文的"中国(CHINA)"。进口国横线上填最终进口国,进口国必须与第三栏目的港的国别一致。凡货物运往欧盟范围内,进口国不明确时,进口国可填EU。

另外,申请单位应授权专人在此栏手签,标上申报地点、日期,并加盖申请单位中英文印章(正副本均须手签并盖章)。手签人手迹须在直属海关注册备案,并保持相对稳定。

此栏日期不得早于发票日期(第十栏)(最早是同日)。盖章时应避免覆盖进口国名称和手签人姓名。本证书一律不得涂改,证书不得加盖校对章。

13. 其他说明

根据信用证要求加具的其他说明,如合同号、信用证号码等,可加在第七栏结束符下空白处。

⏱ 实训任务

🔖 **任务一: 根据下列资料填制产地证。**

宁波摩士轴承厂欲销往瑞士苏黎世一批由本厂生产的轴承,总价5,666.87美元,净重800 KGS,纸箱装,每箱净重100 KGS,由宁波始发,交货条件CIF ZURICH SWITZERLAND。由于瑞士是中国的给惠国,且该产品在给惠范围之内,因此该公司为获得普惠制待遇于出口装运前申领原产地证明。

(一)信用证资料

L/C NO.:CPP0000E

EXPIRY:20191227,CHINA

AMOUNT:USD 5,666.87

APPLICANT:FERNANDO DE BESSA MOREIRA,LDAVIA SA CARNEIRO-Z IND, MAIA I-SEC IX LOTE 29-GUARDA-MOREIRA-4470 MALA

BENEFICIARY:NINGBO MOSS BEARING CO. LTD,640 ZHENLUO ROAD (WEST),ZHENHAI DISTRICT,NINGBO,CHINA

PORT OF SHIPMENT:NINGBO,CHINA

PORT OF DISCHARGE:ZURICH,SWITZERLAND

SHIPMENT DATE:LATEST BY DEC. 1, 2019

COVERING:ROLAMENTOS (BEARINGS),800 KGS AS PER S/C NO. BB3887 NOV.1,2019

SHIPPING MARK:JOSEPHINE/ZURICH/SWITZERLAND/NO.1-UP

REQUIRED DOCUMENTS:

+ GSPORIGINAL CERTIFICATE IMPLYING THE COVERING GOODS PRODUCED IN CHINA，IN TRIPLICATE．

（二）其他资料

INVOICE NO.：INV123

INVOICE DATE：NOV.18，2019

B/L DATE：NOV. 30，2019

VESSEL/VOYAGE：HANJIN OTTAWA V.045E

REFERENCE NO.：G183300023456712

1. Goods Consigned from （exporter's business name, address, country）	Reference No. GENERALIZED SYSTEM OF PREFERENCES CERTIFICATE OF ORIGIN （combined declaration and certificate） FORM A Issued in THE PEOPLE'S REPUBLIC OF CHINA （country）
2. Goods Consigned to （consignee's name, address, country）	See Notes Overleaf
3.Means of Transport and Route (as far as known)	4. For Official Use

5.Item Number	6.Marks and Numbers of Packages	7.Number and Kind of Package; Description of Goods	8.Origin Criterion (see notes overleaf)	9.Gross Weight or Other Quantity	10.Number and Date of Invoice

11.Certification It is hereby certified, on the basis of control carried out, that the declaration by the exporter is correct.	12. Declaration by the Exporter The undersigned hereby declares that the above details and statements are correct; that all the goods were produced in CHINA and that they comply with the origin （country） requirements specified for those goods in the Generalized System for Preferences for goods exported to _____. (importing country)
Place and Date, Signature and Stamp of Certifying Authority	Place and Date, Signature of Authorized Signatory

任务二： 根据下列资料填制产地证。

宁波粮油进出口公司向法国出口一批化学原料酪蛋白36MT，交易条件为CIF。出口公司于2019年2月22日向有关当局申请产地证，并于次日获批。

（一）信用证资料

DOC. CREDIT：IRREVOCABLE

CREDIT NUMBER：3/0146/35

DATE OF ISSUE：20190210

EXPIRY DATE：20190321 PLACE AT CHINA

APPLICANT：F-I-T FRANCE INTERNATIONAL TRADE

        NO. 24 AVENUE HENRI FREVILLE，35200 RENNES-FRANCE

BENEFICIARY：COFCO NINGBO CEREALS AND OILS IMP. AND EXP. CO LTD

        7 FLOOR，NO. 503 DAQING ROAD（NORTH），NINGBO，CHINA

AMOUNT：CURRENCY USD AMOUNT 82,800

AVAILABLE WITH：BY PAYMENT AGAINST DOCUMENTS RECEIVED IN

        COMFORMITY AS PER U INSTRUCTIONS BY PAYMENT

PARTIAL SHIPMENT：ALLOWED

TRANSSHIPMENT：NOT ALLOWED

PORT IN CHARGE：ANY CHINESE PORT

TRANSPORT TO：ROTTERDAM，THE NETHERLANDS

LATEST DATE OF SHIP：20190228

DESCRIPTION OF GOODS：

36 MT INDUSTRIAL CASEIN SECOND GRADE CHINESE ORIGIN ALL SPECIFICATIONS ACCORDING TO BUYER'S CONTRACT REF NO.02980038 DATED FEB. 09，2019 AND PACKED IN MULTIPLY PAPER BAGS LINED WITH POLY STRAP OF 25 KGS NET WEIGHT AT PRICE OF USD 2,300/M. T.（-MOISTURE 12％，MAXIMUM -FAT 02％ MAXIMUM -ASH 03％ MAXIMUM -FREE ACIDITY 100T，MAXIMUM -PROTEIN 80％，MAXIMUM，ORIGIN CHINA）.

CIF ROTTERDAM，SOUTH HOLLAND，THE NETHERLANDS

DOCUMENTS REQUIRED：

+SIGNED COMMERCIAL INVOICE IN TRIPLICATE.

+CERTIFICATE OF ORIGIN SIGNED BY OFFICIAL RECOGNIZED AUTHORTIES IN P. R. CHINA.

+FULL SET OF CLEAN ON BOARD OCEAN BILL OF LADING ISSUED TO ORDER OF APPLICANT NOTIFY ACCOUNTEE AND MARKED FREIGHT PREPAID.

（二）其他资料

INVOICE NO.：BP919A530016

INVOICE DATE：FEB. 20，2019

B/L DATE：FEB. 28，2019

H.S. CODE：35011000.00

CERTIFICATE NO.：CCPIT180018751

MARKS：按标准唛头自行设计

1.Exporter (full name and address)	Certificate No.
	CERTIFICATE OF ORIGIN **OF** **THE PEOPLE'S REPUBLIC OF CHINA**
2.Consignee (full name and address)	
3.Means of Transport and Route	5.For Certifying Authority Use Only
4.Country/Region of Destination	

6.Marks and Numbers	7.Number and Kind of Package；Description of Goods	8.H.S. Code	9.Quantity	10.Number and Date of Invoices

11.Declaration by the Exporter The undersigned hereby declares that the above details and statements are correct；that all the goods were produced in China and that they comply with the Rules of Origin of the People's Republic of China.	12.Certification It is hereby certified that the declaration by the exporter is correct.
—————————————————————— Place and Date，Signature and Stamp of Authorized Signatory	—————————————————————— Place and Date，Signature and Stamp of Certifying Authority

✎**任务三：** 根据下列资料填制产地证。

（一）信用证资料

FROM：ROYAL BANK OF CANADA，MONTREAL BRANCH

TO：BANK OF CHINA，ZHEJIANG BRANCH

FORM OF DOC.：IRREVOCABLE TRANSFERABLE

DOC NO.：DC HMN927739

DATE OF ISSUE：SEP. 24，2019

APPLICABLE RULES：UCP LATEST VERSION

EXPIRY DATE AND PLACE：DEC. 30，2019 IN COUNTRY

OF BENEFICIARIES

APPLICANT：POINT ZERO GIRLS CLUB INC.

NO. 1650 CHABANEL WEST，MONTREAL，QUEBEC

CANADA H4N 3M8

BENEFICIARY：ZHEJIANG CATHAYA INTERNATIONAL CO. LTD

NO. 105 TIYU CHANG ROAD，HANGZHOU，ZHEJIANG

CHINA 310004

DCAMT：USD 147，600.00

PCT CR AMT TOLERANCE：05/05

PARTIAL SHIPMENTS：SEE BELOW

TRANSSHIPMENT：ALLOWED

TAKE CHARGE/RECEIPT/DISP FM：SHANGHAI, CHINA

FINAL DEST/DELIVERY/TRNSP TO：MONTREAL，QUEBEC，CANADA

LATEST DATE OF SHIPMENT：DEC. 25，2019

GOODS：LADY'S SWEATER

ALO099　50％RAYON，32％COTTON，2％SPANDEX

24，000.00 PCS AT USD 6.15/PC FOB SHANGHAI, CHINA

DOCUMENTS REQUIRED：

＋CERTIFICATE OF ORIGIN SHOWING COUNTRY OF ORIGIN.

…

ADDITIONAL CONDITIONS ：

＋ALL DOCUMENTS SHOULD INDICATE L/C NO.L/C DATE AND NAME

OF ISSUING BANK.

（二）其他资料

本批出货数量：14,400 PCS，300 CARTONS

INVOICE NO.：BP919A530016

INVOICE DATE：DEC.11，2019

B/L DATE：DEC.19，2018

VESSEL/VOYAGE：HANJINOTTAWA V.073E

H.S. CODE：61043900

CERTIFICATE NO.：CCPIT181234567

SHIPPING MARKS：

　　POINT ZERO/STYLE NO.：ALO099/ QTY：/N.W.：/G.W.：/MEAS.：/CARTON NO：

1.Exporter	Certificate No.
	CERTIFICATE OF ORIGIN **OF** **THE PEOPLE'S REPUBLIC OF CHINA**
2.Consignee	
3.Means of Transport and Route	5.For certifying authority use only
4.Country/Region of Destination	

6.Marks and Numbers	7.Number and Kind of Package; Description of Goods	8.H.S. Code	9.Quantity	10.Number and Date of Invoices

11.Declaration by the Exporter The undersigned hereby declares that the above details and statements are correct; that all the goods were produced in China and that they comply with the Rules of Origin of the People's Republic of China.	12.Certification It is hereby certified that the declaration by the exporter is correct.
——————————————— Place and Date, Signature and Stamp of Authorized Signatory	——————————————— Place and Date, Signature and Stamp of Certifying Authority

✎**任务四**： 根据以下资料，审核并修改已填制的普惠制产地证明书 FORM A，在已填制的 16 个栏目中，即标号（1）—（16）中找出若干处填制错误，并说明原因。

（一）背景

上海某进出口公司 SHANGHAI ABC I/E CO. 接受服装厂 SHANGHAI SHENGDA GARMENT CO. LTD 委托，代理出口货物 50000 件全棉男衬衫至日本东京。该产品的面料由日本进口商提供，款式也由日本设计师提供，上海工厂加工后返销日本。该外贸公司于 2018 年 3 月 5 日，持填制完毕的普惠制产地证证明申请书一份，普惠制产地证明书 FORM A 一份和商业发票一份、向出入境检验检疫局申请办理普惠制产地证。

（二）商业发票、装箱单的资料

INVOICE NO.：01-00534

INVOICE DATE：MAR. 5，2018

TO：DI BAUE JAPAN INC.

　　7-1 IHONBASHI AKOZAKI-CHO，CHUO KU，TOKYO，JAPAN

ISSUED BY：SHANGHAI ABC I/E COMPANY

　　　　　NO.12345 WANPING ROAD，SHANGHAI，CHINA

SHIPPING MARKS：D.B./TOKYO/NO.1-UP

DESCRIPTIONS：MEN'S 100% COTTON WOVEN SHIRTS

QUANTITY：50,000 PCS /1,500 CTNS/1,500 KGS/10 CBM

（三）补充资料

装运港：SHANGHAI

目的港：TOKYO

船名航次：QIANZHENG HAO V.002

开船日：2018 年 3 月 9 日

签证机构：中华人民共和国上海出入境检验检疫局

贸易方式：来料加工

签证号码：G18000330036

商品编码：62052000.99

（四）已填制的普惠制产地证

1. Goods Consigned from（exporter's business name，address，country）(1) SHANGHAI SHENGDA GARMENT CO. LTD			Reference No.（4） SHZ/00033/0036 **GENERALIZED SYSTEM OF PREFERENCES** **CERTIFICATE OF ORIGIN** （combined declaration and certificate） **FORM A**		
2.Goods Consigned to（consignee's name，address，country）(2) DI BAUE JAPAN INC. 7-1 IHONBASHI AKOZAKI-CHO CHUO KU，TOKYO，JAPAN			Issued in（5）THE PEOPLE'S REPUBLIC OF CHINA （country） See Notes Overleaf		
3.Means of Transport and Route（as far as known）(3) SHIPMENT BY VESSEL FROM SHANGHAI, CHINA TO TOKYO, JAPAN			4. For Official Use（6）		
5.Item Number (7)	6.Marks and Numbers of Packages(8) D.B. TOKYO NO.1-50000	7.Number and Kind of Package；Description of Goods(9) ONE THOUSAND FIVE HUNDRED CARTONS OF MEN'S 100％ COTTON WOVEN SHIRTS	8.Origin Criterion（see notes overleaf）(10) "P"	9.Gross Weight or Other Quantity(11) 1,500 KGS	10. Number and Date of Invoices (12) 01-00543 MAR. 5，2018
11.Certification(13) It is hereby certified，on the basis of control carried out，that the declaration by the exporter is correct. CIQ Shanghai 丁三 MAR.9，2018 --------------- Place and Date，Signature and Stamp of Certifying Authority			12. Declaration by the Exporter The undersigned hereby declares that the above details and statements are correct；that all the goods were produced in CHINA（14）and that they comply （country） with the origin requirements specified for those goods in the Generalized System of Preferences for goods exported to _____ （15）. （importing country） Shanghai ABC I/E Company Shanghai MAR.9，2018 韦明 --------------- Place and Date，Signature of Authorized Signatory (16)		

✎**任务五：** 根据以下资料，审核并修改已填制的普惠制产地证明书 FORM A，在已填制的 16 个栏目中，即标号（1）—（16）中找出若干处填制错误，并说明原因。

（一）信用证、发票、提单资料

ISSUING BANK：DONTUSU COMMERCIAL BANK TOKYO，JAPAN

L/C NO.：KKT5846172

ISSUING DATE：OCT.15，2019

BENEFICIARY：SHANGHAI MACHINERY IMP.& EXP.CORP.(GROUP)

　　　　　　　NO. 726 CHUNGSHAN ROAD E.1.，SHANGHAI，CHINA

APPLICANT：SHITAYA KINZOKU CO. LTD

　　　　　　6-11-7-CHOME UENO TAITO-KU TOKYO，JAPAN

AMOUNT：USD 15,880.00

SHIPMENT：FROM SHANGHAI FOR TRANSPORTATION TO YOKOHAMA

　　　　　FOR 20 FT CONTAINER

COVERING SHIPMENT OF："RABBIT" BRAND SHOVEL WITH WOODEN

　　　　　　　　HANDLE，S501 MH 210 DOZS AND S503 MH 200

　　　　　　　　DOZS AS PER S/C NO. A9700247

TRADE TERM：CIF YOKOHAMA

SHIPPING MARKS：A9700247/YOKOHAMA/NO.1-UP

INVOICE NO.：GD920059

INVOICE DATE：NOV.2，2019

MANUFACTURER：SHANGHAI CHONGMING FARMING TOOL FACTORY

PACKING：1 DOZ/CTN

VESSEL：HANGTUV.0134

CONTAINER NO.：1×20'FCL SCZU7854343

H.S. CODE：82011000.10

CERTIFICATE NO.：G180723451

B/L NO.：GK101024

B/L DATE：NOV.18，2019

ART NO.	UNIT PRICE	N.W.	G.W.	MEAS.
S501 MH	USD 40.00/DOZ	@24.00 KGS/CTN	@25.00 KGS/CTN	@(97×36×23) CBM/CTN
S503 MH	USD 37.40/DOZ	@22.00 KGS/CTN	@23.00 KGS/CTN	@(97×36×25) CBM/CTN

（二）已填制的普惠制产地证

1. Goods Consigned from （exporter's business name，address，country）（1） SHANGHAI MACHINERY IMP. & EXP. CORP. NO.726 CHONGSHAN ROAD E.1.， SHANGHAI，CHINA	Reference No.（4）GD920059 **GENERALIZED SYSTEM OF PREFERENCES CERTIFICATE OF ORIGIN** （combined declaration and certificate） **FORM A**
2.Goods Consigned to (consignee's name, address, country)（2） 6-11-7-CHOME UENO TAITO-KU TOKYO，JAPAN	Issued in（5）THE PEOPLE'S REPUBLIC OF CHINA　　　（country） See Notes Overleaf
3.Means of Transport and Route (as far as known)（3） FROM SHANGHAI TO KOBE BY SEA	4. For official Use（6）

5.Item Number（7）	6.Marks and Numbers of Packages（8）A9700247 YOKOAMA NO.1-410	7. Number and Kind of Package；Description of Goods(9) "RABBIT" BRAND SHOVEL WITH METAL HANDLE 410 CTNS	8.Origin Criterion (see notes overleaf)（10） "P"	9.Gross Weight or Other Quantity（11） 9,850 KGS	10. Number and Date of Invoices（12） SH07/ 2345/12345 NOV. 2, 2019

11.Certification(13) It is hereby certified，on the basis of control carried out，that the declaration by the exporter is correct. THE PEOPLE'S REPUBLIC OF CHINA SHANGHAI CUSTOMS Shanghai OCT. 26，2019　××× ———————————————— Place and Date，Signature and Stamp of Certifying Authority	12. Declaration by the Exporter The undersigned hereby declares that the above details and statements are correct；that all the goods were produced in CHINA（14）and that they comply with 　　　（country） the origin requirements specified for those goods in the Generalized System of Preferences for goods exported to 　　TOKYO　　（15）. 　　（importing country） Shanghai Machinery Imp.& Exp.Corp.(Group) Shanghai OCT. 26，2019 陈浩 ———————————————— Place and Date，Signature of Authorized Signatory（16）

项目七　运输单据填制

实训目标

能够根据有关资料填制海运提单和航空运单。

实训指导

一、海运提单填制说明

不同船公司签发的海运提单的正面格式有所不同,其正面需填制的栏目说明如下。

1. 托运人(shipper)

托运人是委托运输的人,一般是合同的卖方。

信用证方式下,一般填写信用证中的受益人名称和地址。如果信用证受益人未规定地址,也可以不加注地址。如果信用证规定做成第三者提单(third party B/L),也可照办。

托收方式下,以托收的委托人,即卖方为托运人。

2. 收货人(consignee)

此栏又称为抬头栏,应严格按照合同和信用证的有关规定填写。本栏有记名式收货人、不记名式收货人和指示式收货人三种填写方法。

(1) 记名式收货人:此栏填写某人或某企业的具体名称,如信用证条款为"full set of B/L consigned to D.E. Company",则此栏填写"D.E. Company"。这种提单只有指定收货人可以提货,不能转让,流通性差但安全性好。

(2) 不记名式收货人:此栏空白不填或仅填写"to bearer"。这种提单谁持有谁就可以提货,转让时也不必背书,流通性好但风险较大,目前国际上很少使用。

(3) 指示式收货人:提示式的收货人又可分为不记名提示式(to order)和记名提示式(to order of...)两种。

①to order:凭指示或称空白抬头,如信用证条款为"full set of B/L made out to order",则此栏填写"to order"。这种提单需由托运人在提单背面背书,才可以转让。

②to order of...:凭×××指示,这种提单需由指定人在提单背面背书,才可以转让。常见的有:

a. 凭开证行指示,如信用证条款为"full set of B/L made out to our order",our指开证行,此种提单需经银行背书才可转让给买方,有利于开证银行在向买方收汇前牢牢掌握物权。

b. 凭开证申请人指示,如信用证条款为"B/L issued to order of applicant",这种提单需经开证申请人背书才能转让,不利于银行掌握物权。

c. 凭托运人指示,如信用证条款为"full set of B/L made out to order of shipper",这种提单等同于凭提示(to order)提单,在国际贸易中使用非常普遍。

3. 被通知人(notify party)

此栏填写船公司在货物到达目的港时发送到货通知的收件人。

信用证方式下,此栏必须严格按信用证要求填写。如果信用证没有规定被通知人,应将信用证的开证申请人名称、地址填入副本提单的此栏中,而正本的此栏为空白。

托收方式下,此栏一般填写托收的付款人。

4. 提单号码(B/L No.)

提单号码由承运人或其代理人提供,一般列在右上角,便于工作联系和查核,没有编号的提单无效。

5. 前段运输(pre-carriage by)

如果货物需转运,此栏填写第一程船的船名和航次号;如果货物不需转运,此栏空白不填。

6. 收货地点(place of receipt)

如果货物需转运,此栏填写收货的港口名称;如果货物不需转运,此栏空白不填。

7. 船名航次(vessel voy. No.)

如果货物需转运,填写第二程船的船名和航次号;如果货物不需转运,填写该批货物实际所装运的船名和航次号。

8. 装运港(port of loading)

填写货物实际装运的港口名称。如果信用证中对装运港仅作笼统规定(如 China main port)或同时列明几个装运港,应填写实际装运的港口名称。如果货物需转运,填写转运港的名称。

9. 卸货港(port of discharge)

填写货物实际卸下的港口名称,即目的港。

10. 最终目的地(final destination)

填写最终目的地的名称。如果货物的最终目的地是目的港,此栏空白。

11. 唛头、集装箱箱号与封号(marks & Nos., container, seal No.)

填写唛头、集装箱箱号和封号。唛头应与发票和装箱单上的完全一致。如既无唛头,也无集装箱箱号/封号,则填写"N/M"。

12. 件数和包装种类(number and kind of packages)

填写装入集装箱内货物的外包装件数或集装箱个数,分别用阿拉伯数字小写和英文数字大写表示。具体要求如下：

（1）对于包装货物，应注明包装数量和单位，并加大写数量。如 100 纸箱，则此栏填写"100 cartons"和"say one hundred cartons only"。

（2）对于散装货物，例如煤炭、原油等，此栏可加"in bulk"，数量无须加大写。

（3）对于裸装货物，应填件数，并加大写数量。如一台机器或一辆汽车，填"1 unit"，100 头猪则应填"100 heads"等，

（4）如是集装箱运输，由托运人装箱的整箱货可只写集装箱数量，如 2 个集装箱，则此栏填"2 containers"。如要注明集装箱箱内小件数量时，数量前应加"STC（said to contain)"，如"2 containers（STC 100 cartons）"。拼箱货，则按集装箱内小件数量填写。只要海关已对集装箱封箱，承运人对箱内的内容和数量不负责任，提单内应加注"shipper's load & count"（托运人装货并计数）。

（5）如是托盘装运，应填托盘数量，同时用括号加注货物的包装件数，如"3 pallets（STC 45 cartons）"。提单内还应加注"shipper's load & count"。

（6）如是两种或多种包装，件数要显示数字相加的和，种类用"package"表示，并在大写栏内写大写合计数量。

13. 货物名称或货物描述（description of goods）

货物名称应严格按照信用证或发票上的货名和文字填写，可用货物的统称表示。

14. 毛重（gross weight）

填写货物的实际毛重，一般以千克为计量单位。

15. 尺码（measurement）

填写实际货物的体积，一般以立方米为计量单位，小数点后保留 3 位小数。

16. 运费条款（freight and charges）

此栏的填写应按信用证规定并根据成交的价格术语来确定。当使用 CIF 或 CFR 时，应填"freight prepaid"（运费预付）或"freight paid"（运费已付）；当使用 FOB 时，应填"freight collect"（运费待付）或"freight payable at destination"（运费到付）。有时，信用证还要求注明运费的金额，则要填写实际运费支付额。

17. 其他说明

按信用证要求，加注特别说明。如指定船名，强调运费的支付，不显示发票金额、单价、价格等的条款；或强调显示信用证号码、合同号码等的条款；限制使用班轮公会的条款或指定承运人的条款。

18. 正本提单份数（number of original B/L）

提单有正本副本之分。正本提单上印有"ORIGINAL"字样，并注明提单签发日期和签名。正本提单的份数必须符合信用证的要求。如，信用证规定"全套海运提单"（full set

B/L 或 complete set B/L)，按惯例签发三份正本交银行议付。

19.提单签发地点及日期(place and date of issue)

提单签发地点一般为装运港所在城市。

提单签发日期表示货物实际装运的时间或已经接受船方、船代理等有关方面监管的时间。此时间应不迟于信用证或合同规定的最迟装运日期。已装船提单的签发日期视为装运日期。

20.提单的签署(signature)

提单必须经过签署手续后才能生效,有权签署提单的除了船长,还可以是承运人,或由他们授权的代理人。提单签署时应表明签署人的身份,代理人的任何签字必须表明其系代表承运人还是船长签字。

(1)承运人(China Ocean Shipping Company)本人签字。

提单签字处：China Ocean Shipping Company as Carrier。

(2)承运代理人(DEF Shipping Co.)签字。

提单签字处：DEF Shipping Co. as Agent for and/or on behalf of China Ocean Shipping Company as Carrier。

(3)船长(Captain James Brown)签字。

提单签字处：Captain James Brown as Master。

(4)船长代理签字。

提单签字处：DEF Shipping Co. as Agent for and /or on Behalf of Captain James Brown as Master。

📷 实训内容

✎**任务一：** 根据下列资料填制海运提单。

1. APPLICANT：ADH TRADING CO., KARACHI

2. BENEFICIARY：ZHEJIANG LIGHT INDUSTRIAL PRODUCTS IMPORT AND EXPORT CORPORATION

3. EXPIRY DATE：SEP. 15，2019

4. PARTIAL SHIPMENTS：ALLOWED

5. TRANSSHIPMENT：ALLOWED

6. SHIPMENT FROM NINGBO TO KARACHI

7. DESCRIPTION OF GOODS："GOLD ELEPHANT" BRAND WATCH

8. FULL SET OF "SHIPPED ON BOARD" OCEAN BILL OF LADING MADE OUT TO ORDER OF SHIPPER AND BLANK ENDORSED, SHOWING FREIGHT PREPAID AND NOTIFY APPLICANT.

9. QUANTITY OF GOODS：1,000 PCS

10. PACKING IN 40 CTNS

11. THE NAME OF STEAMER：CHANGJIANG　　VOY. NO.：V.231

12. B/L NO.：CJ2651　　　　B/L DATE：SEP. 5，2019

13. GROSS WEIGHT：@16 KGS/CTN　　NET WEIGHT：@15 KGS/CTN

14. MEASUREMENT：0.012 CBM

Shipper	SINOTRANS	B/L No.

中国对外贸易运输总公司
CHINA NATIONAL FOREIGN TRADE TRANSPORTATION CORP.
直运或转船提单
BILL OF LADING
DIRECT OR WITH TRANSSHIPMENT

SHIPPED on board in apparent good order and condition (unless otherwise indicated) the goods or packages specified herein and to be discharged at the mentioned port of discharge or as near thereto as the vessel may safely get and be always afloat.

The weight, measure, marks and numbers, quality, contents and value, being particulars furnished by the Shipper, are not checked by the Carrier on loading.

The Shipper, Consignee and the Holder of this Bill of Lading hereby expressly accept and agree to all printed, written or stamped provisions, exceptions and conditions of this Bill of Lading, including those on the back hereof.

IN WITNESS where of the number of original Bills of Lading stated below have been signed, one of which being accomplished, the other(s) to be void.

Consignee or Order

Notify Address

Pre-carriage by	Place of Loading

Vessel	Port of Transshipment

Port of Discharge	Final Destination

Container, Seal No. or Marks & Nos.	Number & Kind of Packages	Description of Goods	Gross Weight (KGS)	Measurement (CBM)

ABOVE PARTICULARS FURNISHED BY SHIPPER

Freight & Charges			Regarding Transshipment Information Please Contact
Ex. Rrate	Prepaid at	Freight Payable at	Place and Date of Issue
	Total Prepaid	Number of Original B(s)/L	Signed for or on Behalf of the Master as Agent(s)

任务二： 根据下列资料填制海运提单。

1. LETTER OF CREDIT NO.：LC-515

2. EXPIRY DATE：20190315 PLACE IN CHINA

3. APPLICANT：BLUE SKY HOLDINGS LTD HONG KONG，CHINA

4. BENEFICIARY：ZHEJIANG LIGHT INDUSTRIAL PRODUCTS IMPORT AND EXPORT CORPORATION

5. AMOUNT：CURRENCY USD AMOUNT 25,000.00

6. PARTIAL SHIPMENTS：ALLOWED

7. TRANSSHIPMENT：ALLOWED

8. LOADING IN CHARGE：SHANGHAI，CHINA

9. FOR TRANSPORT TO：HAMBURG

10. LATEST DATE OF SHIPMENT：20190228

11. DESCRIPTION OF GOODS：TOYS DETAILS AS PER ORDER NO.P01009 FOB SHANGHAI

12. FULL SET（3/3）OF ORIGINAL CLEAN ON BOARD MARINE BILLS OF LADING MADE OUT TO ORDER OF APPLICANT MARKED "FREIGHT COLLECT" AND NOTIFY APPLICANT.

13. B/L MUST SHOW THIS LETTER OF CREDIT NO.

14. PACKING：TOTAL PACKED IN 200 CARTONS

15. QUANTITY：1,000 PCS

16. BILL OF LADING NO.：YB5008

17. B/L DATE：20190220

18. VESSEL VOY. NO.：SUNFENG V.188

19. CONTAINER NO.：GVDU2041118/SEAL 21281

20. NET WEIGHT：20 KGS/CARTON

21. GROSS WEIGHT：21 KGS/CARTON

22. MEASUREMENT：0.086 CBM/CARTON

Shipper	SINOTRANS	B/L No.

中国对外贸易运输总公司
CHINA NATIONAL FOREIGN TRADE TRANSPORTATION CORP.
直运或转船提单
BILL OF LADING
DIRECT OR WITH TRANSSHIPMENT

SHIPPED on board in apparent good order and condition (unless otherwise indicated) the goods or packages specified herein and to be discharged at the mentioned port of discharge or as near thereto as the vessel may safely get and be always afloat.

The weight, measure, marks and numbers, quality, contents and value, being particulars furnished by the Shipper, are not checked by the carrier on loading.

The Shipper, Consignee and the Holder of this Bill of Lading hereby expressly accept and agree to all printed, written or stamped provisions, exceptions and conditions of this Bill of Lading, including those on the back hereof.

IN WITNESS where of the number of original Bills of Lading stated below have been signed, one of which being accomplished, the other(s) to be void.

Consignee or Order

Notify Address

Pre-carriage by	Place of Loading

Vessel	Port of Transshipment

Port of Discharge	Final Destination

Container, Seal No. or Marks & Nos.	Number & Kind of Packages	Description of Goods	Gross Weight (KGS)	Measurement (CBM)

ABOVE PARTICULARS FURNISHED BY SHIPPER

Freight & Charges	Regarding Transshipment Information Please Contact

Ex. Rate	Prepaid at	Freight Payable at	Place and Date of Issue
	Total Prepaid	Number of original B(s)/L	Signed for or on Behalf of the Master
			as Agent(s)

✎**任务三：** 根据下列资料填制海运提单。

    1. L/C NO. A-12B-34C DATED JAN. 11, 2019

    2. APPLICANT：SUMITOMD CORPORATION, OSAKA

    3. BENEFICIARY：ZHEJIANG ZHONGDA IMPORT & EXPORT GROUP COMPANY, LTD

    4. AMOUNT：CURRENCY USD AMOUNT 28,000.00

    5. PARTIAL SHIPMENTS：ALLOWED

    6. TRANSSHIPMENT：ALLOWED

    7. LOADING IN CHARGE：SHIPMENT FROM CHINESE MAIN PORT

    8. FOR TRANSPORT TO：OSAKA, JAPAN

    9. DESCRIPTION OF GOODS：HALF DRIED APPLE PRUNE DETAILS AS PER SALES CONTRACT NO. FJE2145

    10. PACKING：IN WOODEN CASES, 12 KGS PER CASE

    11. TRADE TERMS：CFR OSAKA

    12. 2/3 SET OF CLEAN ON BOARD OCEAN BILLS OF LADING MADE OUT TO ORDER AND BLANK ENDORSED AND MARKED "FREIGHT PREPAID" AND NOTIFY "SUMITOMD CORPORATION, OSAKA". COMBINED TRANSPORT BILL OF LADING ACCEPTABLE.

    13. 1/3 ORIGINAL B/L AND OTHER SHIPPING DOCUMENTS MUST BE SENT DIRECTLY TO APPLICANT SUMITOMD CORPORATION, OSAKA IN 3 DAYS AFTER B/L DATE, AND SENT BY FAX.

    14. ALL DOCUMENTS MUST BEAR THIS L/C NO.

    15. BILL OF LADING NO.：GSO456   DATE OF B/L：FEB.18, 2019

    16. OCEAN VESSEL VOY. NO.：CHANG GANG V.203984

    17. PORT OF LOADING：SHANGHAI

    18. CONTAINER SEAL NO.：2×20' FCL CY/CY

            TRIU 3672996 KHLU3782939

    19. TOTAL QUANTITY OF GOODS：16,800 KGS

    20. GROSS WEIGHT：15 KGS/CASE

    21. MEASUREMENT：@(20×10×10)CBM/CASE

    22. SHIPPING MARKS：SC/NOS.1-UP/OSAKA/MADE IN CHINA

Shipper					
Consignee or Order		SINOTRANS		B/L No.	
Notify Address		中国对外贸易运输总公司 CHINA NATIONAL FOREIGN TRADE TRANSPORTATION CORP. 直运或转船提单 **BILL OF LADING** **DIRECT OR WITH TRANSSHIPMENT** SHIPPED on board in apparent good order and condition（unless otherwise indicated）the goods or packages specified herein and to be discharged at the mentioned port of discharge or as near thereto as the vessel may safely get and be always afloat. The weight，measure，marks and numbers，quality，contents and value，being particulars furnished by the Shipper，are not checked by the carrier on loading. The Shipper，Consignee and the Holder of this Bill of Lading hereby expressly accept and agree to all printed，written or stamped provisions，exceptions and conditions of this Bill of Lading，including those on the back hereof. IN WITNESS where of the number of original Bills of Lading stated below have been signed，one of which being accomplished，the other（s）to be void.			
Pre-carriage by	Place of Loading				
Vessel	Port of Transshipment				
Port of Discharge	Final Destination				
Container，Seal No. or Marks & Nos.	Number & Kind of Packages	Description of Goods		Gross Weight（KGS）	Measurement（CBM）
ABOVE PARTICULARS FURNISHED BY SHIPPER					
Freight & Charges				Regarding Transshipment Information Please Contact	
Ex. Rate	Prepaid at	Freight Payable at		Place and Date of Issue	
	Total Prepaid	Number of Original B（s）/L		Signed for or on Behalf of the Master as Agent（s）	

任务四：根据下列资料填制航空运单

（一）信用证资料

1. FROM：UFJ BANK，TOKYO

2. TO：BANK OF CHINA，ZHEJIANG BRANCH

3. DATE OF ISSUE：DEC. 28，2019

4. L/C NO.：UF7896

5. EXPIRY DATE AND PLACE：FEB.15，2019 IN CHINA

6. APPLICANT：SAKURA COMPANY，6-2 OHTEMACHI，1-CHOME，CHIYADA-KU，TOKYO

7. BENEFICIARY：ZHEJIANG RONGXIN MEDICINES AND HEALTH PRODUCTS COMPANY，NO. 89 SHAOXING ROAD，SHAOXING，ZHEJIANG，CHINA

8. L/C AMOUNT：USD 22，912.50

9. TAKING CHARGE PLACE：SHANGHAI，CHINA

10. FOR TRANSPORTATION TO：TOKYO，JAPAN

11. LATEST DATE OF SHIPMENT：JAN.31，2019

12. DOCUMENTS REQUIRED：

＋ AWB CONSIGNED TO APPLICANT MARKED FREIGHT PREPAID INDICATING ACTUAL FLIGHT DATE.

（二）其他资料

航空公司 2019 年 1 月 17 日对托运人的航空托运单予以确认：

1. SHIPPER：ZHEJIANG RONGXIN MEDICINES AND HEALTH PRODUCTS COMPANY

2. GOODS：5，250 PCS HOSPITAL UNIFORM

3. FLIGHT NO.：CA1908

4. ACTUAL FLIGHT DATE：JAN.18，2019

5. FROM SHANGHAI AIRPORT TO TOKYO AIRPORT

6. G.W.：1，232 KGS

7. MEAS.：4.20 CBM

8. PACKED IN 88 CARTONS

9. SHIPPING MARKS：S.C./TOKYO/1-88

10. 空运单据由上海佳达航空国际货运代理有限公司（BEST INTERNATIONAL AIR FREIGHT CO. LTD）签发

11. 签发日期：2019 年 1 月 18 日

航空运单
的填制

Shipper's Name and Address	Shipper's Account Number	Not Negotiable

Air Waybill 中国东方航空公司
ISSUED BY CHINA EASTERN AIRLINES
Copies 1，2 and 3 of this Air Waybill are originals and have the same validity

Consignee's Name and Address	Consignee's Account Number	It is agreed that the goods described herein are accepted in apparent good order and condition (except as noted) for carriage SUBJECT TO THE CONDITIONS OF CONTRACT ON THE REVERSE HEREOF, ALL GOODS MAY BE CARRIED BY ANY OTHER MEANS. INCLUDING ROAD OR ANY OTHER CARRIER UNLESS SPECIFIC CONTRARY INSTRUCTIONS ARE GIVEN HEREON BY THE SHIPPER. THE SHIPPER'S ATTENTION IS DRAWN TO THE NOTICE CONCERNING CARRIER'S LIMITATION OF LIABILITY. Shipper may increase such limitation of liability by declaring a higher value for carriage and paying a supplemental charge if required.

Issuing Carrier's Agent Name and City	Accounting Information

Agents IATA Code	Account No.	

Airport of Departure (Addr. of First Carrier) and Requested Routing	Reference Number	Optional Shipping Information

To	By First Carrier	Routing and Destination	To	by	To	by	Currency	CHGS Code	WT/VAL PPD	COLL	Other PPD	COLL	Declared Value for Carriage	Declared Value for Customs

Airport of Destination	Flight/Date	For Carrier Use only	Flight/Date	Amount of Insurance	INSURANCE-If carrier offers insurance and such insurance is requested in accordance with the conditions thereof indicate amount to be insured in figures in box marked "Amount of Insurance".

Handling Information

SCI

No. of Pieces RCP	Gross Weight	Kg lb	Rate Class / Commodity Item No.	Chargeable Weight	Rate / Charge	Total	Nature and Quantity of Goods (incl. Dimensions or Volume)

Prepaid	Weight Charge	Collect	Other Charges
	Valuation Charge		
	Tax		
	Total Other Charges Due Agent		Shipper certifies that the particulars on the face hereof are correct and that insofar as any part of the consignment contains dangerous goods, such part is properly described by name and is in proper condition for carriage by air according to the applicable Dangerous Goods Regulations Charges at Destination.
	Total Other Charges Due Carrier		
			Signature of Shipper or His Agent
Total Prepaid	Total Collect		
Currency Conversion	CC Charges in dest. Currency		Executed on(date) At(place) Signature of Issuing Carrier or as Agent
For Carrier's Use Only at Destination	Charges at Destination	Total Collect Charges	AWB No.

任务五： 根据下列资料填制空运提单。

2019 年 4 月 7 日,南京食品贸易公司(NANJING FOOD TRADING CO. LTD)的货物从南京起运,航班为 FX0910,请根据有关资料制作空运提单。

（一）信用证资料

MAR. 22, 2019 09：18：11　　　　　　　　　　LOGICAL TERMINAL E102

MT S700　　　　ISSUE OF A DOCUMENTARY CREDIT

　　　　　　　　　　　　　　　　　　PAGE 00001

　　　　　　　　　　　　　　　　　　FUNCMSG700

　　　　　　　　　　　　　　　　　　UMR06881051

MSGACKDWS765I AUTH OK，KEY B198081689580FC5，BKCHCNBJ RJHISARI RECORO

BASIC HEADER F　01　BKCHCNBJA940 0588 550628

APPLICATION HEADER 0 700 1057 180320 RJHISARIXXX 7277 977367 020213 1557 N

　　　　　　　＊ ALRAJHI BANKING AND INVESTMENT

　　　　　　　＊ CORPORATION

　　　　　　　＊ RIYADH

　　　　　　　＊（HEAD OFFICE）

USER HEADER SERVICE CODE　　103：　　　（银行盖信用证通知专用章）

　　　　　　BANK. PRIORITY　113：

　　　　　　MSG USER REF.　108：

　　　　　　INFO. FROM CI　115：

SEQUENCE OF TOTAL　　＊27：1 / 1

FORM OF DOC. CREDIT　＊40A：IRREVOCABLE

DOC. CREDIT NUMBER　＊20：0011LC123756

DATE OF ISSUE　31C：20190322

DATE/PLACE EXP.　＊31 D：DATE 180515 PLACE CHINA

APPLICANT　＊50：NEO GENERAL TRADING CO.

　　　　　　P.O.B OX 99552，RIYADH 22766，KSA

　　　　　　TEL：00966-1-4659220　FAX：00966-1-4659213

BENEFICIARY　＊59：NANJING FOOD TRADING CO. LTD

　　　　　　HUARONG MANSION RM2901，NO. 85 GUANJIAQIAO，

　　　　　　NANJING 210005，CHINA

　　　　　　TEL：0086-25-4715004　FAX：0086-25-4711363

AMOUNT　＊32 B：CURRENCY USD AMOUNT 13,260.00

AVAILABLE WITH/BY　＊41 D：ANY BANK IN CHINA，

BY NEGOTIATION

DRAFTS AT...　42 C：AT SIGHT

DRAWEE　42 A：RJHISARI

＊ALRAJHI BANKING AND INVESTMENT

＊CORPORATION

＊RIYADH

＊（HEAD OFFICE）

PARTIAL SHIPMENTS　43P：NOT ALLOWED

TRANSSHIPMENTS　43T：NOT ALLOWED

LOADING ON BOARD　44A：NANJING，CHINA

FOR TRANSPORT TO　44B：DAMMAM PORT，SAUDI ARABIA

LATEST DATE OF SHIPMENT　44C：20190430

GOODS DESCRIPT　45A：

ABOUT 1,700 CARTONS CANNED MUSRHOOM PIECES & STEMS 24 TINS× 425 GRAMS NET WEIGHT （D.W. 227 GRAMS） AT USD 7.80 PER CARTON.ROSE BRAND.

DOCS REQUIRED　46A：

＋SIGNED COMMERCIAL INVOICE IN TRIPLICATE ORIGINAL AND MUST SHOW BREAKDOWN OF THE AMOUNT AS FOLLOWS：FOB VALUE， FREIGHT CHARGES AND TOTAL AMOUNT C AND F.

＋FULL SET AIR WAYBILL EVIDENCING NEO GENERAL TRADING CO. MARKED FREIGHT PREPAID.

＋PACKING LIST IN 1 ORIGINAL PLUS 5 COPIES，ALL OF WHICH MUST BE MANUALLY SIGNED.

＋INSPECTION （HEALTH） CERTIFICATE FROM C. I. Q. （ENTRY-EXIT INSPECTION AND QUARANTINE OF THE PEOPLE'S REP. OF CHINA） STATING GOODS ARE FIT FOR HUMAN BEING.

＋CERTIFICATE OF ORIGIN DULY CERTIFIED BY C. C. P. I. T. STATING THE NAME OF THE MANUFACTURERS OF PRODUCERS AND THAT GOODS EXPORTED ARE WHOLLY OF CHINESE ORIGIN.

＋THE PRODUCTION DATE OF THE GOODS NOT TO BE EARLIER THAN HALF MONTH AT TIME OF SHIPMENT. BENEFICIARY MUST CERTIFY THE

SAME.

+SHIPMENT TO BE EFFECTED BY CONTAINER AND BY REGULARE LINE. SHIPMENT COMPANY'S CERTIFICATE TO THIS EFFECT SHOULD ACCOMPANY THE DOCUMENTS.

ADDITIONAL CONDITIONS 47A：

+ A DISCREPANCY FEE OF USD 50.00 WILL BE IMPOSED ON EACH SET OF DOCUMENTS PRESENTED FOR NEGOTIATION UNDER THIS L/C WITH DISCREPANCY. THE FEE WILL BE DEDUCTED FROM THE BILL AMOUNT.

CHARGES 71B：

+ ALL CHARGES AND COMMISSIONS OUTSIDE KSA ON BENEFICIARIES' ACCOUNT INCLUDING REIMBURSING BANK COMMISSION，DISCREPANCY FEE (IF ANY) AND COURIER CHARGES.

CONFIRMAT INSTR. ＊49：WITHOUT

REIMBURS BANK 53D：

+ ALRAJHI BANKING AND INVESTMENT CORP. RIYADH (HEAD OFFICE)

INSTRUCTIONS TO PAYING BANK 78：

+DOCUMENTS TO BE DESPATCHED IN ONE LOT BY COURIER.

+ ALL CORRESPONDENCE TO BE SENT TO ALRAJHI BANKING AND INVESTMENT CORPORATION RIYADH (HEAD OFFICE)

TRAILER ORDER IS ＜MAC：＞＜PAC：＞＜ENC：＞＜CHK：＞＜TNG：＞＜PDE：＞

MAC：E55927A4

CHK：7B505952829A

HOB：

（二）补充资料

商品毛重：19,074.44 KGS

体积：36.85 CBM

Rate Class 运价分类代号：M

Rate/Charge 费率：20.61

Other Charge 其他费用：AWC(运单费)50.00

999 | | 999

Shipper's Name and Address	Shipper's Account Number

Not Negotiable
Air Waybill
Issued by

中国国际航空公司
AIR CHINA
BEIJING CHINA

Copies 1, 2 and 3 of this Air Waybill are originals and have the same validity.

Consignee's Name and Address	Consignee's Account Number

It is agreed that the goods described herein are accepted in apparent good order and condition (except as noted) for carriage SUBJECT TO THE CONDITIONS OF CONTRACT ON THE REVERSE HEREOF, ALL GOODS MAY BE CARRIED BY ANY OTHER MEANS. INCLUDING ROAD OR ANY OTHER CARRIER UNLESS SPECIFIC CONTRARY INSTRUCTIONS ARE GIVEN HEREON BY THE SHIPPER. THE SHIPPER'S ATTENTION IS DRAWN TO THE NOTICE CONCERNING CARRIER'S LIMITATION OF LIABILITY.
Shipper may increase such limitation of liability by declaring a higher value for carriage and paying a supplemental charge if required.

Issuing Carrier's Agent Name and City

Accounting Information

Agents IATA Code	Account No.

Airport of Departure (Addr. of First Carrier) and Requested Routing

Reference Number   Optional Shipping Information

To	By First Carrier	Routing and Destination	To	by	To	by	Currency	CHGS Code	WT/VAL		Other		Declared Value for Carriage	Declared Value for Customs
									PPD	COLL	PPD	COLL		

Airport of Destination	Flight/Date	For Carrier Use only	Flight/Date	Amount of Insurance	INSURANCE-If carrier offers insurance and such insurance is requested in accordance with the conditions thereof indicate amount to be insured in figures in box marked "Amount of Insurance".

Handling Information

SCI

No. of Pieces RCP	Gross Weight	Kg lb	Rate Class / Commodity Item No.	Chargeable Weight	Rate / Charge	Total	Nature and Quantity of Goods (incl. Dimensions or Volume)

Prepaid	Weight Charge	Collect	Other Charges
	Valuation Charge		
	Tax		
	Total Other Charges Due Agent		Shipper certifies that the particulars on the face hereof are correct and that insofar as any part of the consignment contains dangerous goods, such part is properly described by name and is in proper condition for carriage by air according to the applicable Dangerous Goods Regulations Charges at Destination.
	Total Other Charges Due Carrier		

Signature of Shipper or His Agent

Total Prepaid	Total Collect
Currency Conversion Rates	CC Charges in dest. Currency

Executed on(date)   At(place)   Signature of Issuing Carrier or as Agent

For Carrier's Use Only at Destination	Charges at Destination	Total Collect Charges

AWB No.

任务六： 根据以下资料，审核并修改已填制的提单，在已填制的 20 个栏目中，即标号（1）—（20）中找出若干处填制错误，并说明原因。

（一）国际货运委托书

国际货运委托书

Shipper's Letter of Instruction

Shipper（托运人） SHANGHAI MACHINE CO. LTD NO.1223 JIDI ROAD, MINHANG, SHANGHAI, CHINA 291197	发票编号 19EX07	贸易方式 G.T.	收汇方式 L/C
	可否转船 否	运费方式 到付	提单份数 3
	可否分批 否	装运期限 20190618	有效期限 20190620

Consignee（收货人） TO ORDER OF HONGKONG & SHANGHAI BANK JAKARTA BRANCH	收货地点 MINHANG	装货港 SHANGHAI	卸货港 JAKARTA
	目的地 Final Destination for the Merchant JAKARTA,INDONESIA		

Notified Party（通知方） PT ANTA TIRTA KIRANA JI.GREEN GARDEN BLICK Z4 JAKARTA 11520 INDONESIA	交货地点 Place of Delivery JAKARTA,INDONESIA		运输条款 CY/CY
	集装箱类别和数量	拼箱号	装箱方式 DOOR/DOOR
	20′ 40′ × 4 45′′	40HT 40HC 20HT	

Marks & Nos.	Kind of Packages	Description of Goods	Gross Weight	Measurement
JAKARTA MADE IN CHINA	13 WOODEN CASES	CO-EXTRUSION FILM BLOWING LINE MODEL：SM-65-80-3E-1800	29,900 KGS	185 CBM

配载要求和备注：
1. 6 月 16 日上门装箱并安排熏蒸
2. 运费到付,杂费预付
3. 指定货运代理公司 ABC COMPANY
所填全部属实并愿遵守承运人的一切载运章程。
WE HEREBY CERTIFIES THAT THE PARTICULARS ON THE FACE HEREOF ARE CORRECT AND AGREES CONDITIONS OF CARRIAGE OF THE CARRIER.

托运人（公章）：上海机械有限公司　　托运日期：20190609　　经办人：王晓路

（二）配舱资料

船名及航次：KUO FU V.5065

关单号：CMAGLXFF98560

装船日：JUN.18，2019

开船日：JUN.20，2019

起运港：SHANGHAI

卸货港：JAKARTA

（三）装箱资料

集装箱号、封号：CGMU4289466/2248269/40′

ECMU4143706/2248268/40′

FSCU4036720/2248364/40′

TGHU4532523/2257014/40′

件数：13 PACKAGES

毛重：29,900 KGS

体积：175 CBM

（四）已填制的提单

Shipper(1) SHANGHAI MACHINE CO. LTD NO.1223 JIDI ROAD, MINHANG, SHANGHAI, CHINA 291197	SINOTRANS B/L NO.：CMAGLXFF98560(9) 中国对外贸易运输总公司 CHINA NATIONAL FOREIGN TRADE TRANSPORTATION CORP. 直运或转船提单 BILL OF LADING DIRECT OR WITH TRANSSHIPMENT

Consignee or Order(2) TO ORDER OF HONGKONG & SHANGHAI BANKJAKARTA BRANCH	

SHIPPED on board in apparent good order and condition （unless otherwise indicated） the goods or packages specified herein and to be discharged at the mentioned port of discharge or as near thereto as the vessel may safely get and be always afloat.

Notify Address(3) PT ANTA TIRTA KIRANA JI.GREEN GARDEN BLICK Z4 JAKARTA 11520 INDONESIA	

The weight，measure，marks and numbers，quality，contents and value，being particulars furnished by the Shipper，are not checked by the carrier on loading.

Pre-carriage by	Place of Loading(5) SHANGHAI
Vessel(4) KUO FU V.5065	Port of Transshipment (7)
Port of Discharge(6) JAKARTA	Final Destination(8)

The Shipper, Consignee and the Holder of this Bill of Lading hereby expressly accept and agree to all printed，written or stamped provisions, exceptions and conditions of this Bill of Lading, including those on the back hereof.

IN WITNESS where of the number of original Bills of Lading stated below have been signed，one of which being accomplished，the other(s) to be void.

Container，Seal No. or Marks & Nos. (10) JAKARTA MADE IN CHINA 4×40' FCL	Number & Kind of Packages (11) 13 WOODEN CASES	Description of Goods (12) CO-EXTRUSION FILM BLOWING LINE MODEL：SM-65-80-3E-1800 CY/CY (15)	Gross Weight (KGS) (13) 29,900	Measurement (CBM) (14) 185

ABOVE PARTICULARS FURNISHED BY SHIPPER	

Freight & Charges OCEAN FREIGHT COLLECT (16) OTHER CHG COLLECT (17)	Regarding Transshipment Information Please Contact

Ex. Rate	Prepaid at	Freight Payable at	place and Date of Issue SHANGHAI JUN. 20,2019 (19)
	Total Prepaid	Number of Original B(s)/L THREE (18)	Signed for or on Behalf of the Master (20) CHINA NATIONAL FOREIGN TRADE TRANSPORTATION CORP. as Agent(s)

任务七： 根据下面相关资料指出下列海运提单中错误的地方。

（一）相关资料

买方：QINGDAO ECONOMIC TRADE INT'L CO. LTD

　　　NO. 19，ZHUZHOU ROAD，QINGDAO

卖方：VICTOR MACHINERY INDUSTRY CO. LTD

　　　NO.338，BA DE STREET，SHU LIN CITY，TAIBEI

　　　TEL/FAX：886-2-26689666/26809123

信用证对海运提单的要求：

　　＋FULL SET（INCLUDING 3 ORIGINALS AND 3 NON-NEGOTIABLE COPIES）OF CLEAN ON BOARD OCEAN BILLS OD LADING MARKED "FREIGHT PREPAID" MADE OUT TO ORDER AND BLANK ENDORSED NOTIFYING APPLICANT WITH ITS FULL NAME AND ADDRESS.

发票号：FU1011103

提单号：KEETAO100933

船名、航次：YM HORIZON UT018NCNC

装船日期：MAY 10，2019

装运港：TAIWAN MAIN PORT

目的港：QINGDAO

唛头：E.T.I

　　　QINGDAO

　　　NOS.1-2

货物描述：ONE COMPLETE STE OF SHEET CUTTER

毛重：15,600 KGS

体积：51 CBM

包装：PACKED IN TWO WOODEN CASES

贸易术语：CIF QINGDAO

（二）已填制的海运提单

Shipper Insert Name，Address and Phone TO ORDER	B/L No. KEETAO100935
Consignee Insert Name，Address and Phone VICTOR MACHINERY INDUSTRY CO. LTD NO.338，BA DE STREET，SHU LIN CITY，TAIBEI TEL/FAX：886-2-26689666/26809123	**E** EASY LINK OCEAN FREIGHT FORWARDER CO.LTD 迅通海運承攬運送股份有限公司 TEL：(02) 2562-7299 FAX：(02) 2568-4558 海攬（基）字第1041號 台北市南京東路2段8號10樓-1 **BILL of LADING**
Notify Party Insert Name，Address and Phone VICTOR MACHINERY INDUSTRY CO. LTD NO.338，BA DE STREET，SHU LIN CITY，TAIBEI TEL/FAX：886-2-26689666/26809123	

Ocean Vessel Voy. No. YM HORIZON UT018NCNC	Port of Loading QINGDAO
Port of Discharge KEELUNG	Port of Destination

Marks & Nos. Container / Seal No.	No. of Containers or Packages	Description of Goods	Gross Weight	Measurement
E.T.I QINGDAO NOS.1-5	5 WOODEN CASES	ONE COMPLETE OF SHEET CUTTER FREIGHT COLLECT	15,600 KGS	51 CBM

Description of Contents for Shipper's Use Only（Not Part of This B/L Contract）

Total Number of Containers and/or Packages（in words）
SAY TWO WOODEN CASES ONLY

Ex. Rate：	Prepaid at	Payable at QINGDAO	Place and Date of Issue QINGDAO MAY 13，2019
	Total Prepaid	No. of Original B(s)/L THREE（3）	Signed for the Carrier EASY LINK OCEAN FREIGHT FORHARDER CO. LTD TONY

LADEN ON BOARD THE VESSEL YM HORIZON UT018NCNC

DATE：MAY 13，2019   BY：EASY LINK OCEAN FREIGHT FORHARDER CO. LTD

TONY

项目八　商业汇票填制

实训目标

能够根据有关资料填制商业汇票。

实训指导

商业汇票各栏目的内容填制如下。

1. 出票条款

又称出票依据。信用证业务中,如信用证有具体规定的,则必须按信用证规定填写;如信用证没有规定的,则填开证行名称与地址、信用证号码、开证日期。

在托收业务中,一般应加具货物的名称、数量、启运港、目的港及合同号码等,并注明"for collection",如"drawn under contract No.123 against shipment of 200 M/T peanut from Ningbo to Sydney"。

2. 年息

这一栏由结汇银行填写,用以清算企业与银行间利息费用。出口公司不必填写此栏目。

3. 号码

即汇票号码,一般都以相应的发票号码兼作汇票号码。

4. 汇票金额

汇票上应填上小写金额和大写金额。汇票小写金额填在"exchange for"后,金额数保留两位小数。汇票大写金额填在"the sum of"后,要求顶格写,以防有人故意在汇票金额上做手脚。

在填制汇票金额时,应注意以下几点。

(1)信用证有规定的,则按信用证有关规定填写。如信用证规定汇票金额为发票金额的97%,那么假如发票金额为 USD 1,000.00,汇票金额则填 USD 97.00,其差额3%一般为应付的佣金。这种做法通常用于中间商代开信用证的场合。

(2)信用证没有规定的,则汇票金额与发票金额一致。

(3)如信用证规定部分信用证付款,部分托收,则分做两套汇票:信用证项下支款的按信用证允许的金额填制,以银行为付款人;其余部分为托收项下汇票的金额,以客户为付款人;两者之和等于发票金额。

(4)汇票上的金额大、小写必须一致。

5. 出票日期和出票地点

出票地点一般是出口商所在地,一般事先已印好,无须现填。

出票地点后的横线填出票日期。在信用证方式下,一般以议付日期作为出票日期;托收方式下,该日期按托收行寄单日期填写。该日期一般由银行代填,需用英文,不能全部用阿拉伯数字。

6. 汇票付款期限

汇票付款期限分即期和远期两种。按不同的付款期限填制:

(1) 即期付款,只需在横线上用"＊＊＊"或"——"或"×××"表示,也可直接打上"at sight",但不能留空。

(2) 远期付款,按信用证的规定填入相应的付款期限。

托收方式下的汇票付款期限,除表明即期或远期的期限外,还要在期限前注明具体的托收种类,如"D/P at sight"或"D/P at ××× days after sight"或"D/A at ××× days after sight"。

7. 受款人

又称收款人,也称汇票抬头人,具体写法有三种。

(1) 限制性抬头。

例如,"仅付给甲公司(pay A Co. only)"或"付给甲公司,不准转让(pay A Co., not transferable)"。这种汇票不能经背书进行转让。

(2) 指示式抬头。

例如,"付给甲公司或其指定人(pay A Co. or order;pay to the order of A Co.)"。这种载有指示性抬头的汇票可以经过背书转让。

(3) 来人抬头。

即在汇票上不指定收款人名称,而只写明"付给持票人(pay holder)"或"付给来人(pay bearer)"字样。

我国《票据法》规定不记载收款人名称的汇票是无效的。目前出口业务中使用最广泛的是指示式抬头,汇票的格式上也基本印好"pay to the order of ×××",这里的"×××"是汇票的记名收款人,通过他的背书,汇票可以转让。

在信用证方式下,汇票中受款人这一栏目中填写的应是银行名称和地址,一般都是议付行的名称和地址。究竟要哪家银行作为受款人,这要看信用证中是否有具体的规定。

在托收方式下,一般以托收行(出口地银行)作为收款人。

8. 付款人

又称受票人。在信用证方式下,汇票的付款人应按照信用证的规定填写;若信用证中未规定付款人,则填写开证行。在托收方式下,一般以进口商作为汇票的付款人。

9. 出票人

一般填出口企业,包括企业全称和负责人的签字盖章。在可转让信用证情况下,出票人也有可能为信用证的第二受益人。

10. 汇票份数

汇票在没有特殊规定时,都打两张,一式两份。汇票一般都在醒目的位置上印着"1""2"字样,表示第一联和第二联。汇票的第一联和第二联在法律效力上无区别。第一联生效则第二联自动作废,第二联生效则第一联自动作废,即付一不付二,付二不付一。

⏱ 实训任务

✎ **任务一**: 根据下列资料填制汇票。

(一)信用证资料

ISSUING BANK:BANK OF CHINA,SEOUL BRANCH

ADVISING BANK:BANK OF CHINA, QINGDAO BRANCH

L/C NO.:810080000797 DATED NOV.07, 2019

EXPIRY DATE:JAN. 15, 2020 PLACE IN CHINA

BENEFICIARY:QINGHE LIGHT IND. PROD. IMP. & EXP. CORP

                NO. 55 YINGBIN RD., QINGDAO, CHINA

APPLICANT:SUNKUONG LIMITED

              (HSRO) C. P. O.BOX 1780, SEOUL, REPUBLIC OF KOREA

L/CAMOUNT:USD AMOUNT 67,050.00

PLS. /NEG. TOL,(%):05/05

AVAILABLE WITH/BY:ADVISING BANK BY NEGOTIATION

DRAFTS AT:120 DAYS AFTER THE DATE OF SHIPMENT FOR 100 PCT OF

              THE INVOICE VALUE

DRAWEE:BKCHKRSE

        * BANK OF CHINA,SEOUL BRANCH

        * SEOUL

QUANTITY 5 PCT MORE OR LESS ARE ALLOWED.

LATEST DATE OF SHIPMENT:DEC. 31, 2019

PRESENTATION PERIOD:DOCUMENTS TO BE PRESENTED WITHIN 15 DAYS

              AFTER THE DATE OF SHIPMENT, BUT WITHIN

              THE VALIDITY OF THE CREDIT.

（二）发票资料

INVOICE NO.：81609D3030

INVOICE DATE：DEC.19，2019

QUANTITY OF GOODS：9,400 DOZ

UNIT PRICE：USD 7.45/DOZ CIF BUSAN

（三）其他资料

B/L DATE：DEC. 25，2019

凭

Drawn under ---------------------------------

信用证或购买证第　　　号

L/C or A/P No. ---------------------------------

日期　　年　　月　　日

Dated ---------------------------------

按　　　息　　　付　　　款

Payable with interest @ _____% per annum

号码	汇票金额		中国青岛	年　月　日
No.-----------Exchange for			Qingdao, China	-------------20...

见票　　　　　　　　　　　日　后（本　汇　票　之　副　本　未　付）　付

At _____ sight of this FIRST of Exchange　（Second of exchange being unpaid）

Pay to the order of_____或其指定人

金额

The sum of

此致

To ---------------------------------

✎**任务二**：根据下列资料填制汇票。

ISSUING BANK：THE BANK OF TOKYO LTD

NAGOYA OFFICE P.O.BOX 240，NAGOYA-NAKA，

NAGOYA 460-91，JAPAN

PLACE AND DATE OF L/C：NAGOYA OCT. 6，2019

L/C NO.：123A-456

BENEFICIARY：ZHEJIANG KINGTEX TRADING CO. LTD

NO.165 ZHONGHE ZHONG ROAD, HANGZHOU，CHINA

ADVISING BANK：BANK OF CHINA, ZHEJIANG BRANCH

AMOUNT：USD 13,700.00

PARTIAL SHIPMENTS：ALLOWED

COVERING：T-SHIRTS

ITEM.50402-A　5,000 PCS AT USD 1.60

ITEM.50430-B　3,000 PCS AT USD 1.90

TRADE TERMS：FOB C2 KOBE

　　CREDIT AVAILABLE WITH FREELY NEGOTIABLE BY ANY BANK BY NEGOTIATION AGAINST PRESENTATION OF THE DOCUMENTS DETAILED HEREIN AND OF YOUR DRAFTS AT SIGHT FOR 98％ INVOICE COST DRAWN ON THE BANK OF TOKYO，LTD，NEW YORK AGENCY，NEW YORK，N.Y.

　　货物实际分三批装，第一批（ITEM 50402-A，1000 件；ITEM 50430-B，1000 件）于 2019 年 11 月 30 日装运完毕。出口方于 2019 年 12 月 5 日交单议付。发票号码为 ZJ201811。

凭
Drawn under ------------------------------------

信用证或购买证第　　　　号
L/C or A/P No. ------------------------------------

日期　　年　　月　　日
Dated ------------------------------------

按　　　息　　　付　　　款
Payable with interest @ _____% per annum

号码　　　　　汇票金额　　　　　　　中国杭州　　　　　年　　月　　日
No. ------------Exchange for ▆▆▆▆▆ Hangzhou, China ----------------20...

见票　　　　　　　　　　　日 后（本 汇 票 之 副 本 未 付）　付
At ----------- sight of this FIRST of Exchange　（Second of exchange being unpaid）

Pay to the order of_____或其指定人

金额
The sum of ▆▆▆▆▆▆▆▆▆▆▆▆▆▆▆▆▆▆
▆▆▆▆▆▆▆▆▆▆▆▆▆▆▆▆▆▆▆▆

此致
To --------------------------------.

--------------------------------.

✎**任务三：　根据下列资料填制汇票。**

THE SELLER：SHANGHAI JINHAI IMPORT & EXPORT CO. LTD

THE BUYER：ANTAK DEVELOPMENT LTD

TERMS OF PAYMENT：20％T/T BEFORE SHIPMENT AND 80％ L/C AT SIGHT

DESCRIPTION OF GOODS：MEN'S COTTON WOVEN SHIRTS

　　　　　　　　　AT USD 25.00/DOZ CFR SINGAPORE

L/C NO. 123456 DATED AUG. 18，2019 ISSUED BY BANK OF CHINA，
　　　SINGAPORE BRANCH

EXPIRY DATE AND PLACE：OCT.15，2019 IN CHINA

ADVISING BANK：BANK OF CHINA，SHANGHAI BRANCH

WE OPEN THIS IRREVOCABLE DOCUMENTARY CREDIT FAVOURING YOURSELVES AVAILABLE AGAINST YOUR DRAFT AT SIGHT BY NEGOTIATION WITH ADVISING BANK ON US.

B/L DATED：SEP. 28，2019

INVOICE NO. ：SHGM70561

凭
Drawn under　------------------------------

信用证或购买证第　　　号
L/C or A/P No.　------------------------------

日期　年　月　日
Dated　------------------------------

按　息　付　款
Payable with interest @ _____% per annum

号码　　汇票金额　　　中国上海　　　年　月　日
No.-----------Exchange for　　　　　Shanghai, China　--------------200…

见票　　　　　　日　后　（ 本 汇 票 之 副 本 未 付 ） 付
At　-----------　sight of this FIRST of Exchange　(Second of exchange being unpaid)

Pay to the order of_____或其指定人

金额
The sum of

此致
To　------------------------------

🔖**任务四：** 根据下列资料填制汇票。

L/C NO. A-12B-34C DATED NOV.11，2019

ISSUING BANK：ISREAL DISCOUNT BANK OF NEW YORK，NEW YORK BRANCH

APPLICANT：THE ABCDE GROUP，INC.

BENEFICIARY：ZHEJIANG TEXTILES IMPORT&EXPORT CORPORATION

AMOUNT：USD 5,390.00

COVERING：100％ COTTON CUSHIONS

DRAFTS TO BE DRAWN AT 30 DAYS AFTER SIGHT DRAWN ON US BY NEGOTIATION WITH ANY BANK IN CHINA

OTHER TERMS AND CONDITIONS：INVOICE NOT TO SHOW ANY
  COMMISSION BUT TO SHOW TOTAL CFR NEW YORK USD 5,500.00
COMMISSION OF 2％ TO SHOW ONLY ON BILL OF EXCHANGE
INVOICE NO.：12346

提示：上述来证在发票和汇票的金额上做出了与常规不同的规定。通常,发票中显示佣金而汇票中不显示(如任务二)。本证要求发票不显示佣金而汇票中显示佣金。在汇票中显示佣金并不是在金额上加上佣金,而是在汇票中注明汇票金额已扣除2％佣金。如果汇票金额含2％的佣金,就与发票金额相等,造成汇票金额大于信用证金额。这本身是 UCP600 规定所不允许的,另外会在实际中形成买方支付两个2％的佣金。

凭
Drawn under -------------------------------
信用证或购买证第　　　号
L/C or A/P No. -------------------------------
日期　　年　　月　　日
Dated -------------------------------
按　　息　　付　　款
Payable with interest @ _____% per annum
号码　　　　汇票金额　　　　　　中国杭州　　　　年　　月　　日
No.------------Exchange for　　　　　　Hangzhou, China ------------20…
见票　　　　　　　　　日　后　(本 汇 票 之 副 本 未 付) 　付
At _____ sight of this FIRST of Exchange　(Second of exchange being unpaid)
Pay to the order of_____或其指定人
金额
The sum of

此致
To -------------------------------

🔖**任务五**：根据以下资料,审核并修改已填制的汇票,在已填制的 11 个栏目中,即标号(1)—(11)中找出若干处填制错误,并说明原因。

(一)信用证资料
BENEFICIARY：HAINING ABC LEATHER GOODS CO. LTD
  HUANGHE ROAD, HAINING 314400, CHINA
APPLICANT：GRAPHIC IMAGE
  NO. 305 SPAGNOLI ROAD, MELVILLE, NEW YORK, 11747 USA
EXPIRY DATE：20190205 FOR NEGOTIATION
ISSUING BANK：CITIBANK OF NEW YORK, NEW YORK BRANCH

DRAFTS TO BE DRAWN AT 30 DAYS AFTER SIGHT ON ISSUING BANK FOR 90% OF INVOICE VALUE.

YOU ARE AUTHORIZED TO DRAWN UNDER ROYAL BANK OF NEW YORK FOR DOCUMENTARY IRREVOCABLE CREDIT NO. 742863 DATED JAN. 15，2019.

（二）提单、商业发票资料

发票号：IN34567

发票金额：USD 108,000.00 FOB SHANGHAI

起运地：SHANGHAI，CHINA

目的地：NEW YORK，USA

装船日期：JAN. 26，2019

开船日期：JAN. 27，2019

发票签发人：HAINING ABC LEATHER GOODS CO. LTD,姚小兵

（三）已填制的汇票

凭

Drawn under ROYAL BANK OF NEW YORK（1）

信用证或购买证第　　　号
L/C or A/P No. 742863 （2）

日期　　年　　月　　日
Dated JAN.15，2019 （3）

按　　息　　付　　款
Payable with interest @ _____% per annum

号码　　　汇票金额　　　　　　　中国海宁　　　年　月　日
No. IN34567(4) Exchange for (5) USD108,000.00 Haining, China JAN. 25 (6) 2019

见票　　　　　　　　日　后 （本 汇 票 之 副 本 未 付）　付
At XXX(7) sight of this FIRST of Exchange （Second of exchange being unpaid）

Pay to the order of BANK OF CHINA, ZHEJIANG BRANCH (8) 或其指定人

金额
The sum of UNITED STATES DOLLARS ONE HUNDRED AND EIGHT THOUSAND ONLY (9)

此致
To: (10) ROYAL BANK OF NEW YORK

(11) HAINING ABC LEATHER GOODS CO. LTD

姚小兵

任务六：根据下面相关资料，指出下列进口单据中错误的地方，并改正。

（一）相关资料

卖方：LA GUYENNOISE GROUP，3 RUE DES ANCIENS COMBATTANTS 33460 SOUSSANS FRANCE （授权签字人：MAITY）

买方：TIANJIN LINBEICHEN COMMERCE AND TRADE CO. LTD，NO. 81 JINGSAN ROAD，TIANJIN，CHINA （授权签字人：林晓婉）

货物描述：12,000 PCS OF BOTTLED WINE

PACKING IN 2000 WOODEN CASES

开证行：BANK OF CHINA，TIANJIN BRANCH

信用证号：LC18231679

开证日期：MAY 15，2019

汇票金额：EUR 83,340.00

付款期限：即期

提单日期：JULY 1，2019

议付行：BANQUE NATIONALE PARIS

发票号：LBC2018015

（二）已填制的汇票

BILL OF EXCHANGE

Drawn under ___BANQUE NATIONALE PARIS___

L/C No. _____LC18231670_____

Dated _____MAY 15, 2019_____

No.___LBC2013015___ Exchange for ___€83,430.00___ Paris Date: ___JUNE 23, 2019___

At___30 DAYS AFTER___ sight of this FIRST of Exchange (Second of Exchange being unpaid)

pay to the order of___BANK OF CHINA, TIANJIN BRANCH_____

The sum of SAY EURO EIGHTY THREE THOUSAND FOUR HUNDRED AND THIRTY

ONLY

To: BANQUE NATIONALE PARIS

TIANJIN LINBEICHEN COMMERCE AND TRADE CO. LTD

Laura

项目九　其他常用结汇单据填制

实训目标

能够根据有关资料填制检验证书、装船通知、受益人证明、船公司证明等单据。

实训指导

受益人证明、船公司证明、装运前检验证书等附属单据名称多样，内容、制作格式五花八门。制作附属单据时，出单者可采用自己设计的单据格式，也可用白纸或印有出单者英文信头的信纸打印，显示对应的发票编号和进口商要求的单据名称。

一、检验证书填制说明

1. 外贸企业或生产企业出具的检验检疫证书填制

外贸企业或生产企业出具的检验检疫证书各栏目填制如下。

第 1 栏：填写出口公司或生产企业名称和地址。

第 2 栏：填写检验证书名称，如品质检验证书、数量检验证书。证件的名称视检验检疫的内容而定。但应注意证件名称及所列项目和检验检疫结果应与出口合同和信用证规定相符。

第 3 栏：填写发票号码。

第 4 栏：填写检验证书的日期。该日期不能迟于装运日期。

第 5 栏：填写商品名称。

第 6 栏：填写唛头；如无唛头，填 N/M。

第 7 栏：填写计算单价时使用的带有计量单位的数量和（或）提单及其他运输单据相同栏目中最大包装的件数。

第 8 栏：填写净重和（或）毛重。

第 9 栏：填写检验结果。

第 10 栏：出口公司或生产企业经办人签字并加盖公章。

```
┌─────────────────────────────────────────────────────────────┐
│       1. THE NAME AND ADDRESS OF BENEFICIARY/FACTORY          │
│                2. INSPECTION CERTIFICATE                      │
│                                         3. NO.：              │
│                                         4. DATE：             │
│  5. COMMODITY：                                               │
│  6. SHIPPING MARKS：                                          │
│  7. QUANTITY：                                                │
│  8. WEIGHT：                                                  │
│  9. RESULTS OF INSPECTION：                                   │
│                                                              │
│                                         10. SIGNATURE         │
└─────────────────────────────────────────────────────────────┘
```

检验证书样式

2．检验检疫机构出具的检验检疫证书填制

检验检疫机构出具的检验检疫证书的大部分栏目的填写方法和外贸企业或生产企业出具的检验检疫证书基本一致，不同点有以下几个方面。

（1）编号由检验机构编制，不填发票号码。

（2）增加发货人和收货人两个栏目。发货人（consignor）：一般为出口人，即信用证受益人。受货人（consignee）：一般为进口人，即信用证开证申请人；也可只填"to whom it may concern（致有关当事人/敬启者）"。

（3）由检验机构经办人签字并加盖公章。

二、装船通知填制说明

装船通知一般包括以下内容，各栏目填制如下。

1．出口公司名称和地址

填写出口公司名称和地址。一般分两行打印，名称一行，地址一行。

2．单据名称

如信用证对名称有具体规定的，则按信用证规定填写。

有关装船通知性质的单据名称，常见的有："Shipping Advice""Shipment Advice" "Advice of Shipment""Insurance Declaration""Beneficiary's Certified Copy of Fax" "Declaration of Shipment"等。不同名称的装船通知，内容上也有所不同。

3．通知对象

通知对象也称为抬头，按信用证规定填写，如买方、保险公司、开证行等。

4．参考号码

包括信用证号码、发票号码、预约保险单号码等。若抬头为买方指定的保险公司，则应同时注明预约保险单号码。

装船通知
的填制

5. 通知内容

通知内容主要包括所发运货物的品名、数量、金额、运输工具名称、开航日期、起运港、目的港、运输标志等。此外,通知中还可能出现包装说明、ETD(船舶预离港时间)、ETA(船舶预抵港时间)、ETC(预计开始装船时间)等内容。如信用证提出具体项目要求,应按信用证规定填写。

6. 填制时间

填装船通知的填制日期,该时间不能早于装船通知的发出时间。

装船通知的发出时间不能超过信用证约定的时间。约定的时间常见的有两种情形:(1)以小时为准(within 24/48 hours);(2)以天为准(within 2 days after shipment date)。

如果信用证未对装船通知的出单日期做出明确规定,或要求装船后立即通知,一般要求出口商在货物离开起运地后 3 个工作日内向进口商发出装船通知,即提单日后 3 个工作日内。

如果是 FOB、CFR、FCA、CPT 这些由买方办理保险的术语,需要当日发出装船通知。

7. 其他说明

按信用证的要求,加注的一些其他说明。

8. 签署

装船通知可以不签署,但如果信用证要求提供"已证实的装船通知",则受益人必须在该装船通知上进行签字盖章。

---

1. NAME & ADDRESS OF EXPORTER
2. 单据名称

3. TO: 6. DATE:
        4. RE：L/C NO. …   INVOICE NO. … (OPEN POLICY NO. …)

5.

WE HEREBY INFORMED YOU THAT THE GOODS UNDER THE ABOVE MENTIONED
CREDIT HAVE BEEN SHIPPED. THE DETAILS OF SHIPMENT ARE STATED BELOW.

COMMODITY:

QUANTITY:

INVOICE VALUE：

OCEAN VESSEL/ SHIPPED PER S.S.：

DATE OF SHIPMENT：

PORT OF LOADING：

PORT OF DESTINATION：

MARKS：

7. 特殊条款

                                                                8. SIGNATURE

装船通知样式

三、受益人证明填制说明

受益人证明填制一般包括以下内容。

1. 出口公司名称和地址

一般分两行填写，名称一行，地址一行。

2. 单据名称

按 L/C 规定填，如 Beneficiary's Certificate，Beneficiary's Statement，Beneficiary's Declaration。

3. 抬头栏

类似这样的公开证明或声明，抬头可采用笼统填法，即"致有关当事人（to：whom it may concern）"。

4. 日期

即受益人证明填制日期，应与证明的内容符合。

例如：提单日期是 3 月 12 日，受益人证明的有关内容为"We hereby certify that one set of non-negotiable shipping decuments has been airmailed to the applicant within 2 days after the shipment date"，那么受益人证明填制日期不能早于 3 月 12 日，当然也不能晚于交单日期，最好在 3 月 12 日至 3 月 14 日之间。

5. 参考号码

填写信用证号码、发票号码等。

6. 证明内容

根据信用证填制，但有时应对所用时态作相应变化。主要是将来时态变成完成时态。

例如：信用证条款规定"Beneficiary's certificate certify that all the packages to be lined with waterproof paper and bound with two iron straps outside"，那么受益人证明应作成"We hereby certify that all the packages have been lined with waterproof paper and bound with two iron straps outside"。

7. 其他说明

按信用证的要求，加注的一些其他说明。

8. 签署

受益人证明必须要有出口公司签署才能生效。

受益人证明一般不分正、副本。若信用证要求正本，可在单据名称的正下方打上"ORIGINAL"字样。

```
┌─────────────────────────────────────────────────────────────┐
│                                                              │
│        1. NAME & ADDRESS OF BENEFICIARY                      │
│                                                              │
│           2. BENEFICIARY'S CERTIFICATE                       │
│                                                              │
│      3. TO：WHOM IT MAY CONCERN              4. DATE：        │
│                                                              │
│            5. RE：L/C NO. ... INVOICE NO. ...                │
│                                                              │
│      6. WE HEREBY CERTIFY THAT...                            │
│                                                              │
│                                                              │
│                                            7. SIGNATURE      │
│                                                              │
└─────────────────────────────────────────────────────────────┘
```

受益人证明样式

四、船公司证明填制说明

各家船公司出具的船公司证明的格式虽不一样,但通常包括以下主要内容。

1. 出证日期和地址

一般为签发提单的日期和地址。

2. 船名和提单号

表明本次运输的运载船舶及其提单号。

3. 单据名称

按信用证规定填写。

4. 抬头人

一般都笼统打印"to：whom it may concern"。

5. 证明内容

按照信用证要求,根据实际做出相应证明。

6. 出证人签章

应与提单签单人一致,通常为承运货物的船公司或其代理人、外轮代理公司或承担联运业务的外运公司等。

⊙ 实训任务

✎ **任务一：** 根据下列资料填制检验证书。

（一）信用证资料

L/C NO.：704-3000401

DATE OF ISSUE：AUG. 26，2019

EXPIRY DATE：OCT. 15，2019

APPLICANT：MOKADI TRASING CO. LTD

　　　　　　12-1 THIMOSONE SHINMACHI, KOKURAMINAMI-KU, KITAKYUSHU

　　　　　　CITY, JAPAN

BENEFICIARY：HANGZHOU DAHUA MEDICINES AND HEALTH PRODUCTS

　　　　　　I/E CORPORATION

　　　　　　NO. 25 HUSHU ROAD，HANGZHOU，CHINA

DOCUMENTS REQUIRED：

　　＋INSPECTION CERTIFICATE OF QUALITY ISSUED BY MANUFACTURER

　　…

COVERING SHIPMENT OF NET 6.12 MT OF CHLOROPHYLL PASTE LOT NO.

　　9327（CHLOROPHYLL IN CONTENTS：13％ MIN. EXTINCTION RATIO：

　　3.7％ MAX.）AT USD 3，600.00 PER MT S/C NO.93002-P008 PRODUCED BY

　　LINQU FACTORY，35 QIANQING ROAD，SHAOXING CHINA

（二）其他资料

PACKING IN IRON DRUM OF 170 KGSEACH

SHIPPING MARKS：M.T./YOKOHAMA/NO.1-UP

INVOICE NO.：MH201910

INVOICE DATE：SEP. 12，2019

货物于 2019 年 9 月 20 日装运完毕。

LINQU FACTORY

NO. 35 QIANQING ROAD, SHAOXING, CHINA

INSPECTION CERTIFICATE OF QUALITY

NO.:

DATE:

COMMODITY:

SHIPPING MARKS:

QUANTITY:

WEIGHT:

RESULTS OF INSPECTION:

_____

Authorized Signature

任务二： 根据下列资料填制装船通知、受益人证明。

L/C NO.：513179/WL

DATE OF ISSUE：JULY 18，2019

EXPIRY DATE：NOV. 15，2019 PLACE IN CHINA

LATEST SHIPMENT：OCT. 30，2019

ISSUING BANK：HABIB BANK LIMITED CENTRAL BR. 2-HA, KARACHI PAKISTAN

APPLICANT：JEVAN TRADING CO.

      NO. 15 MARVI BLGH. MARRIO ROAD, P.O. BOX 4666，KARACHI-78000

BENEFICIARY：GUANGHUA LIGHT INDUSTRIAL PRODUCTS IMP. AND EXP. CORP.

      NO. 62 JIANGXI ROAD，HANGZHOU，CHINA

COMMODITY：LOVELY BRAND ALARM CLOCKS 720 PCS AT USD 2.00 PER

      PC FOBKARACHI

SHIPPING MARKS：ABDOLTAH/KARACHI/NO.1-UP

PACKING IN CARTONS OF 24 PCS EACH

G.W.：424 KGS N.W.：369 KGS

SHIPMENT：FROM NINGBO TO KARACHI ON OCT. 28，2018 BY S. S.

      LONGXING V.11

B/L NO.：BL123

INVOICE NO：GLI201907

INVOICE DATE：OCT. 20，2019

DOCUMENTS REQUIRED：

  +ALL SHIPMENTS UNDER THIS CREDIT MUST BE ADVISED BY YOU IMMEDIATELY AFTER SHIPMENT DIRECT TO EASTERN FEDERAL UNION INSURANCE CO. LTD QUNAR HOUSE，M.A. JINNAH ROAD，KARACHI AND TO THE OPENERS，REFERRING TO THEIR COVER NOTE NO. 099421/94/GAL/JEVAN AND A COPY OF SHIPMENT ADVICE IS REQUIRED.

  +6 COPIES OF INVOICE WITH 2 COPIES OF NON-NEGOTIABLE BILLS OF LADING TO BE SENT DIRECT TO AGENTS PAKISTAN GENERAL TRADER，P. O. BOX 5520 KARACHI IMMEDIATELY AFTER SHIPMENT BY REGISTERED POST AND BENEFICIARY'S CERTIFICATE TO THIS EFFECT MUST ACCOMPANY DOCUMENTS.

GUANGHUA LIGHT INDUSTRIAL PRODUCTS IMP. AND EXP. CORP.

NO. 62 JIANGXI ROAD, HANGZHOU, CHINA

SHIPMENT ADVICE

TO：   DATE：

RE：L/C NO.   INVOICE NO.   COVER NOTE NO.

WE HEREBY INFORMED YOU THAT THE GOODS UNDER THE ABOVE MENTIONED CREDIT HAVE BEEN SHIPPED. THE DETAILS OF SHIPMENT ARE STATED BELOW.

COMMODITY：

QUANTITY：

INVOICE VALUE：

OCEAN VESSEL/SHIPPED PER S.S.：

DATE OF SHIPMENT：

PORT OF LOADING：

PORT OF DESTINATION：

MARKS：

Authorized Signature

GUANGHUA LIGHT INDUSTRIAL PRODUCTS IMP. AND EXP. CORP.
NO. 62 JIANGXI ROAD, HANGZHOU, CHINA

BENEFICIARY'S CERTIFICATE

TO：   DATE：

        RE：L/C NO.   INVOICE NO.

WE HEREBY CERTIFY THAT

_____
Authorized Signature

🔗**任务三：** 根据下列资料填制检验证书、装船通知、受益人证明。

（一）信用证资料

APPLICANT：CHAMUNDI TEXTILES(SILK MILLS) LTD

        NO. 56 OHTEMACHI，1-CHOME，CHIIYADA-KU，YOKOHAMA，JAPAN

BENEFICIARY：ZHEJIANG RAIN TEXTILES CO. LTD

        RM1808，WEST LAKE INTERNATION MANSION，

        NO. 235 WENER ROAD，HANGZHOU，CHINA

MERCHANDISE：MULBERRY RAW SILK 80 CARTONS

COUNRTY OF ORIGIN：CHINA

CIF VALUE：USD 99,033.68

PACKED IN SEAWORTHY CARTONS

DOCUMENTS REQUIRED：

+ INSPECTION CERTIFICATE OF QUALITY ISSUED BY THE ENTRY-EXIT INSPECTION AND QUARANTINE OF THE PEOPLE'S REPUBLIC OF CHINA EVIDENCING THAT THE GOODS HAVE BEEN INSPECTED AND FOUND TO BE IN COMPLIANCE WITH THE CONTRACT.

+BENEFICIARY'S STATEMENT STATING THAT THEY HAVE SENT ONE FULL SET OF N/N DOCUMENTS REQUIRED BY L/C TO THE APPLICANT VIA DHL WITHIN 2 DAYS AFTER SHIPMENT.

+BENEFICIARY'S CERTIFIED COPY OF FAX TO THE APPLICANT(FAX NO. 0098-2-23456) ADVISING MERCHANDISE, SHIPMENT DATE, GROSS WEIGHT, NET WEIGHT, INVOICE VALUE, NAME AND VOYAGE OF VESSEL, CARRIER'S NAME, PORT OF LOADING AND PORT OF DISCHARGE IMMEDIATELY AFTER THE DATE OF SHIPMENT.

...

ADDITIONAL CONDITIONS:

+ ALL DOCUMENTS MUST BE MADE OUT IN THE NAME OF THE APPLICANT UNLESS OTHERWISE STIPULATED BY THE L/C.

+ ALL DOCUMENTS MUST INDICATE OUR L/C NUMBER AND ISSUING BANK NAME: THE BANK OF TOKYO-MITSUBISHI UFJ, LTD. 2-7-1, MARUNOUCHI, CHIYODA-KU, TOKYO, JAPAN.

（二）其他资料

S/C NO.: SC 9802

N.W.: 2,397.91 KGS

G.W.: 2,640.00 KGS

MEASUREMENT: 8.240 CBM

DATE OF INSPECTION: JAN.10, 2018

DATE OF SHIPMENT: JAN.12, 2018

CARRIER: AHEAD LOGISTICS CO. LTD

PORT OF LOADING: SHANGHAI

PORT OF DESTINATION: YOKOHAMA

NAME AND VOYAGE OF VESSEL: HYUNDAI VLADIVOSTOK V.526W

INVOICE NO.: 0C01A0120185

INVOICE DATE: JAN.3, 2018

SHIPPING MARKS: CTL/YOKOHAMA/NO.1-UP

（三）检验证书

CIQ

中华人民共和国出入境检验检疫
ENTRY-EXIT INSPECTION AND QUARANTINE
OF THE PEOPLE'S REPUBLIC OF CHINA
INSPECTION CERTIFICATE OF QUALITY

发货人
Consignor _____

收货人
Consignee _____

品名
Commodity _____

报检数量/重量
Quantity/Weight Declared _____

包装种类及数量
Number and Type of Package _____

运输工具
Means of Conveyance _____

标记及号码
Marks & Nos. _____

检验结果
Results of Inspection _____

	签证地点	签证日期
印章	Place of Issue	Date of Issue
Official Stamp	授权签字人	签名
	Authorized Officer	Signature

我们已尽所知和最大能力实施上述检验，不能因我们签发本证书而免除卖方或其他方面根据合同和法律所承担的产品种类责任和其他责任。All inspections are carried out conscientiously to the best of our knowledge and ability. This certificate does not in any respect absolve the seller and other related parties from his contractual and legal obligations especially when product quality is concerned.

（四）装船通知

ZHEJIANG RAIN TEXTILES CO. LTD

RM1808，WEST LAKE INTERNATION MANSION

NO. 235 WENER ROAD，HANGZHOU，CHINA

SHIPPING ADVICE

TO：   DATE：

RE：L/C NO.   INVOICE NO.

WE HEREBY INFORMED YOU THAT THE GOODS UNDER THE ABOVE MENTIONED CREDIT HAVE BEEN SHIPPED. THE DETAILS OF SHIPMENT ARE STATED BELOW.

COMMODITY：

QUANTITY：

INVOICE VALUE：

OCEAN VESSEL/ SHIPPED PER S.S.：

DATE OF SHIPMENT：

PORT OF LOADING：

PORT OF DESTINATION：

MARKS：

Signature

（五）受益人证明

ZHEJIANG RAIN TEXTILES CO. LTD

RM1808，WEST LAKE INTERNATION MANSION

NO.235 WENER ROAD, HANGZHOU，CHINA

BENEFICIARY'S STATEMENT

TO：   DATE：

RE：L/C NO.   INVOICE NO.

WE HEREBY CERTIFY THAT...

— — — — — — — — — —

✎ **任务四：** 阅读下列信用证并指出制作相应单据时应注意的问题。

JAN. 31，2019 15：23：46   LOGICAL TERMINAL E102

MT S700   ISSUE OF A DOCUMENTARY CREDIT

PAGE 00001

FUNCMSG700

UMR06607642

MSGACK DWS765I AUTH OK，KEY B110106173BAOC53B，BKCHCNBJ BNPA＊＊＊＊

RECORO

BASIC HEADER F 01 BKCHCNBJA940 0542 725524

APPLICATION HEADER 0 700 1122180129 BNPACAMMXXX 4968 839712 190130 0028 N

＊ BNP PARIBAS (CANADA)

＊ MONTREAL

USER HEADER   SERVICE CODE   103：

BANK. PRIORITY   113：

MSG USER REF.   108：   （银行盖信用证通知专用章）

INFO. FROM CI   115：

SEQUENCE OF TOTAL   ＊27：1/1

FORM OF DOC. CREDIT   ＊40A：IRREVOCABLE

DOC. CREDIT NUMBER   ＊20：63211020049

DATE OF ISSUE   31C：20190129

EXPIRY   ＊31D：DATE 20190410 PLACE IN BENEFICIARY'S COUNTRY

APPLICANT   ＊50：FASHION FORCE CO. LTD

240 ST. GEORGE STREET, OTTAWA, CANADA

BENEFICIARY   * 59: HANGZHOU SICODA TEXTILE GARMENT CO. LTD

RM2901, YELLOW DRAGON MANSION,

NO.85 SHUGUANG ROAD, HANGZHOU, CHINA

AMOUNT   * 32B: CURRENCY USD AMOUNT 32,640

AVAILABLE WITH/BY   * 41D: ANY BANK BY NEGOTIATION

DRAFTS AT... 42C: AT SIGHT

DRAWEE   42A: BNPACAMMXXX

* BNP PARIBAS (CANADA)

* MONTREAL

PARTIAL SHIPMENTS   43P: NOT ALLOWED

TRANSSHIPMENT   43T: ALLOWED

LOADING ON CHARGE   44A: CHINA

FOR TRANSPORT TO   44B: MONTREAL

LATEST DATE OF SHIPMENT   44C: 20190325

DESCRIPT OF GOODS   45A:

SALES CONDITIONS: CIF MONTREAL/CANADA

SALES CONTRACT NO. F01LCB18127

LADIES COTTON BLAZER (100% COTTON, 40SX20/140X60)

STYLE NO.	PO NO.	QTY/PCS	USD/PC
46-301A	10337	2,550	12.80

DOCUMENTS REQUIRED   46A:

+ COMMERCIAL INVOICES IN 3 COPIES SIGNED BY BENEFICIARY'S REPRESENTATIVE.

+CANADA CUSTOMS INVOICES IN 4 COPIES.

+FULL SET OF ORIGINAL MARINE BILLS OF LADING CLEAN ON BOARD PLUS 2 NON-NEGOTIABLE COPIES MADE OUT OR ENDORSED TO ORDER OF BNP PARIBAS (CANADA) MARKED FREIGHT PREPAID AND NOTIFY APPLICANT'S FULL NAME AND ADDRESS.

+DETAILED PACKING LISTS IN 3 COPIES.

+COPY OF CERTIFICATE OF ORIGIN FORM A.

+COPY OF EXPORT LICENCE.

+BENEFICIARY'S LETTER STATING THAT ORIGINAL CERTIFICATE OF

ORIGIN FORM A, ORIGINAL EXPORT LICENCE, COPY OF COMMERCIAL INVOICE, DETAILED PACKING LISTS AND A COPY OF BILL OF LADING WERE SENT DIRECT TO APPLICANT BY COURIER WITHIN 5 DAYS AFTER SHIPMENT. THE RELEATIVE COURIER RECEIPT IS ALSO REQUIRED FOR PRESENTATION.

+ COPY OF APPLICANT'S FAX APPROVING PRODUCTION SAMPLES BEFORE SHIPMENT.

+LETTER FROM SHIPPER ON THEIR LETTERHEAD INDICATING THEIR NAME OF COMPANY AND ADDRESS, BILL OF LADING NUMBER, CONTAINER NUMBER AND THAT THIS SHIPMENT, INCLUDING ITS CONTAINER, DOES NOT CONTAIN ANY NON-MANUFACTURED WOODEN MATERIAL, DUNNAGE, BRACING MATERIAL, PALLETS, CRATING OR OTHER NON-MANUFACTURED WOODEN PACKING MATERIAL.

+ INSPECTION CERTIFICATE ORIGINAL SINGED AND ISSUED BY FASHION FORCE CO. LTD STATING THE SAMPLES OF FOUR STYLE GARMENTS HAS BEEN APPROVED, WHICH SEND THROUGH DHL BEFORE 15 DAYS OF SHIPMENT.

+INSURANCE POLICY OR CERTIFICATE IN 1 ORIGINAL AND 1 COPY ISSUED OR ENDORSED TO THE ORDER OF BNP PARIBAS (CANADA) FOR THE CIF INVOICE PLUS 10 PERCENT COVERING ALL RISKS, INSTITUTE STRIKES, INSTITUTE WAR CLAUSES AND CIVIL COMMOTIONS CLAUSES. ADDITIONAL CONDITIONS. 47A:

+IF DOCUMENTS PRESENTED ARE FOUND BY US NOT TO BE UN FULL COMPLIANCE WITH CREDIT TERMS. WE WILL ASSESS A CHARGE OF USD 55.00 PER SET OF DOCUMENTS.

+ALL CHARGES IF ANY RELATED TO SETTLEMENTS ARE FOR ACCOUNT OF BENEFICIARY.

+3 PCT MORE OR LESS IN AMOUNT AND QUANTITY IS ALLOWED.

+ ALL CERTIFICATES/LETTERS/STATEMENTS MUST BE SIGNED AND DATED.

+FOR INFORMATION ONLY, PLEASE NOTE AS OF JANUARY 4, 1999 THAT ALL SHIPMENTS FROM CHINA THAT ARE PACKED WITH UNTREATED WOOD WILL BE BANNED FROM CANADA DUE TO THE THREAT POSED BY THE ASIAN

LONGNORNED BEETLE.

+THE CANADIAN GOVERNMENT NOW INSIST THAT EVERY SHIPMENT ENTERING CANADA MUST HAVE THE ABOVE DOCUMENTATION WITH THE SHIPMENT.

+ BILL OF LADING AND COMMERCIAL INVOICE MUST CERTIFY THE FOLLOWING: THIS SHIPMENT, INCLUDING ITS CONTAINER DOES NOT CONTAIN ANY NON-MANUFACTURED WOODEN MATERIAL, DUNNAGE, BRACING MATERIAL PALLETS, CRATING OR OTHER NON MANUFACTURED WOODEN PACKING MATERIAL.

+BENEFICIARY'S BANK ACCOUNT NO. 07773108201140121

CHARGES 71B:

+OUTSIDE COUNTRY BANK CHARGES TO BE BORNE BY THE BENEFICIARY

+OPENING BANK CHARGES TO BE BORNE BY THE APPLICANT

CONFIRMATION * 49: WITHOUT

INSTRUCTIONS 78:

+WE SHALL COVER THE NEGOTIATING BANK AS PER THEIR INSTRUCTIONS.

+FORWARD DOCUMENTS IN ONE LOT BY SPECIAL COURIER PREPAID TO BNP PARIBAS (CANADA) 1981 MCGILL COLLECE AVE. MONTREAL QC H3A 2W8 CANADA.

SEND. TO REC. INFO. 72:

THIS CREDIT IS SUBJECT TO UCP FOR DOCUMENTARY CREDIT 2007 REVISION ICC PUBLICATION 600 AND IS THE OPERATIVE INSTRUMENT.

TRAILER ORDER IS <MAC: > <PAC: > <ENC: > <CHK: > <TNG: > <
PDE: >
MAC: F344CA36
CHK: AA6204FFDFC2

项目十　开证申请书填制

☑ 实训目标

能够根据有关资料填制开证申请书。

💼 实训指导

开证申请书通常为一式两联,申请人除填写正面内容外,还须签具背面的"开证申请人承诺书"。开证申请书其正面各栏目的内容填制如下。

1. To

致 _____ 行。填写开证行名称。

2. Date

填写申请开证日期。

3. Issue by

（1）airmail,以信开的形式开立信用证。选择此种方式,开证行以航邮将信用证寄给通知行。

（2）brief advice by teletransmission,以简电开的形式开立信用证。选择此种方式,开证行将信用证主要内容以电讯方式预先通知受益人,银行承担必须使其生效的责任,但简电本身并非信用证的有效文本,不能凭以议付或付款,银行随后寄出的"证实书"才是正式的信用证。

（3）express delivery,以信开的形式开立信用证。选择此种方式,开证行以快递（如DHL）的方式将信用证寄给通知行。

（4）teletransmission（which shall be the operative instrument）,以全电开的形式开立信用证。选择此种方式,开证行将信用证的全部内容加注密押后发出,该电讯文本为有效的信用证正本。如今大多用"全电开证"的方式开立信用证。

4. Credit No.

信用证号码,由银行填写。

5. Date and Place of Expiry

信用证有效期及地点,地点填受益人所在国家。

6. Applicant

填写开证申请人名称及地址。

7. Beneficiary（Full Name and Address）

填写受益人全称和详细地址。

8. Advising Bank

填写通知行名称及地址。

9. Amount

填写信用证金额,分别用数字小写和文字大写。

10. Parital Shipments

分批装运。填写跟单信用证项下是否允许分批装运。

11. Transshipment

转运。填写跟单信用证项下是否允许货物转运。

12. Loading on Board/Despatch/Taking in Charge at/from

填写装运港。

13. Not Later Than

填写最后装运期。

14. For Transportation to

填写目的港。

15. FOB, CFR, CIF, or Other Terms

价格条款,根据合同内容选择或填写价格条款。

16. Credit Available with

填写此信用证可由_____银行即期付款、承兑、议付、延期付款,即押汇银行(出口地银行)名称。

如果信用证为自由议付信用证,银行可用"any bank in...(地名/国名)"表示。

如果该信用证为自由议付信用证,而且对议付地点也无限制时,可用"any bank"表示。

(1) Sight Payment:勾选此项,表示开具即期付款信用证。

(2) Acceptance:勾选此项,表示开具承兑信用证。

(3) Negotiation:勾选此项,表示开具议付信用证。

(4) Deferred Payment at:勾选此项,表示开具延期付款信用证。

如果开具这类信用证,需要写明延期多少天付款,例如:at 60 days from payment confirmation(60天承兑付款),at 60 days from B/L date(提单日期后60天付款)等。

17. Against the documents detailed herein and beneficiary's draft(s) for _____% of invoice value at _____sight drawn on_____.

此项为汇票信息。大意为:

连同下列单据和受益人按发票金额_____%,作成期限为_____天,付款人为_____的汇票。

注意延期付款信用证不需要选择连同此单据。

"at_____sight"为付款期限。如果是即期,需要在"at_____sight"之间填"＊＊"或"－－",不能留空。"drawn on"为指定付款人。

注意汇票的付款人应为开证行或指定的付款行。

18. Documents Required：(Marked with ×)

信用证需要提交的单据(用"×"标明)。

(1) 经签字的商业发票一式_____份,标明信用证号和合同号_____。

(2) 全套清洁已装船海运提单,制作成空白抬头、空白背书,注明"运费［ ］到付/［ ］已付",［ ］标明运费金额,并通知_____。

(3) 航空运单/承运收据/铁路运单,收货人为_____,注明"运费［ ］到付/［ ］已付",［ ］标明运费金额,并通知_____。

(4) 保险单/保险凭证一式_____份,按发票金额的_____％投保,注明赔付地在_____,以汇票同种货币支付,空白背书,投保_____。

(5) 装箱单/重量证明一式_____份,注明每一包装的数量、毛重和净重。

(6) 数量/重量证书一式_____份,由_____出具。

(7) 品质证书一式_____份,由［ ］制造商/［ ］公众认可的检验机构［ ］或其他_____出具。

(8) 产地证一式_____份,由_____出具。

(9) 经受益人证实的、以传真/电传方式通知申请人的装船证明副本,该证明须在装船后_____小时内发出,并通知［ ］船名［ ］航班号［ ］车厢号,装运日期,货物数量、重量和金额。

(10) 其他单据(若有)。

19. Description of Goods

货物描述。包括:商品名称、型号、规格,数量,单价等内容。

20. Additional Instructions

附加条款,是对以上各条款未述之情况的补充和说明,且包括对银行的要求等。此项内容根据实际需要填写。

(1) 开证行以外的所有银行费用由受益人负担。

(2) 单据须在运输单据出具日后_____天内提交,但不得超过信用证有效期。

(3) 第三方为托运人不可接受,简式/背面空白提单不可接受。

(4) 数量及信用证金额允许有_____％的增减。

(5) 所有单据必须用快递一次性提交给开证行。

(6) 其他条款(若有)。

⊙ 实训任务

✎**任务一： 根据下列资料，填制开证申请书。**

（一）合同条款

2019 年 6 月 25 日，浙江晨林进出口公司（ZHEJIANG CHENLIN IMP. & EXP. CO. LTD，NO.118 HEMU ROAD，HANGZHOU，CHINA）从 LLUE PLUS CO. LTD （NO. 667 HANNAMDONG YOUNGSAN-KU， SEOUL， REPUBLIC OF KOREA）进口 MEN'S WIND BREAKER 一批，达成以下主要合同条款。

（1）Commodity：LADY'S SWEATER，STYLE NO. HL290.

（2）Quantity：2,000 PCS，3% MORE OR LESS ALLOWED.

（3）Packing：IN CARTONS 50 PCS EACH.

（4）Unit Price：USD 35.6/PC CIF NINGBO.

（5）Amount：USD 71,200.00.

（6）Time of Shipment：NOT LATER THAN OCT. 30, 2019.

　　Port of Loading：BUSAN，REPUBLIC OF KOREA.

　　Port of Destination：NINGBO，CHINA.

　　Partial Shipment：ALLOWED.

　　Transshipment：PROHIBITED.

（7）Insurance：TO BE COVERED BY THE SELLER FOR 120% INVOICE VALUE COVERING WPA AND WAR RISK AS PER CIC OF PICC DATED 19810101.

（8）Payment：BY IRREVOCABLE LETTER OF CREDIT AT SIGHT TO REACH THE SELLER NOT LATER THAN JULY 5，2019，VALID FOR NEGOTIATION IN REPUBLIC OF KOREA UNTIL THE 15TH DAY AFTER TIME OF SHIPMENT.

（二）其他资料

（1）合同号码：CL876567。

（2）浙江晨林进出口公司国际商务单证员李丽于 2019 年 7 月 1 日向中国银行浙江分行办理申请电开信用证手续，通知行是 KOOKMIN BANK，SEOUL，REPUBLIC OF KOREA。

（3）涉及的单据份数均为一式三份。

（4）要求韩国客户提供产地证，并在装运后 48 小时内发出装船通知。

IRREVOCABLE DOCUMENTARY CREDIT APPLICATION

To： Date：

☐Issue by airmail ☐With brief advice by teletransmission ☐Issue by express delivery ☐Issue by teletransmission（which shall be the operative instrument）	Credit No. Date and Place of Expiry
Applicant	Beneficiary（full name and address）
Advising Bank	Amount

Partial Shipments ☐allowed☐not allowed	Transshipment ☐allowed☐not allowed	Credit Available with ☐sight payment
Loading on board/despatch/taking in charge at/from Not later than For transportation to		☐acceptance ☐negotiation ☐deferred payment at against the documents detailed herein
☐FOB ☐CFR ☐CIF ☐or other terms _____		☐and beneficiary's draft(s) for __ % of invoice value at_____ drawn on _____

Documents Required：（marked with ×）

1.（ ）Signed commercial invoice in ____ copies indicating L/C No. and Contract No. _____ .

2.（ ）Full set of clean on board Bills of Lading made out to order and blank endorsed，marked "freight 〔 〕 to collect /〔 〕 prepaid 〔 〕 showing freight amount" notifying _____ .

3.（ ）Airway bills/cargo receipt/railway bills consigned to _____ showing "freight〔 〕 to collect/〔 〕 prepaid 〔 〕 showing freight amount" notifying _____ .

4.（ ）Insurance Policy/Certificate in ____ copies for ____ % of the invoice value showing claims payable in _____ in currency of the draft，blank endorsed，covering _____ _____ .

5.（ ）Packing List/Weight Memo in ____ copies indicating quantity，gross and net weights of each package.

6.（ ）Certificate of Quantity/Weight in _____ copies issued by_____ .

7.（ ）Certificate of Quality in ____ copies issued by 〔 〕 manufacturer/〔 〕 public recognized survey 〔 〕 or _____ .

8.（ ）Certificate of origin in ____copies issued by____ .

9.（ ）Beneficiary's certified copy of fax/telex despatched to applicant within____ hours after shipment advising 〔 〕name of vessel/〔 〕flight NO. /〔 〕wagon NO.，date，quantity，weight and value of shipment.

10.（ ）Other documents，if any.

Description of Goods：

Additional Instructions：

1.（ ）All banking charges outside the opening bank are for beneficiary's account.

2.（ ）Documents must be presented within ____ days after date of issuance of the transport documents but within the validity of this credit.

3.（ ）Third party as shipper is not acceptable，Short Form/Blank back B/L is not acceptable.

4.（ ）Both quantity and credit amount ____ % more or less are allowed.

5.（ ）All documents must be sent to issuing bank by courier/speed post in one lot.

6.（ ）Other terms，if any.

任务二： 根据下列资料，填制开证申请书。

（一）合同条款

2019 年 8 月 20 日，上海清河进出口公司（SHANGHAI QINGHE IMP. & EXP. CO. LTD, NO. 118 CHANGXING ROAD, SHANGHAI, CHINA）从 RIQING IMPORT AND EXPORT COMPANY（P.O.BOX 2341, NAGOYA, JAPAN）进口一批 MEN'S WIND BREAKER，达成以下主要合同条款。

（1）Commodity：MEN'S WIND BREAKER，STYLE NO. YM082 KHAKI.

（2）Quantity：2,500 PCS.

（3）Packing：IN CARTONS 50 PCS EACH.

（4）Unit Price：USD 20.00/PC FOB NAGOYA.

（5）Amount：USD 50,000.00.

（6）Time of Shipment：ON OR BEFORE DEC. 30，2019.

　　　 Port of Loading：NAGOYA，JAPAN.

　　　 Port of Destination：SHANGHAI, CHINA.

　　　 Partial Shipment：ALLOWED.

　　　 Transshipment：PROHIBITED.

（7）Insurance：TO BE COVERED BY THE BUYER.

（8）Payment：BY IRREVOCABLE LETTER OF CREDIT AT 120 DAYS AFTER SIGHT TO REACH THE SELLER NOT LATER THAN SEP.20，2019，VALID FOR NEGOTIATION IN REPUBLIC OF KOREA UNTIL THE 15TH DAY AFTER TIME OF SHIPMENT.

（二）其他资料

（1）合同号码：HL20180315。

（2）上海清河进出口公司国际商务单证员李丽于 2019 年 8 月 31 日向中国银行上海分行办理申请电开信用证手续，通知行是 BANK OF TOKYO-MITSUBISHI UFJ, LTD，THE NAGOYA。

（3）要求日本客户在装运后 48 小时内发出装船通知。

（4）所需单据：

＋经签字的商业发票一式五份，标明信用证号和合同号。

＋全套清洁已装船海运提单，制作成凭托运人指示的抬头、空白背书，注明"运费已付"，并通知开证申请人。

＋装箱单一式五份，注明每一包装的数量、毛重和净重。

＋产地证正本一份副本二份，由权威机构出具。

IRREVOCABLE DOCUMENTARY CREDIT APPLICATION

To：   Date：

☐Issue by airmail ☐With brief advice by teletransmission ☐Issue by express delivery ☐Issue by teletransmission（which shall be the operative instrument）	Credit No.
	Date and place of expiry
Applicant	Beneficiary（full name and address）
Advising Bank	Amount

Partial Shipments ☐allowed☐not allowed	Transshipment ☐allowed☐not allowed	Credit available with ☐sight payment

Loading on board/despatch/taking in charge at/from
Not later than
For transportation to
☐FOB   ☐CFR   ☐CIF
☐or other terms _____

☐acceptance
☐negotiation
☐deferred payment at
against the documents detailed herein
☐and beneficiary's draft(s) for __ ％ of invoice value
at_____ drawn on _____

Documents Required：（marked with ×）

1.（   ）Signed commercial invoice in _____ copies indicating L/C No. and Contract No. _____ .
2.（   ）Full set of clean on board Bills of Lading made out to order and blank endorsed，marked "freight ［   ］ to collect /［   ］ prepaid ［   ］ showing freight amount" notifying _____ .
3.（   ）Airway bills/cargo receipt/railway bills consigned to _____ showing "freight ［   ］ to collect/［   ］ prepaid ［   ］ showing freight amount" notifying _____ .
4.（   ）Insurance Policy/Certificate in _____ copies for _____ ％ of the invoice value showing claims payable in _____ in currency of the draft，blank endorsed，covering _____ _____ .
5.（   ）Packing List/Weight Memo in _____ copies indicating quantity，gross and net weights of each package.
6.（   ）Certificate of Quantity/Weight in _____ copies issued by_____ .
7.（   ）Certificate of Quality in _____ copies issued by ［   ］ manufacturer/［   ］ public recognized survey ［   ］ or_____ .
8.（   ）Certificate of origin in _____ copies issued by_____ .
9.（   ）Beneficiary's certified copy of fax/telex despatched to applicant within_____ hours after shipment advising ［   ］name of vessel/［   ］flight NO. /［   ］wagon NO.，date，quantity，weight and value of shipment.
10.（   ）Other documents，if any.

Description of Goods：

Additional Instructions：

1.（   ）All banking charges outside the opening bank are for beneficiary's account.
2.（   ）Documents must be presented within _____ days after date of issuance of the transport documents but within the validity of this credit.
3.（   ）Third party as shipper is not acceptable，Short Form/Blank back B/L is not acceptable.
4.（   ）Both quantity and credit amount _____ ％ more or less are allowed.
5.（   ）All documents must be sent to issuing bank by courier/speed post in one lot.
6.（   ）Other terms，if any.

任务三： 根据下列资料，审核开证申请书。

（一）合同条款

2018 年 6 月 20 日,上海华联皮革制品有限公司(SHANGHAI HUALIAN LEATHER GOODS CO. LTD, 156 CHANGXING ROAD, SHANGHAI, CHINA)向 SVS DESIGN PLUS CO. LTD (1-509 HANNAMDONG YOUNGSAN-KU, SEOUL, REPUBLIC OF KOREA)出口一批 DOUBLE FACE SHEEPSKIN,达成以下主要合同条款。

（1）Commodity：DOUBLE FACE SHEEPSKIN，COLOUR CHESTNUT.

（2）Quantity：3,175.25 SQFT.

（3）Packing：IN CARTONS.

（4）Unit Price：USD 7.40/SQFT CIF INCHON.

（5）Amount：USD 23,496.85.

（6）Time of Shipment：During NOV. 2019.

　　　　Port of Loading：SHANGHAI, CHINA.

　　　　Port of Destination：INCHON, REPUBLIC OF KOREA.

　　　　Partial Shipment：ALLOWED.

　　　　Transshipment：PROHIBITED.

（7）Insurance：TO BE COVERED BY THE BUYER.

（8）Payment：BY IRREVOCABLE LETTER OF CREDIT AT 45 DAYS AFTER SIGHT TO REACH THE SELLER NOT LATER THAN JUNE 24，2019，VALID FOR NEGOTIATION IN CHINA UNTIL THE 15TH DAY AFTER TIME OF SHIPMENT.

（9）Document：

＋ SIGNED COMMERCIAL INVOICE IN 3 FOLD.

＋ SIGNED PACKING LIST IN 3 FOLD.

＋FULL SET OF CLEAN ON BOARD OCEAN B/L IN 3/3 ORIGINALS ISSUED TO ORDER OF ISSUING BANK "FREIGHT PREPAID" AND NOTIFY THE APPLICANT.

＋CERTIFICATE OF ORIGIN IN 1 ORIGINAL AND 1 COPY ISSUED BY THE CHAMBER OF COMMERCE IN CHINA.

＋ INSURANCE POLICY/CERTIFICATE IN DUPLICATE ENDORSED IN BLANK FOR 110％ INVOICE VALUE COVERING ALL RISKS AND WAR RISKS OF CIC OF PICC (19810101).SHOWING THE CLAIMING CURRENCY IS THE SAME AS THE CURRENCY OF CREDIT .

（二）相关资料

（1）信用证号码：MO722111057。

（2）合同号码：SP20180415。

（3）SVS DESIGN PLUS CO. LTD 国际商务单证员金浩于 2019 年 6 月 23 日向 KOOKMIN BANK，SEOUL，REPUBLIC OF KOREA 办理申请电开信用证手续，通知行是 BANK OF CHINA，SHANGHAI BRANCH。

IRREVOCABLE DOCUMENTARY CREDIT APPLICATION

TO：BANK OF CHINA   Date：JUNE 25，2019

Beneficiary(full name and address) SVS DESIGN PLUS CO. LTD 1-509 HANNAMDONG YOUNGSAN-KU， SEOUL，REPUBLIC OF KOREA	L/C No. MO722111059 Contract No.SP20180415
	Date and place of expiry of the credit NOV. 15，2019 in CHINA

Partial Shipment not allowed	Transshipment allowed	Issued by teletransmission（which shall be the operative instrument）
Loading on board/dispatch/taking in charge at/from INCHON, REPUBLIC OF KOREA Not later than OCT. 31，2019 For transportation to SHANGHAI，CHINA		Amount（both in figures and words） EUR 23,496.85 SAY EURO TWENTY THREE THOUSAND FOUR HUNDRED NINETY SIX POINT EIGHTY FIVE ONLY
Description of Goods： DOUBLE FACE SHEEPSKIN COLOUR CHESTNUT 3,175.25 SQFT Packing：IN GUNNY BAGS		Credit Available with ANY BANK IN CHINA by negotiation against the documents detailed herein and beneficiary's draft for 100％ of the invoice value AT SIGHT drawn on US.
		CFR

Documents Required：（marked with ×）

1.（×）Signed Commercial invoice in 5 copies indicating invoice No.，contract No.

2.（×）Full set of clean on board ocean Bill of Lading made out to order and blank endorsed，marked "freight"[×]to collect /[ ]prepaid [×]showing freight amount notify the applicant.

3.（×）Insurance Policy/Certificate in 2 copies for 120％ of the invoice value showing claims payable in China in currency of the draft, blank endorsed，covering [×]Ocean Marine Transportation/ [ ]Air Transportation /[ ] Over Land transportation All risks.

4.（×）Packing List/Weight Memo in 5 copies indication quantity/gross and net weights for each package and packing conditions as called for by the L/C.

5.（ ）Certificate of Quantity/Weight in____ copies issued by an independent surveyor at the loading port，indicating the actual surveyed quantity/weight of shipped goods as well as the packing condition.

6.（ ）Certificate of Quality in____ copies issued by[ ] manufacturer/[ ] public recognized survey/ [ ] or____.

7.（ ）Beneficiary's Certified copy of FAX dispatched to the accountee within____ after shipment advising [ ] name of vessel/[ ] date, quantity, weight and value of shipment.

8.（ ）Beneficiary's Certificate certifying that extra copies of the documents have been dispatched according to the contract terms.

9.（ ）Shipping Company's Certificate attesting that the carrying vessel is chartered or booked by accountee or their shipping agents.

10.（×）Other documents, if any：

a) Certificate of Origin in 3 copies issued by authorized institution.

Additional Instructions： …
Advising Bank： KOOKMIN BANK，SEOUL，REPUBLIC OF KOREA

综合实训

项目一　信用证方式 FOB 下出口单据填制

☑ 实训目标

　　能够根据相关资料填制信用证方式 FOB 下的出口单据：商业发票、装箱单、一般原产地证书、出境货物检验检疫申请单、出口货物报关单、海运提单、装船通知、受益人证明、商业汇票。

⏱ 实训任务

📖 实训指导
项目一

　🔗 **任务：请根据下述资料填制单据。**

（一）销售合同

ZHEJIANG COCO CO. LTD

NO. 110 TIYU CHANG ROAD, HANGZHOU, CHINA

SALES CONTRACT

TO：YAGI AND CO. LTD TOKYO BRANCH　　　　　NO.：20190001

　　SEC：417 SUMISEI NIHONBASHI　　　　　　　DATE：APRIL 24，2019

　　KOAMICHO BLDG. 14-1 KOAMICHO　　　　　　Tel. 78556431

　　NIHONBASHI CHUO-KU TOKYO，JAPAN

Dear Sirs，

　　We hereby confirm having sold to you the following goods on terms and conditions as specified below：

Shipping Marks	Description of Goods	Quantity	Unit Price	Amount
N/M	T-SHIRTS 504002-A 504002-B	 5,000 PCS 3,000 PCS	FOB SHANGHAI USD 1.34/PC USD 1.34/PC	 USD 6,700.00 USD 4,020.00
TOTAL：		8,000 PCS		USD 10,720.00

1. Terms of Payment：L/C AT SIGHT，PAYABLE BY NEGOTIATION WITH ANY BANK

2. Port of Loading：SHANGHAI, CHINA

3. Port of Destination：JAPANESE PORT

4. Latest Date of Shipment：MAY 25，2019

5. Partial Shipment：ALLOWED，Transshipment：NOT ALLOWED

6. Insurance：TO BE COVERED BY THE BUYERS

7. 5 PCT MORE OR LESS IN QUANTITY AND AMOUNT IS ALLOWED

THE BUYER：   THE SELLER：

YAGI AND CO. LTD TOKYO BRANCH   ZHEJIANG COCO CO. LTD

　　　　　　JOHN   王斌

（二）信用证

APPLICATION HEADER：MIZUHO BANK LTD. TOKYO

SEQUENCE OF CREDIT：1/1

FORM OF DOC. CREDIT：IRREVOCABLE

DOC. CREDIT NUMBER：30-0031-152303

DATE OF ISSUE：20190428

EXPIRY：DATE 20190601 PLACE NEGOTIATING BANK

APPLICANT：YAGI AND CO. LTD TOKYO BRANCH

　　　　　SEC：417 SUMISEI NIHONBASHI

　　　　　KOAMICHO BLDG. 14-1 KOAMICHO

　　　　　NIHONBASHI CHUO-KU TOKYO JAPAN

BENEFICIARY：ZHEJIANG COCO CO. LTD

　　　　　　NO. 110 TIYU CHANG ROAD HANGZHOU CHINA

AMOUNT：CURRENCY USD AMOUNT 10,836.58

POS./NEG. TOL.(%)：05/05

AVAILABLE WITH/BY：ANY BANK

　　　　　　　BY NEGOTIATION

DRAFTS AT...：BENEFICIARY'S DRAFT(S)

　　　　　AT SIGHT

　　　　　FOR FULL INVOICE COST

DRAWEE：MIZUHO BANK LTD. TOKYO

PARTIAL SHIPMENTS：ALLOWED

TRANSSHIPMENT：PROHIBITED

LOADING IN CHARGE：SHANGHAI PORT

FOR TRANSPORT TO...：JAPANESE PORT

LATEST DATE OF SHIP.：20190525

DESCRIPT. OF GOODS：T-SHIRTS

CONTRACT NO.	ITEM	QUANTITY	UNIT PRICE
20190001	504002-A	5,000 PCS	USD 1.34
20190001	504002-B	3,000 PCS	USD 1.34

FOB SHANGHAI PORT

DOCUMENTS REQUIRED：

+SIGNED COMMERCIAL INVOICE IN 2 COPIES, STATING APPLICANT'S REFER NO.IM417H1533.

+3/3 SET OF CLEAN ON BOARD MARINE BILLS OF LADING AND/OR COMBINED. TRANSPORT B/L MADE OUT TO ORDER OF YAGI AND CO. LTD, NOTIFY APPLICANT，INDICATING CREDIT NUMBER，EACH MARKED FREIGHT COLLECT.

+PACKING LIST IN 2 COPIES.

+CERTIFICATE OF ORIGIN ISSUED BY CCPIT.

+BENEFICIARY'S CERTIFICATE IN 2 COPIES WITH RELATIVE COURIER RECEIPT STATING THAT：2 SETS OF TYPED AND SIGNED NON-NEGOTIABLE SHIPPING DOCUMENTS HAVE BEEN SENT TO ACCOUNTEE BY COURIER WITHIN 2 DAYS AFTER SHIPMENT.

ADDITIONAL COND.：

+5 PCT MORE OR LESS IN QUANTITY AND AMOUNT IS ALLOWED.

+INVOICE TO BE SPECIFIED COUNTRY OF ORIGIN.

+INVOICE TO BE STATED FOLLOWS：BREAKDOWN FOR EACH ITEM，TOTAL NET/GROSS WEIGHT.

+PACKING LIST TO BE STATED FOLLOWS：QUANTITY FOR EACH ITEM IN EACH CARTON.

+SHIPPING ADVICE SHOULD BE SENT BEFORE TYPED INVOICE AND PACKING LIST，B/L DIRECTLY TO ACCOUNTEE BY FAX（NO. 813-3667-4130）（ATTN. MR. INAGAKI SEC. 382）WITHIN 24 HOURS AFTER SHIPMENT

ADVISING L/C NO./VESSEL VOY. NO./OPEN COVER NO./QUANTITY/ AMOUNT/B/L NO. BY SHIPPER.

+SHIPMENT SHOULD BE EFFECTED BY CONTAINER VESSEL. SHIPMENT MUST BE EFFECTED THRU AIT CORP., SHANGHAI OFFICE（ATTN：MR. ZHOU JIE TEL：021-5356-0651）AND CLEAN ON BOARD MULTIMODAL TRANSPORT B/L OF AIT CORP. IS ALSO ACCEPTABLE.

+INSURANCE HAS BEEN EFFECTED BY APPLICANT.

DETAILS OF CHARGES：ALL BANK CHARGES OUTSIDE JAPAN ARE FOR THE BENEFICIARY'S ACCOUNT

PRESENTATION PERIOD：DOCUMENT MUST BE PRESENTED WITHIN 15 DAYS AFTER THE DATE OF SHIPMENT BUT WITHIN THE VALIDITY OF THIS CREDIT.

CONFIRMATION：WITHOUT

INSTRUCTIONS TO THE NEGOTIATING BANK：

+ UPON RECEIPT OF THE ORIGINAL DOCUMENTS IN ORDER，WE SHALL REIMBURSE YOU BY REMITTING THE AMOUNT CLAIMED TO YOUR DESIGNATED ACCOUNT.

+ ALL DOCUMENTS MUST BE AIRMAILED TO US IN ONE LOT BY REGISTERED MAIL.

+A DISCREPANCY FEE WILL BE DEDUCTED/CHARGED IF DOCUMENTS ARE PRESENTED WITH DISCREPANCIES.

+NEGOTIATING BANK MUST FORWARD NEGOTIATED DOCUMENTS TO MIZUHO BANK，LTD，HEAD OFFICE(ADDRESS：UCHISAIWAICHO, CHOME, CHIYODA-KU，TOKYO，JAPAN).

（三）补充资料

1. 商业发票号码为：IVO346

2. 商业发票的日期：2019 年 5 月 8 日

3. 合同日期：2019 年 4 月 24 日

4. 船名：XINGXING V.123

5. 装船日期：2019 年 5 月 15 日

6. 目的港：东京（TOKYO）

7. 提单号码：AIT123

8. 预约保险单号码：OC123

9. 商品：T-SHIRT 504002A，5,000 PCS 装成 50 个纸箱，每箱 100 件，每箱净重 5.5
KGS，毛重 5.6 KGS，箱子的规格为 30 cm×40 cm×50 cm，单价 USD 1.34。

T-SHIRT 504002B，3,000 PCS 装成 30 个纸箱，每箱 100 件，每箱净重 5.8 KGS，毛
重 5.9 KGS，箱子的规格为 30 cm×40 cm×50 cm，单价 USD 1.34。

拼箱，装入 20 英尺集装箱，集装箱号码为 COSCO771120。

10. H.S. CODE：6206.4000

11. 报检单位登记号：1255667743

12. 报检单编号：E20180000000001234

13. 生产单位注册号：3452338654

14. 发货人人民币账号：089877

15. 外币账号：MY567890012

16. 海关编号：×××20190001244566

17. 境内货源地：浙江杭州

18. 产地证编号：CCPIT180011143

（四）单据

1. 商业发票

ZHEJIANG COCO CO. LTD

NO.110 TIYU CHANG ROAD，HANGZHOU，CHINA

COMMERCIAL INVOICE

TO：

INV. NO.：＿＿＿＿＿＿＿＿

DATE：＿＿＿＿＿＿＿＿

S/C NO.：＿＿＿＿＿＿＿

L/C NO.：＿＿＿＿＿＿＿

FROM＿＿＿＿＿＿＿＿＿＿　TO ＿＿＿＿＿＿＿＿＿＿

MARKS & NOS.	DESCRIPTION OF GOODS	QUANTITY	UNIT PRICE	AMOUNT

TOTAL AMOUNT：

＿＿＿＿＿＿＿＿＿＿

2. 装箱单

ZHEJIANG COCO CO. LTD.

NO. 110 TIYU CHANG ROAD, HANGZHOU, CHINA

PACKING LIST

TO：

INV. NO.：_____

DATE：_____

S/C NO.：_____

L/C NO.：_____

CASE NO.	MARKS & NOS.	QUANTITY & DESCRIPTION OF GOODS	G. W. (KGS)	N. W. (KGS)	MEAS. (CBM)
TOTAL：					

TOTAL：

3. 一般原产地证书

1.Exporter	Certificate No.			
2.Consignee	**CERTIFICATE OF ORIGIN** **OF** **THE PEOPLE'S REPUBLIC OF CHINA**			
3.Means of Transport and Route	5.For certifying authority use only			
4. Country/Region of Destination				
6.Marks and Numbers	7. Number and Kind of Package; Description of Goods	8. H.S. Code	9.Quantity	10.Number and Date of Invoice

11.Declaration by the Exporter	12.Certification
The undersigned hereby declares that the above details and statements are correct; that all the goods were produced in China and that they comply with the Rules of Origin of the People's Republic of China.	It is hereby certified that the declaration by the exporter is correct.
—————————————————— Place and Date, Signature and Stamp of Authorized Signatory	—————————————————— Place and Date, Signature and Stamp of Certifying Authority

4.出境货物检验检疫申请单

中华人民共和国海关

出境货物检验检疫申请

申请单位(加盖公章):　　　　　　　　　　　　　＊编号:＿＿＿＿＿＿＿＿

申请单位登记号:　　　联系人:　　电话:　　　申请日期:　　年　月　日

发货人	(中文)	
	(外文)	
收货人	(中文)	
	(外文)	

货物名称(中/外文)	H.S.编码	产地	数/重量	货物总值	包装种类及数量

运输工具名称号码		贸易方式		货物存放地点	
合同号		信用证号		用途	
发货日期		输往国家(地区)		许可证/审批号	
起运地		到达口岸		生产单位注册号	

集装箱规格、数量及号码

合同、信用证订立的检验检疫条款或特殊要求	标记及号码	随附单据(画"√"或补填)	
		□合同 □信用证 □发票 □换证凭单 □装箱单 □厂检单	□包装性能结果单 □许可/审批文件 □ □ □

需要证单名称(画"√"或补填)		＊检验检疫费	
□品质证书　　　__正__副 □重量证书　　　__正__副 □数量证书　　　__正__副 □兽医卫生证书　__正__副 □健康证书　　　__正__副 □卫生证书　　　__正__副 □动物卫生证书　__正__副	□植物检疫证书　　__正__副 □熏蒸/消毒证　　__正__副 □出境货物换证凭单__正__副 □ □ □ □	总金额 (元人民币)	
		计费人	
		收费人	

申请人郑重声明:	领取证单	
1.本人被授权申请检验检疫。 　2.上列填写内容正确属实,货物无伪造或冒用他人的 厂名、标志、认证标志,并承担货物质量责任。 　　　　　　　　　　　　签名:＿＿＿＿＿	日期	
	签名	

注:有"＊"号栏由海关填写

5. 出口货物报关单

预录入编号：

海关编号：

中华人民共和国海关出口货物报关单

（××海关）

页码/页数：

境内发货人	出境关别	出口日期	申报日期	备案号
境外收货人	运输方式	运输工具名称及航次号	提运单号	
生产销售单位	监管方式	征免性质	许可证号	
合同协议号	贸易国（地区）	运抵国（地区）	指运港	离境口岸
包装种类	件数	毛重（千克）	净重（千克）	成交方式	运费	保费	杂费
随附单证及编号							
标记唛码及备注							
项号 商品编号 商品名称及规格型号		数量及单位	单价/总价/币制	原产国（地区）	最终目的国（地区）	境内货源地	征免
报关人员 报关人员证号 电话		兹申明对以上各项承担如实申报、依法纳税之法律责任。		海关批注及签章			
申报单位		申报单位（盖章）					

6. 海运提单

Shipper		SINOTRANS B/L No.
Consignee or Order		中国对外贸易运输总公司 **CHINA NATIONAL FOREIGN TRADE TRANSPORTATION CORP.** 直运或转船提单 **BILL OF LADING** **DIRECT OR WITH TRANSSHIPMENT**
Notify Address		SHIPPED on board in apparent good order and condition（unless otherwise indicated）the goods or packages specified herein and to be discharged at the mentioned port of discharge or as near thereto as the vessel may safely get and be always afloat. The weight, measure, marks and numbers, quality, contents and value, being particulars furnished by the Shipper, are not checked by the carrier on loading.
Pre-carriage by	Place of Loading	The Shipper, Consignee and the Holder of this Bill of Lading hereby expressly accept and agree to all printed, written or stamped provisions, exceptions and conditions of this Bill of Lading, including those on the back hereof.
Vessel	Port of Transshipment	IN WITNESS where of the number of original Bills of Lading stated below have been signed, one of which being accomplished, the other(s) to be void.
Port of Discharge	Final Destination	

Container, Seal No. or Marks & Nos.	Number & Kind of Packages	Description of Goods	Gross Weight (KGS)	Measurement (CBM)

ABOVE PARTICULARS FURNISHED BY SHIPPER

Freight & Charges			Regarding Transshipment Information Please Contact
Ex. Rate	Prepaid at	Freight Payable at	Place and Date of Issue
	Total Prepaid	Number of Original B(s)/L	Signed for or on Behalf of the Master as Agent(s)

7. 装船通知

ZHEJIANG COCO CO. LTD
NO. 110 TIYU CHANG ROAD, HANGZHOU, CHINA
SHIPPING ADVICE

TO: DATE:

RE: L/C NO.   INVOICE NO.   COVER NOTE NO.

WE HEREBY INFORMED YOU THAT THE GOODS UNDER THE ABOVE MENTIONED CREDIT HAVE BEEN SHIPPED. THE DETAILS OF SHIPMENT ARE STATED BELOW.

COMMODITY:

QUANTITY:

INVOICE VALUE:

OCEAN VESSEL/SHIPPED PER S.S.:

DATE OF SHIPMENT:

PORT OF LOADING:

PORT OF DESTINATION:

MARKS:

                                              Signature

8. 受益人证明

ZHEJIANG COCO CO. LTD

NO. 110 TIYU CHANG ROAD，HANGZHOU，CHINA

BENEFICIARY'S CERTIFICATE

TO：   DATE：

RE：L/C NO.   INVOICE NO.

WE HEREBY CERTIFY THAT...

_____

9. 商业汇票

凭

Drawn under   -

信用证或购买证第   号

L/C or A/P No. -

日期   年   月   日

Dated -

按   息   付   款

Payable with interest @ _____% per annum

号码   汇票金额   中国杭州   年   月   日

No. - - - - - - - - - Exchange for ▓▓▓▓ Hangzhou, China - - - - - - - - - - - - - - 20...

见票   日   后（ 本 汇 票 之 副 本 未 付 ） 付

At - - - - - - - - -   sight of this FIRST of Exchange （ Second of exchange being unpaid ）

Pay to the order of_____或其指定人

金额

The sum of ▓▓▓▓▓▓▓▓▓▓▓▓▓▓▓▓▓▓▓▓

▓▓▓▓▓▓▓▓▓▓▓▓▓▓▓▓▓▓▓▓▓▓▓

此致

To -

- -

项目二 信用证方式 CFR 下出口单据填制

☑ 实训目标

能够根据相关资料填制信用证方式 CFR 下的出口单据：商业发票、装箱单、海运出口托运单、普惠制产地证、出境货物检验检疫申请单、出口货物报关单、海运提单、受益人证明、商业汇票。

⏱ 实训任务

🔗任务：请根据下述资料填制单据。

（一）销售合同

SHANGHAI GARDEN PRODUCTS IMP. AND EXP. CO. LTD

NO. 27 ZHONGSHAN DONGYI ROAD, SHANGHAI, CHINA

SALES CONTRACT

TO：LAIKI PERAGORA ORPHANIDES LTD   NO.：E03FD121

NO. 020 STRATIGOU TIMAGIA AVE.   DATE：JAN. 01，2019

6046，LARNAKA，CYPRUS

Dear Sirs，

We hereby confirm having sold to you the following goods on terms and conditions as specified below：

Shipping Mark	Description of Goods	Quantity	Unit Price	Amount
L.P.O.L. DOC. NO.186/06/10014 MADE INCHINA NO.1-325	WOODEN FLOWER STANDS WOODEN FLOWER POTS	350 PCS 600 PCS	CFR LIMASSOL PORT USD8.90/ PC USD5.00/PC	USD 3,115.00 USD 3,000.00
Total：		950 PCS		USD 6,115.00

1. Terms of Payment：L/C AT SIGHT BY NEGOTIATION WITH ANY BANK

2. Port of Loading：SHANGHAI, CHINA

3. Port of Destination：LIMASSOL PORT

4. Latest Date of Shipment：FEB. 14，2019

5. Partial Shipment and Transshipment：ALLOWED

6. Insurance：TO BE COVERED BY THE BUYER

THE BUYER：   THE SELLER：

LAIKI PERAGORA ORPHANIDES LTD   SHANGHAI GARDEN PRODUCTS IMP.

AND EXP. CO. LTD

JOHNSON   王燕

（二）信用证

ISSUING BANK：CYPRUS POPULAR BANK LTD，LARNAKA

ADVISING BANK：BANK OF CHINA，SHANGHAI BRANCH

SEQUENCE OF TOTAL   ＊27：1/1

FORM OF DOC. CREDIT   ＊40A：IRREVOCABLE

DOC. CREDIT NUMBER   ＊20：186/06/10014

DATE OF ISSUE   31C：20190105

EXPIRY   ＊31D：DATE20190228 PLACE CHINA

APPLICANT   ＊50：LAIKI PERAGORA ORPHANIDES LTD

NO. 020 STRATIGOU TIMAGIA AVE.

6046，LARNAKA, CYPRUS

BENEFICIARY   ＊59：SHANGHAI GARDEN PRODUCTS IMP. AND EXP. CO. LTD

NO. 27 ZHONGSHAN DONGYI ROAD，SHANGHAI，CHINA

AMOUNT   ＊32B：CURRENCY USD AMOUNT 6,115.00

POS. /NEG. TOL.（%）   39A：05/05

AVAILABLE WITH/BY   ＊41D：ANY BANK BY NEGOTIATION

DRAFT AT...   42C：AT SIGHT

DRAWEE   ＊42D：LIKICY2NXXX

CYPRUS POPULAR BANK LTD

LARNAKA

PARTIAL SHIPMENTS   43P：ALLOWED

TRANSSHIPMENT   43T：ALLOWED

LOADING IN CHARGE   44A：SHANGHAI PORT

FOR TRANSPORT TO...   44B：LIMASSOL PORT

LATEST DATE OF SHIP MENT   44C：20190214

DESCRIPT. OF GOODS   45A：

WOODEN FLOWER STANDS AND WOODEN FLOWER POTS

AS PER S/C NO. E03FD121.

CFR LIMASSOL PORT, INCOTERMS 2010

DOCUMENTS REQUIRED 46A:

+ COMMERCIAL INVOICE IN QUADRUPLICATE ALL STAMPED AND SIGNED BY BENEFICIARY CERTIFYING THAT THE GOODS ARE OF CHINESE ORIGIN AND THAT THE CONTENT IS TRUE AND CORRECT.

+ FULL SET OF CLEAN ON BOARD BILL OF LADING MADE OUT TO ORDER OF SHIPPER AND BLANK ENDORSED, MARKED FREIGHT PREPAID AND NOTIFY APPLICANT, INDICATING L/C NO.

+ PACKING LIST IN TRIPLICATE SHOWING PACKING DETAILS SUCH AS CARTON NO. AND CONTENTS OF EACH CARTON.

+ GSP CERFIFICATE OF ORIGIN FORM A ISSUED AND/OR VISAED BY COMPETENT AUTHORITIES.

+ CERTIFICATE STAMPED AND SIGNED BY BENEFICIARY STATING THAT THE ORIGIAL INVOICE AND PACKING LIST HAVE BEEN DISPATCHED TO THE APPLICANT BY COURIER SERVISE 2 DAYS BEFORE SHIPMENT.

ADDITIONAL COND. 47A:

+ EACH PACKING UNIT BEARS AN INDELIBLE MARK INDICATING THE COUNTRY OF ORIGIN OF THE GOODS. PACKING LIST TO CERTIFY THIS.

+ INSURANCE IS BEING ARRANGED BY THE BUYER.

+ A USD50.00 DISCREPANCY FEE, FOR BENEFICIARY'S ACCOUNT, WILL BE DEDUCTED FROM THE REIMBURSEMENT CLAIM FOR EACH PRESENTATION OF DISCREPANT DOCUMENTS UNDER THIS CREDIT.

+ THIS CREDIT IS SUBJECT TO THE U. C. P. FOR DOCUMENTARY CREDITS (2007 REVISION) I.C.C., PUBLICATION NO. 600.

DETAILS OF CHARGES 71B: ALL BANK CHARGES OUTSIDE CYPRUS ARE FOR THE ACCOUNT OF THE BENEFICIARY.

PRESENTATION PERIOD 48: WITHIN 15 DAYS AFTER THE DATE OF SHIPMENT BUT WITHIN THE VALIDITY OF THE CREDIT

CONFIRMATION *49: WITHOUT

INSTRUCTION 78: ON RECEIPT OF DOCUMENTS CONFIRMING TO THE TERMS OF THIS DOCUMENTARY CREDIT, WE UNDERTAKE TO REIMBURSE YOU IN THE CURRENCY OF THE CREDIT IN ACCORDANCE WITH YOUR INSTRUCTIONS,

WHICH SHOULD INCLUDE YOUR UID NUMBER AND THE ABA CODE OF THE
  RECEIVING BANK.

（三）相关资料

1. 发票号码：06SHGD3029

2. 发票日期：2019 年 2 月 9 日

3. 提单号码：SHYZ042234

4. 提单日期：2019 年 2 月 12 日

5. 船名：LT USODIMARE

6. 航次：V.021W

7. 集装箱号码：FSCU3214999 1×20'FCL，CY/CY

8. 集装箱封号：1295312

9. 商品：

木花架，WOODEN FLOWER STANDS，H.S.CODE：44219090，中国制造

QUANTITY：350 PCS，USD 8.90/PC，2 PCS/箱，共 175 箱。纸箱尺码：66 cm×
22 cm×48 cm，毛重：11 KGS/箱，净重：9 KGS/箱。

木花桶，WOODEN FLOWER POTS，H.S.CODE：44219090，中国制造

QUANTITY：600 PCS，USD 5.00/PC，4 PCS/箱，共 150 箱。纸箱尺码：42 cm×
42 cm×45 cm，毛重：15 KGS/箱，净重：13 KGS/箱。

10. 受益人证明签发日期：2019 年 2 月 10 日

11. 报检单位联系电话：88776655

12. 上海园林用品进出口有限公司（7712312342）

13. 报检单编号：E20180000000007856

14. 国际运费：900 美元

15. 海关编号：××××20180000000089

16. 境内货源地：上海

17. 报关人员：陈列，电话：87865544

（四）单据

1. 商业发票

(1) Issuer：		上海园林用品进出口有限公司 SHANGHAI GARDEN PRODUCTS IMP. AND EXP. CO. LTD No. 27 Zhongshan Dongyi Road，Shanghai，China	
(2) To：		**COMMERCIALINVOICE**	
		(4) NO.	(5) Date
(3) Transport Details： From　　　To Partial Shipments： Transshipment： By		(6) Terms of Payment	(7) L/C No.
		(8) Country of Origin	
(9) Marks & Nos.	(10) Description of Goods	(11) Quantity	(12) Unit Price	(13) Amount
Total：(14)				
(15)				
			(16) Signature	

2. 装箱单

Issuer	上海园林用品进出口有限公司 SHANGHAI GARDEN PRODUCTS IMP. AND EXP. CO. LTD	
To	No. 27 Zhongshan Dongyi Road，Shanghai，China **PACKING LIST**	
	Invoice No.	Date

Marks & Nos.	Description of Goods； Kind and Number of Package	Gross Weight	Net Weight	Measurement

3.海运出口托运单

海运出口托运单

托运人 Shipper				
编号 No.			船名 S/S	
目的港 For				
唛头 Marks & Nos.	件数 Quantity	货名 Description of Goods	重量(千克)Weight(kilos)	
			净 Net	毛 Gross
共计件数(大写) Total Number of Packages in Writing			运费付款方式 Mode of Freight Payment	
运费计算 Freight Charges		尺码 Measurement		
备注 Remarks				
抬头 Order of		可否转船 Transshipment	可否分批 Partial Shipments	
通知 Notify		装运期 Time of Shipment	有效期 Expiry Date	提单张数 Copies of B/L
		金额 Amount		
收货人 Consignee		银行编号 Bank No.	信用证号 L/C No.	

制单　　　　月　　　　日

4. 普惠制产地证

(1) Goods Consigned from (exporter's business name, address，country) (2) Goods Consigned to (consignee's name, address, country)	Reference No. GENERALIZED SYSTEM OF PREFERENCES **CERTIFICATE OF ORIGIN** （combined declaration and certificate） **FORM A** Issued in THE PEOPLE'S REPUBLIC OF CHINA （country） See Notes Overleaf
(3) Means of Transport and Route (as far as known)	(4) For Official Use

(5) Item Number	(6) Marks and Numbers of Packages	(7) Number and Kind of Package；Description of Goods	(8) Origin Criterion (see notes overleaf)	(9) Gross Weight or Other Quantity	(10) Number and Date of Invoices

(11) Certification It is hereby certified，on the basis of control carried out，that the declaration by the exporter is correct.	(12) Declaration by the exporter The undersigned hereby declares that the above details and statements are correct；that all the goods were produced in CHINA and that they comply with the （country） origin requirements specified of those goods in the Generalized System of Preferences for goods exported to ＿＿＿＿＿＿＿＿ . （importing country）
＿＿＿＿＿＿＿＿＿＿＿＿＿＿＿＿＿＿ Place and Date，Signature and Stamp of Certifying Authority	＿＿＿＿＿＿＿＿＿＿＿＿＿＿＿＿＿＿ Place and Date，Signature of Authorized Signatory

5.出境货物检验检疫申请单

中华人民共和国海关

出境货物检验检疫申请

申请单位(加盖公章)：　　　　　　　　　　　　　　　　　＊编号：＿＿＿＿＿＿＿＿＿

申请单位登记号：　　　　联系人：　电话：　　　　　　申请日期：　　年　月　日

发货人	(中文)					
	(外文)					
收货人	(中文)					
	(外文)					
货物名称(中/外文)	H.S.编码	产地	数/重量	货物总值	包装种类及数量	

运输工具名称号码		贸易方式		货物存放地点	
合同号		信用证号		用途	
发货日期		输往国家(地区)		许可证/审批号	
起运地		到达口岸		生产单位注册号	

集装箱规格、数量及号码	

合同、信用证订立的检验检疫条款或特殊要求	标记及号码	随附单据(画"√"或补填)	
		□合同 □信用证 □发票 □换证凭单 □装箱单 □厂检单	□包装性能结果单 □许可/审批文件 □ □ □

需要证单名称(画"√"或补填)		＊检验检疫费
□品质证书　　　__正__副 □重量证书　　　__正__副 □数量证书　　　__正__副 □兽医卫生证书　__正__副 □健康证书　　　__正__副 □卫生证书　　　__正__副 □动物卫生证书　__正__副	□植物检疫证书　__正__副 □熏蒸/消毒证　　__正__副 □出境货物换证凭单__正__副 □ □ □ □	**总金额** (元人民币) 计费人 收费人

申请人郑重声明： 　1.本人被授权申请检验检疫。 　2.上列填写内容正确属实,货物无伪造或冒用他人的厂名、标志、认证标志,并承担货物质量责任。 　　　　　　　　　　　　签名：＿＿＿＿＿	领取证单	
	日期	
	签名	

注：有"＊"号栏由海关填写

6. 出口货物报关单

中华人民共和国海关出口货物报关单

（××海关）

预录入编号： 　　　　　　　海关编号： 　　　　　　　　　　　　　　　　　页码/页数：

境内发货人	出境关别	出口日期	申报日期	备案号
境外收货人	运输方式	运输工具名称及航次号	提运单号	
生产销售单位	监管方式	征免性质	许可证号	
合同协议号	贸易国（地区）	运抵国（地区）	指运港	离境口岸
包装种类	件数	毛重（千克）	净重（千克）	成交方式	运费	保费	杂费
随附单证及编号							
标记唛码及备注							
项号 商品编号	商品名称及规格型号	数量及单位	单价/总价/币制	原产国（地区）	最终目的国（地区）	境内货源地	征免
报关人员 报关人员证号	电话	兹申明对以上内容承担如实申报、依法纳税之法律责任。	海关批注及签章	
		签名		
申报单位		申报单位（签章）		

177

7. 海运提单

Shipper	SINOTRANS	B/L No.
	中国对外贸易运输总公司	
Consignee or Order	**CHINA NATIONAL FOREIGN TRADE TRANSPORTATION CORP.**	
	直运或转船提单	
	BILL OF LADING	
Notify Address	**DIRECT OR WITH TRANSSHIPMENT**	
	SHIPPED on board in apparent good order and condition (unless otherwise indicated) the goods or packages specified herein and to be discharged at the mentioned port of discharge or as near thereto as the vessel may safely get and be always afloat.	

Pre-carriage by	Place of Loading	The weight, measure, marks and numbers, quality, contents and value, being particulars furnished by the Shipper, are not checked by the carrier on loading.
Vessel	Port of Transshipment	The Shipper, Consignee and the Holder of this Bill of Lading hereby expressly accept and agree to all printed, written or stamped provisions, exceptions and conditions of this Bill of Lading, including those on the back hereof.
Port of Discharge	Final Destination	IN WITNESS where of the number of original Bills of Lading stated below have been signed, one of which being accomplished, the other(s) to be void.

Container, Seal No. or Marks & Nos.	Number & Kind of Packages	Description of Goods	Gross Weight (KGS)	Measurement (CBM)

ABOVE PARTICULARS FURNISHED BY SHIPPER			
Freight & Charges			Regarding Transshipment Information Please Contact
Ex. Rate	Prepaid at	Freight Payable at	Place and Date of Issue
	Total Prepaid	Number of Original B/L	Signed for or on Behalf of Themaster
			as Agent(s)

8. 受益人证明

SHANGHAI GARDEN PRODUCTS IMP. AND EXP. CO. LTD

No. 27 Zhongshan Dongyi Road，Shanghai，China

BENEFICIARY'S CERTIFICATE

TO：   DATE：

RE：L/C NO.   INVOICE NO.

WE HEREBY CERTIFY THAT...

9. 商业汇票

凭

Drawn under   ------------------------------------

信用证或购买证第   号

L/C or A/P No. ------------------------------------

日期   年   月   日

Dated ---

按   息   付   款

Payable with interest @ _____% per annum

号码   汇票金额   中国上海   年   月   日

No. -------------Exchange for   Shanghai, China   ----------------20...

见票   日   后   （ 本 汇 票 之 副 本 未 付 ）   付

At ------------   sight of this FIRST of Exchange   （ Second of exchange being unpaid ）

Pay to the order of_____ 或其指定人

金额

The sum of

此致

To ------------------------------------

项目三 信用证方式 CIF 下出口单据填制

实训目标

能够根据相关资料填制信用证方式 CIF 下的出口单据：商业发票、装箱单、订舱委托书、投保单、保险单、出境货物检验检疫申请单、出口货物报关单、海运提单、装船通知、受益人证明、商业汇票。

实训任务

任务：请根据下述资料填制单据。

（一）销售合同

CHINA SHENZHEN SEZ FOREIGN TRADE（GROUP）CORP.

NO. 2 ZHONG XING RD., SHENZHEN, CHINA.

SALES CONTRACT

TO：KINGROCK DEVELOPMENT LIMITED

RM.1203 12/F CAPTITOL CENTER

NO. 5-19 JARDINE'S BAZAAR

CAUSEWAY BAY, HONG KONG, CHINA

NO.：（00）A01-E246

DATE：APRIL 24，2019

Tel. 77886655

Dear Sirs,

We hereby confirm having sold to you the following goods on terms and conditions as specified below：

Shipping Mark	Description of Goods	Quantity	Unit Price	Amount
T.C. SINGAPORE NO.1-6000	SODIUM SULPHATE ANHYDROUS	300 M/T	CIF SINGAPORE USD 91.00/MT	USD 2,7300.00
Total：		300 M/T		USD 2,7300.00

1. Terms of Payment：BY L/C AGAINST BENEFICIARY'S DRAFT（S）AT 30 DAYS DRAWN ON THE ISSUING BANK

2. Port of Loading：ZHANJIANG,CHINA

3. Port of Destination：SINGAPORE

4. Latest Date of Shipment：NOV.10，2019

5. Partial Shipments：NOT ALLOWED

   Transshipment：NOT ALLOWED

6. Insurance：TO BE COVERED BY THE SELLERS FOR 110% OF CIF VALUE，COVERING WAR RISK AND ALL RISKS

7. 3 PCT MORE OR LESS IN QUANTITY AND AMOUNT IS ALLOWED

THE BUYER：   THE SELLER：

KINGROCK DEVELOPMENT LIMITED   CHINA SHENZHEN SEZ FOREIGN

                                 TRADE（GROUP）CORP.

        JINKONG   陈成

（二）信用证

DATE：OCT.18，2019

TO：BANK OF CHINA SHENZHEN BRANCH, SHENZHEN, GUANGDONG, CHINA

FROM：ABN HONG KONG/MAIN BRANCH/IB DC DEPT. ALGEMENE BANK NEDERLAND N.V. HONG KONG

OUR IRREVOCABLE DOCUMENTARY CREDIT NO.：CW02705

EXPIRY DATE：NOV.20，2019

APPLICANT：KINGROCK DEVELOPMENT LIMITED

       RM.1203 12/F CAPTITOL CENTER, NO. 5-19 JARDINE'S BAZAAR, CAUSEWAY BAY, HONG KONG

BENEFICIARY：CHINA SHENZHEN SEZ FOREIGN TRADE（GROUP）CORP.

       NO. 2 ZHONG XING RD.，SHENZHEN, GUANGDONG, CHINA

AMOUNT：USD 27,300.00（SAY U.S.D TWENTY SEVEN THOUSAND THREE HUNDRED AND 00/100 ONLY）

CREDIT AVAILABLE WITH ANY BANK, BY NEGOTIATION, AGAINST PRESENTATION OF BENEFICIARY'S DRAFT(S) AT 30 DAYS, DRAWN ON US IN DUPLICATE FOR 100 PERCENT OF THE NET INVOICE VALUE, SHOWING NUMBER AND DATE OF CREDIT, ACCOMPANIED BY THE DOCUMENTS DETAILED BELOW：

+COMMERCIAL INVOICE IN TRIPLICATE IN ENGLISH INDICATING THE CREDIT NUMBER, DULY SIGNED BY BENEFICIARIES ON CIF BASIS.

   +FULL SET OF MARINE BILLS OF LADING IN TRIPLICATE TO ORDER MARKED FREIGHT PERPAID ENDORSED IN BLANK, NOTIFY：STARRY

INTER-TRADE (FAR EAST) PTE LTD.

+INSURANCE POLICY /CERTIFICATE ENDORSED IN BLANK FOR 110％ CIF VALUE，COVERING：WAR RISK AND ALL RISKS.

+SIGNED PACKING LIST IN TRIPLICATE.

+ COPY BRIEF TELEX SENT TO APPLICANT ADVISING SHIPMENT DETAILS WITHIN 3 DAYS AFTER SHIPMENT EFFECTED.

+BENEFICIARY'S CERT. CERTIFYING THAT ONE FULL SET OF NON-NEGOTIABLE SHIPPING DOCUMENTS HAS BEEN SENT TO APPLICANT BY COURIER SERVICE WITHIN 7 DAYS AFTER SHIPMENT EFFECTED.

COVERING SHIPMENT OF：

300 M/T OF SODIUM SULPHATE ANHYDROUS AT USD 91.00/MT CIF SINGAPORE

SHIPMENT/DESPATCH/TAKING IN CHARGE FROM/AT ZHANJIANG，CHINA

TO SINGAPORE

LATEST SHIPMENT/DELIVERY DATE：NOV.10，2019

PARTIAL SHIPMENTS：NOT ALLOWED

TRANSSHIPMENT：NOT ALLOWED

SPECIAL CONDITIONS：

+AMOUNT AND QUANTITY 3 PCT MORE OR LESS ALLOWABLE.

+PACKING IN PLASTIC LINED PLASTIC WOVEN BAGS OF 50 KGS NET EACH. PACKING LIST TO EVIDENCE SAME REQUIRED.

+DOCUMENTS IN COMBINED FORM ARE NOT ALLOWED.

+DOCUMENTS TO BE PRESENTED WITHIN 20 DAYS AFTER THE DATE OF ISSUANCE OF THE SHIPPING DOCUMENT(S) BUT WITHIN THE VALIDITY OF THE CREDIT.

+ALL BANK CHARGES OUTSIDE HONG KONG ARE FOR THE ACCOUNT OF BENEFICIARY.

INSTRUCTIONS：

+ALL DOCUMENTS TO BE FORWARDED BY THE NEGOTIATING BANK IN ONE COVER BY REGISTERED AIRMAIL TO US AT 14TH FLOOR，UNITED CENTRE，95 QUEENSWAY，CENTRAL，HONG KONG.ATTENTION I/B DEPT. UNLESS OTHERWISE STATED.

+FOR THE ADVISING BANK：WITHOUT ADDING YOUR CONFIRMATION. PLEASE ACKNOWLEDGE RECEIPT.

+REIMSURSEMENT：UPON RECEIPT OF YOUR DOCUMENTS IN CONFORMITY WITH THE CREDIT TERMS，WE SHALL REIMBURSE YOU AS INSTRUCTED.

THIS CABLE IS THE OPERATIVE CREDIT INSTRUMENT AND IS ISSUED SUBJECT

TO UNIFORM CUSTOMS AND PRACTICE FOR DOCUMENTARY CREDIT，2007 REVISION，ICC PUBLICATION NO. 500. NO MAIL CONFIRMATION IS TO FOLLOW.

（三）补充资料

1. 发票号码.：KG1213

2. 发票日期：2019 年 10 月 25 日，签发人：陈成

3. 装箱单签发日期：2019 年 10 月 25 日，签发人：陈成

4. 总净重：305,000 KGS

5. 总毛重：306,220 KGS

6. 总包装数：6,100 BAGS

7. 总体积：278 CBM

8. 提单号码：SP-004

9. 提单签发日：NOV. 5，2019

10. 提单签发地点：ZHANJIANG

11. 船名：HUANG LONG V.11

12. H.S.编码：28331100.00

13. 报检单位联系电话：65774433

14. 报检单位登记号：8765432109

15. 报检单编号：E20190000000009012

16. 生产厂家：深圳化工厂

17. 报关人员：温理，电话：67854983

18. 国际运费：1,000 美元

19. 保险费：560 美元

20. 海关编号：×××20190000007685

21. 境内货源地：深圳

（四）单据

1. 商业发票

Issuer	中国深圳特区外贸集团公司 CHINA SHENZHEN SEZ FOREIGN TRADE (GROUP) CORP. NO. 2 ZHONG XING RD., SHENZHEN, CHINA **COMMERCIAL INVOICE**	
To	NO.	Date
Transport Details：	S/C NO.	L/C NO.
Partial Shipments：		
Transshipment：	Terms of Payment	
From To		
Vessel		

Marks & Nos.	Description of Goods； Kind and Number of Package	Quantity	Unit price	Amount

2. 装箱单

中国深圳特区外贸集团公司

CHINA SHENZHEN SEZ FOREIGN TRADE（GROUP）CORP.

NO. 2 ZHONG XING RD.，SHENZHEN，CHINA

PACKING   LIST

(1) Seller	(3) Invoice No.	(4) Invoice Date
	(5) From	(6) To
	(7) Total Packages（in words）	
(2) BUYER	(8) Marks & Nos.	

(9)C/Nos. (10) Nos. & Kinds of Packages. (11) Item (12) Qty. (13) G.W. (14) N.W. (15) Meas

(16)

(17) Issued By：

(18) Signature

3. 订舱委托书

出 口 货 物 订 舱 委 托 书			日期　月　日	
(1)发货人	(4)信用证号码			
	(5)开证银行			
	(6)合同号码		(7)成交金额	
	(8)装运口岸		(9)目的港	
(2)收货人	(10)转船运输		(11)分批装运	
	(12)信用证有效期		(13)装运期限	
	(14)运费		(15)成交条件	
	(16)公司联系人		(17)电话/传真	
(3)通知人	(18)公司开户行		(19)银行账号	
	(20)特别要求			

(21)标记唛码	(22)货号规格	(23)包装件数	(24)毛重	(25)净重	(26)数量	(27)单价	(28)总价
	(29)总件数	(30)总毛重	(31)总净重	(32)总尺码		(33)总金额	

(34)备注

4. 投保单

中保财产保险有限公司浙江分公司

THE PEOPLE'S INSURANCE (PROPERTY) COMPANY OF CHINA，LTD

ZHEJIANG BRANCH

进出口货物运输保险投保单

APPLICATION FORM FOR I/E MARINE CARGO INSURANCE

被保险人 Insured's Name				
发票号码(出口用)或合同号码(进口用) Invoice No. or Contract No.	包装数量 Quantity	保险货物项目 Description of Goods		保险金额 Amount Insured

装载运输工具　　　　　　　航次、航班或车号　　　开航日期
Per Conveyance_____　Voy. No.　_____　Slg. Date_____

自　　　　　　　至　　　　　　　转运地　　　　　　　赔款地
From_____　To_____　Via_____　Claim Payable at_____

承保险别　　　　　　　　　　标记唛码
Conditions &./or　　　　　　Shipping Marks
Special Coverage

投保人签章及公司名称、电话、地址
Applicant's Signature and Co.'s Name，Add. and Tel. No.

备注：

投保日期
Date

保险公司填写　　　报单号：　　　　费率：　　　　核保人：

187

5. 保险单

中保财产保险有限公司

The People's Insurance (Property) Company of China，Ltd

发票号码	保险单号次
Invoice No.	Policy No.

海洋货物运输保险单
MARINE CARGO TRANSPORTATION INSURANCE POLICY

被保险人 Insured	

中保财产保险有限公司(以下简称本公司)根据被保险人的要求,及其所缴付约定的保险费,按照本保险单承担险别和背面所载条款与下列特别条款承保下列货物运输保险,特签发本保险单。

This policy of insurance witnesses that the People's Insurance (Property) Company of China，Ltd (hereinafter called "the Company"), at the request of the Insured and in consideration of the agreed premium paid by the Insured, undertakes to insure the undermentioned goods in transportation subject to conditions of the policy as per the clauses printed overleaf and other special clauses attached hereon.

保险货物项目 Description of Goods	包装 Packing	单位 Unit	数量 Quantity	保险金额 Amount Insured

承保险别 Conditions	货物标记 Marks of Goods

总保险金额 Total Amount Insured	

保费 Premium		载运输工具 Per Conveyance S.S.		开航日期 Slg. on or abt.	
起运港 From			目的港 To		

所保货物,如发生本保险单项下可能引起索赔的损失或损坏,应立即通知本公司下述代理人查勘。如有索赔,应向本公司提交保险单正本(本保险单共有　　份正本)及有关文件。如一份正本已用于索赔,其余正本则自动失效。

In the event of loss or damage which may result in acclaim under this policy, immediate notice must be given to the Company's agent as mentioned hereunder. Claims, if any, one of the original policy which has been issued in　　original(s) together with the relevant documents shall be surrendered to the Company. If one of the original policy has been accomplished, the others to be void.

赔款偿付地点 Claim Payable at		中保财产保险有限公司浙江分公司 The People's Insurance (Property) Company of China，Ltd Zhejiang Branch Authorized Signature
日期 Date		在 At	
地址 Address		

6.出境货物检验检疫申请单

中华人民共和国海关
出境货物检验检疫申请

申请单位(加盖公章)：   * 编号：_____

申请单位登记号：   联系人：   电话：   申请日期：   年 月 日

发货人	(中文)					
	(外文)					
收货人	(中文)					
	(外文)					

货物名称(中/外文)	H.S.编码	产地	数/重量	货物总值	包装种类及数量

运输工具名称号码		贸易方式		货物存放地点	
合同号		信用证号		用途	
发货日期		输往国家(地区)		许可证/审批号	
起运地		到达口岸		生产单位注册号	

集装箱规格、数量及号码	

合同、信用证订立的检验检疫条款或特殊要求	标记及号码	随附单据(画"√"或补填)	
		□合同 □信用证 □发票 □换证凭单 □装箱单 □厂检单	□包装性能结果单 □许可/审批文件 □ □ □

需要证单名称(画"√"或补填)		* 检验检疫费	
□品质证书　__正__副 □重量证书　__正__副 □数量证书　__正__副 □兽医卫生证书　__正__副 □健康证书　__正__副 □卫生证书　__正__副 □动物卫生证书　__正__副	□植物检疫证书　__正__副 □熏蒸/消毒证　__正__副 □出境货物换证凭单__正__副 □ □ □ □	总金额 (元人民币)	
		计费人	
		收费人	

申请人郑重声明：	领取证单	
1.本人被授权申请检验检疫。 　2.上列填写内容正确属实,货物无伪造或冒用他人的厂名、标志、认证标志,并承担货物质量责任。 　　　　　　　　　签名:_____	日期	
	签名	

注：有"＊"号栏由海关填写

7. 出口货物报关单

预录入编号：　　　　　海关编号：　　　　　　　　　　　　　　　　　　页码/页数：

中华人民共和国海关出口货物报关单

（××海关）

境内发货人		出境关别	出口日期	申报日期	备案号
境外收货人		运输方式	运输工具名称及航次号	提运单号	
生产销售单位		监管方式	征免性质	许可证号	
合同协议号		贸易国（地区）	运抵国（地区）	指运港	离境口岸
包装种类	件数	毛重（千克）	净重（千克）	成交方式	运费	保费	杂费
随附单证及编号					
标记唛码及备注					
项号	商品编号	商品名称及规格型号	数量及单位	单价/总价/币制	原产国（地区）	最终目的国（地区）	境内货源地	征免
报关人员	报关人员证号	电话	兹申明对以上内容承担如实申报、依法纳税之法律责任。	海关批注及签章	
申报单位				申报单位（签章）	

8. 海运提单

Shipper	![SINOTRANS] B/L No.
Consignee or Order	中国对外贸易运输总公司 **CHINA NATIONAL FOREIGN TRADE TRANSPORTATION CORP.** 直运或转船提单 **BILL OF LADING DIRECT OR WITH TRANSSHIPMENT**
Notify Address	SHIPPED on board in apparent good order and condition (unless otherwise indicated) the goods or packages specified herein and to be discharged at the mentioned port of discharge or as near thereto as the vessel may safely get and be always afloat.

Pre-carriage by	Place of Loading	The weight, measure, marks and numbers, quality, contents and value, being particulars furnished by the Shipper, are not checked by the carrier on loading.
Vessel	Port of Transshipment	The Shipper, Consignee and the Holder of this Bill of Lading hereby expressly accept and agree to all printed, written or stamped provisions, exceptions and conditions of this Bill of Lading, including those on the back hereof.
Port of Discharge	Final Destination	IN WITNESS where of the number of original Bills of Lading stated below have been signed, one of which being accomplished, the other(s) to be void.

Container, Seal No. or Marks & Nos.	Number & Kind of Packages	Description of Goods	Gross Weight (KGS)	Measurement (CBM)

ABOVE PARTICULARS FURNISHED BY SHIPPER		
Freight & Charges		Regarding Transshipment Information Please Contact

Ex. Rate	Prepaid at	Freight Payable at	Place and Date of Issue
	Total Prepaid	Number of Original B/L	Signed for or on Behalf of the Master as Agent(s)

9. 装船通知

CHINA SHENZHEN SEZ FOREIGN TRADE（GROUP）CORP.

NO. 2 ZHONG XING RD.，SHENZHEN，CHINA

SHIPPING ADVICE

TO：   DATE：

RE：L/C NO.   INVOICE NO.

WE HEREBY INFORMED YOU THAT THE GOODS UNDER THE ABOVE MENTIONED CREDIT HAVE BEEN SHIPPED. THE DETAILS OF SHIPMENT ARE STATED BELOW.

COMMODITY：

QUANTITY：

INVOICE VALUE：

OCEAN VESSEL/SHIPPED PER S.S.：

DATE OF SHIPMENT：

PORT OF LOADING：

PORT OF DESTINATION：

MARKS：

Signature

10. 受益人证明

CHINA SHENZHEN SEZ FOREIGN TRADE（GROUP）CORP.

NO. 2 ZHONG XING RD.，SHENZHEN，CHINA

BENEFICIARY'S CERTIFICATE

TO：WHOM IT MAY CONCERN   DATE：

RE：L/C NO.   INVOICE NO.

WE HEREBY CERTIFY THAT...

- - - - - - - - - - - - -

11. 商业汇票

凭

Drawn under -

信用证或购买证第   号

L/C or A/P No. -

日期   年   月   日

Dated -

按   息   付   款

Payable with interest @ _____% per annum

号码   汇票金额   中国深圳   年   月   日

No. - - - - - - - -Exchange for [   ] Shenzhen, China - - - - - - - - - - - - - -20...

见票   日 后（ 本 汇 票 之 副 本 未 付 ）   付

At - - - - - - - - - - - sight of this FIRST of Exchange （ Second of exchange being unpaid ）

Pay to the order of_____或其指定人

金额

The sum of

此致

To - .

- .

- -

项目四　信用证方式 FOB 下结汇单据填制

📋 实训目标

　　能够根据有关资料填制信用证方式 FOB 下整套结汇单据：商业发票、普惠制产地证、海运提单、装船通知、受益人证明。

⊘ 实训任务

🔗**任务：　请根据下述资料填制单据。**

　　（一）信用证资料

FROM：UBI BANCA（UNIONE DI BANCHE ITALIANE）S.C.P.A. BERGAMO

TO：BANK OF CHINA LIMITED, ZHEJIANG BRANCH

DATE OF ISSUE：20191113

L/C NO.：0946CIM2002454R0

EXPIRY DATE AND PLACE：20190309 CHINA

APPLICANT：CALZEDONIA S.P.A.

　　　　　　VIA MONTE BALDO 20 37062 DOSSOBUONO DI VILLAFRANCA VR

BENEFICIARY：ZHEJIANG CHUBO TRADING CO. LTD

　　　　　　NO.35 HUSHU ROAD, HANGZHOU, CHINA

L/C AMOUNT：USD 733,920.00

POS./NEG.TOL(%)：05/05

AVAILABLE WITH/BY：BANCA REGIONALE EUROPEA SPA(UBI BANC GROUP),

　　　　　　　　PAVIA（MAIN BRANCH）, BY DEF. PAYMENT

DEFERRED PAYM. DET.：PAYMENT AT 60 DAYS FROM TRANSPORT

　　　　　　　　DOCUMENTS DATE

PARTIAL SHIPMENTS：ALLOWED

TRANSSHIPMENT：ALLOWED

PORT OF LOADING：SHANGHAI, CHINA

PORT OF DISCHARGE：VENEZIA, ITALY

LATEST DATE OF SHIP.：20190222

DESCRIP. OF GOODS：CLOTHING

PO NO.	ART.CODE	QUANTITY	TOT.VALUE	DATE OF SHIPMENT
2000004151	CL020A	8,940 PCS	USD 108.174,00	30/11/2019
2000004661	CL020A	8,940 PCS	USD 108.174,00	30/11/2019
2000004552	AI018S	10,000 PCS	USD 192.072,00	22/02/2020
2000004577	CM020A	30,000 PCS	USD 325.500,00	25/12/2019

TATAL AMOUNT: USD 733.920,00

INCOTERMS 2000: FOB SHANGHAI

DOCUMENTS REQUIRED:

+ COMMERCIAL INVOICE DULY SIGNED AND DATED EVIDENCING THAT INVOICE AND SHIPPED GOODS ARE IN CONFORMITY WITH ORDERS NO. 2000004151/4661/4552/4577: ORIGINAL AND 2 COPIES.

+ 2/3 ORIGINAL BILL OF LADING ISSUED TO THE ORDER OF CALZEDONIA S.P.A. MARKED FREIGHT COLLECT NOTIFY APPLICANT.

+ GSP CERTIFICATE OF ORIGIN FORM A ISSUED AND/OR VISAED BY COMPETENT AUTHORITIES: 4 COPIES.

+ BENEFICIARY'S CERTIFICATE ATTESTING THAT: 1/3 ORIGINAL BILL OF LADING, ORIGINAL CERTIFICATE OF ORIGIN, ORIGINAL CERTIFICATE OF ORIGIN FORM A AND ONE COPY OF ALL OTHER DOCUMENTS WERE SENT DIRECTLY TO: CALZEDONIA S.P.A., VIA SPINETTI 1, 37050 VALLESE DI OPPEANO C/A SIG. RA FRANCESCA ROTONDI C/O UFFICIO IMPORT-EXPORT.

+ COPY OF FAX SENT BY BENEFICIARY TO APPLICANT WITHIN SHIPMENT DATE SHOWING ALL DETAILS OF DELIVERY FOR INSURANCE PURPOSES.(FAX REPORT MUST BE INCLUDED.)

ADDITIONAL COND.:

+ ALL DOCUMENTS MUST BE WORDED IN ENGLISH.

+ ALL DOCUMENTS MUST REPORT OUR L/C NUMBER AND ISSUING BANK NAME: BANCA REGIONALE EUROPEA SPA.

+ NO DRAFT IS REQUIRED, IF ANY IT WILL RETURNED TO YOU AND EUR 50.00 OUR CHARGES DEDUCTD FROM PAYMENT.

+ ONE EXTRACOPY OF ALL DOCUMENTS IS REQUIRED FOR ISSUING BANK'S FILE. IF NOT PRESENTED EUR 10.00 WILL BE DEDUCTED FROM PROCEEDS.

+ PENALTY FOR POSSIBLE DELAYS: 10 PERCENT DISCOUNT FOR

DELIVERIES FROM 7 DAYS AFTER LAST DELIVERY DATE，TILL 14 DAYS AFTER LAST DELIVERY DATE. 20 PERCENT DISCOUNT FOR DELIVERIES FROM 15 DAYS AFTER LAST DELIVERY DATE，TILL 40 DAYS AFTER LAST DELIVERY DATE.

（二）其他资料

INVOICE NO.：BP919A520301

INVOICE DATE：2019/12/22

出仓单显示：PO NO. 2000004577 ART. CODECM020A 5,500 PCS 80 CTNS

SHIPPING MARKS：CALZEDONIA/VERONA/NO.1-80

S/C NO.：ZSD095010339

B/L NO.：SIN7890

VESSEL VOY.：VICTORY V.090

ON BOARD DATE：20191224

ETA DATE：20200116

G.W.：416 KGS

N.W.：352.30 KGS

MEASUREMENT：3.936 CBM

货物完全中国原产。出口公司于 2019 年 12 月 22 日向有关当局申请产地证,当日获批。

提示：本批出运货物为 PO NO. 2000004577 的货物,请注意发票的批注内容为：

INVOICE AND SHIPPED GOODS ARE IN CONFORMITY WITH ORDERS NN. 2000004577。

（三）单据

1. 商业发票

浙江楚帛贸易有限公司

ZHEJIANG CHUBO TRADING CO. LTD

NO. 35HUSHU ROAD，HANGZHOU，CHINA

COMMERCIAL   INVOICE

To：		No.
		Date
		S/C No.

From	To

Drawn Under

L/C No.   Date

Marks & Nos.	Description of Goods Kind & Number of Package	Quantity	Unit Price	Amount

2. 普惠制产地证

(1) Goods Consigned from (exporter's business name, address, country)	Reference No.
	GENERALIZED SYSTEM OF PREFERENCES **CERTIFICATE OF ORIGIN** (combined declaration and certificate) FORM A Issued in THE PEOPLE'S REPUBLIC OF CHINA (country)
(2) Goods Consigned to (consignee's name, address, country)	
	See Notes Overleaf

(3) Means of Transport and Route (as far as known)	(4) For Official Use

(5) Item Number	(6) Marks and Numbers of Packages	(7) Number and Kind of Packages; Description of Goods	(8) Origin Criterion (see notes overleaf)	(9) Grossweight or Other Quantity	(10) Number and Date of Invoices

(11) Certification	(12) Declaration by the Exporter
It is hereby certified, on the basis of control carried out, that the declaration by the exporter is correct.	The undersigned hereby declares that the above details and statements are correct; that all the goods were produced in CHINA and that they comply with the (country) origin requirements specified of those goods in the Generalized System of Preferences for goods exported to _____. (importing country)
_____ Place and Date, Signature and Stamp of Certifying Authority	_____ Place and Date, Signature of Authorized Signatory

3. 海运提单

Shipper	SINOTRANS		B/L No.
Consignee or Order	中国对外贸易运输总公司 CHINA NATIONAL FOREIGN TRADE TRANSPORTATION CORP. 直运或转船提单 **BILL OF LADING** **DIRECT OR WITH TRANSSHIPMENT**		
Notify Address	SHIPPED on board in apparent good order and condition (unless otherwise indicated) the goods or packages specified herein and to be discharged at the mentioned port of discharge or as near thereto as the vessel may safely get and be always afloat.		

Pre-carriage by	Place of Loading	The weight, measure, marks and numbers, quality, contents and value, being particulars furnished by the Shipper, are not checked by the carrier on loading.
Vessel	Port of Transshipment	The Shipper, Consignee and the Holder of this Bill of Lading hereby expressly accept and agree to all printed, written or stamped provisions, exceptions and conditions of this Bill of Lading, including those on the back hereof.
Port of Discharge	Final Destination	IN WITNESS where of the number of original Bills of Lading stated below have been signed, one of which being accomplished, the other(s) to be void.

Container, Seal No. or Marks & Nos.	Number & Kind of Packages	Description of Goods	Gross Weight (KGS)	Measurement (CBM)

ABOVE PARTICULARS FURNISHED BY SHIPPER			
Freight & Charges			Regarding Transshipment Information Please Contact
Ex. Rate	Prepaid at	Freight Payable at	Place and Date of Issue
	Total Prepaid	Number of Original B/L	Signed for or on Behalf of the Master as Agent(s)

4. 装船通知

浙江楚帛贸易有限公司

ZHEJIANG CHUBO TRADING CO. LTD

NO. 35 HUSHU ROAD，HANGZHOU，CHINA

SHIPPING ADVICE

TO：   DATE：

RE：L/C NO.   INVOICE NO.

WE HEREBY INFORMED YOU THAT THE GOODS UNDER THE ABOVE MENTIONED CREDIT HAVE BEEN SHIPPED. THE DETAILS OF SHIPMENT ARE STATED BELOW.

COMMODITY：

QUANTITY：

INVOICE VALUE：

OCEAN VESSEL/ SHIPPED PER S.S.：

ETD DATE：

ETA DATE：

PORT OF LOADING：

PORT OF DESTINATION：

MARKS：

Signature

5．受益人证明

浙江楚帛贸易有限公司

ZHEJIANG CHUBO TRADING CO. LTD

NO. 35HUSHU ROAD，HANGZHOU，CHINA

BENEFICIARY'S CERTIFICATE

TO：   DATE：

RE：L/C NO.   INVOICE NO.

WE HEREBY CERTIFY THAT...

_ _ _ _ _ _ _ _ _ _ _

项目五　信用证方式 CIF 下结汇单据填制

实训目标

　　能够根据有关资料填制信用证方式 CIF 下整套结汇单据：商业发票、装箱单、保险单、一般原产地证书、装船前检验证书、船公司证明、海运提单、装船通知、受益人证明、商业汇票。

实训任务

：　请根据下述资料填制单据。

（一）信用证资料

FROM：NATIONAL BANK LIMITED, DHAKA（MOHAKHALI BRANCH）

TO：WACHOVIA BANK, NA, SHANGHAI

DATE OF ISSUE：20190719

L/C NO.：094709060309

EXPIRY DATE AND PLACE：20190826 CHINA

APPLICANT：AFG APPARELS LTD.

　　　　　　JOYNABARI, HEMAYETPUR, SAVAR, DHAKA, BANGLADESH

BENEFICIARY：ZHEJIANG FANTA TRADING CO. LTD

　　　　　　NO. 158 ZHONGSHAN ZHONG ROAD, HANGZHOU, CHINA

L/C AMOUNT：USD 48,513.00

POS./NEG.TOL（%）：03/03

AVAILABLE WITH/BY：ANY BANK IN CHINA BY NEGOTIATION

DRAFTS AT：120 DAYS SIGHT

DRAWEE：OURSELVES

PARTIAL SHIPMENTS：ALLOWED

TRANSSHIPMENT：ALLOWED

TAKING CHARGE PLACE：ANY PORT OF CHINA

FINAL DESTINATION：CHITTAGONG SEAPORT

LATEST DATE OF SHIP.：20190805

DESCRIP. OF GOODS：FABRIC FOR 100PCT EXPORT ORIENTED READYMADE

　　GARMENTS INDUSTRY AS PER BENEFICIARY'S PROFORMA INVOICE

NO.OCL-09043-CK02-V4 DTD.15JUL18 AS UNDER

DESCRIPTION	COLOR	QTY YDS	U/PRICE USD/YD	TOTAL AMT. IN USD
100PCT COTTON TWILL	STONE	8,950	1,57	
S/D,16X12/108X56	OLIVE	8,450	1,57	
WD：57/58″	BLACK	13,500	1,57	
STYLE NO.S/33335				
TOTAL： CIF CHITTAGONG		30,900 YDS		48,513.00

DOCUMENTS REQUIRED：

+SIGNED COMMERCIAL INVOICES IN OCTUPLICATE CERTIFYING MERCHANDISE ARE STRICTLY IN ACCORDANCE WITH THE PROFORMA INVOICE AS STATED ABOVE.

+PACKING LIST REQUIRED IN 5 COPIES.

+FULL SET OF CLEAN SHIPPED ON BOARD OCEAN BILL OF LADING DRAWN OR ENDORSED TO THE ORDER OF NATIONAL BANK LIMITED, MOHAKHALI BRANCH 9-MOHAKHALI C/A, DHAKA, BANGLADESH SHOWING FREIGHT PREPAID AND NOTIFY L/C APPLICANT AND US GIVING FULL NAME AND ADDRESS.

+CERTIFICATE OF ORIGIN REQUIRED FROM CHAMBER OF COMMERCE STATING MERCHANDISE TO BE OF CHINA ORIGIN.

+ INSURANCE POLICY/CERTIFICATE IN DUPLICATE ENDORSED IN BLANK FOR 120% INVOICE VALUE, COVERING ALL RISKS AND WAR RISK OF CIC OF PICC (1/1/1981) INDICATING L/C NO AND MARKED INSURANCE PREMIUM.

CHARGES 71B：ALL CHARGES AND COMMISSIONS ARE FOR ACCOUNT OF

+SHIPMENT UNDER THIS CREDIT MUST BE ADVISED BY BENEFICIARY DIRECT TO M/S PRAGATI INSURANCE LTD, BANGABANDHU AVENUE BRANCH 13,B.B. AVENUE, DHAKA-1000, BANGLADESH QUOTING THEIR COVER NOTE NO. PIL/BBA/MC-0164/07/2009 DTD 16JUL09 GIVING FULL DETAILS OF SHIPMENT. A COPY OF THIS ADVICE MUST ACCOMPANY EACH SET OF SHIPPING DOCS.

ADDITIONAL CONDITIONS：

01—L/C AUTHORISATION FORM NO.N8LAB-46109

IRC NO.BA-124933

H.S. CODE NO.5407.52.00

IMPORT UNDER EXPORT L/C NO.1572603 DTD 13JUL18

OUR L/C NO. 094709060309 DTD 19JUL18 MUST APPEAR IN ALL DOCS.

02－SHIPMENT/TRANSSHIPMENT ON FLAG VESSEL OF IRAQ/LIBYA/ISRAEL/CUBA PROHIBITED.

03－DISCREPANT DOCS MUST NOT BE NEGOTIATED.

04－NEGOTIATING BANK MUST FORWARD DOCS TO NATIONAL BANK LIMITED，MOHAKHALI BRANCH 9-MOHAKHALI C/A，DHAKA，BANGLADESH IN TWO SEPARATE LOTS BY COURIER SERVICES.

05－ONE SET OF NON-NEGOTIABLE COPY OF DOCS TO BE SENT THE APPLICANT WITHIN 7 DAYS AFTER SHIPMENT BY COURIER，COURIER RECEIPT MUST ACCOMPANY WITH SHIPPING DOCS.

06－SHORT FORM/STALE/CHARTERED PARTY/BLANK BACKED/THIRD PARTY BL/FCR/FBL NOT ACCEPTABLE.

07－IN CASE OF DISCREPANT/COLLECTION DOCS AN AMOUNT OF USD 50,00 AND SWIFT CHARGES USD 50,00 WILL BE DEDUCTED FROM BILL VALUE AT THE TIME OF SETTLEMENT OF THE BILL.

08－BENEFICIARY MUST CERTIFY THAT INVOICE PRICE IS NET AND DOES NOT INCLUDE ANY COMMISSION FOR THEIR AGENT IN BANGLADESH.

09－PRE-SHIPMENT INSPECTION CERTIFICATE ISSUED BY SGS/LLOYDS/OR ANY INTERNATIONAL REPUTED ORGANISATION/BENEFICIARY/ MANUFACTURER ACCEPTABLE.

10－INTEREST FOR THE ACTUAL USANCE PERIOD TO BE PAID AT LIBOR BY THE APPLICANT.

11－MATURITY DATE TO BE COUNTED FROM THE DATE OF NEGOTIATION.

12－CONTINUOUS LENGTH OF FABRICS MUST NOT BE LESS THAN 20 YDS. A CERTIFICATE TO THIS EFFECT SHOULD ACCOMPANY SHIPPING DOCS.

（二）其他资料

1. 发票号：9109H69R038

2. 发票日期：20190721

3. 销售合同号：09EJFR039

4 出口公司有权签字人：百灵

5. 出仓单显示：

STONE8950YDS　114BALES

OLIVE8450YDS　107BALES

BLACK13500YDS　171BALES

6. 装运港：青岛

7. 船名：YM UTILITY V.0004M

8. 包装数量：392 BALES

9. 净重：11,432.1 KGS

10. 毛重.：11,628.2 KGS

11. 尺寸：23.520 CMB

12. 唛头：

AFG APPARELS LTD

CHITTAGONG，BANGLADESH

COLOR：

QTY：YDS

C/T NO.：

13. 产地：

14. 货物指装 1×20′集装箱　FCL

15. 装运日：20190723

16. 集装箱号：HJCU8430166

17. 铅封号：S/6046374

18. SHIPPER'S LOAD AND COUNT

19. 提单号：HJSCTAOI18391305

20. 保险费率：0.12％

21. 出口公司于 2019 年 7 月 21 日向有关当局申请产地证,并当日获批

（三）单据

1. 商业发票

浙江纺大贸易有限公司

ZHEJIANG FANTA TRADING CO. LTD

NO. 158 ZHONGSHAN ZHONG ROAD，HANGZHOU，CHINA

COMMERCIAL INVOICE

To：			No.	
			Date	
			L/C No.	
			S/C No.	
From		To		
Marks & Nos.	Description of Goods； Kind & No. of Packages		Quantity	Unit Price	Amount

2. 装箱单

浙江纺大贸易有限公司

ZHEJIANG FANTA TRADING CO. LTD

NO. 158 ZHONGSHAN ZHONG ROAD，HANGZHOU，CHINA

PACKING LIST

To：		No.：		
		Date：		
Marks & Nos.	Quantity and Descriptions of Goods	Net Weight	Gross Weight	Measurement

3. 保险单

中国人民保险公司××分公司
海洋货物运输保险单

发票号次	第一正本	保险单号次
INVOICE NO.	**THE FIRST ORIGINAL**	POLICY NO.

中国人民保险公司(以下简称本公司)根据_____(以下简称被保险人)的要求,由被保险人向本公司缴付约定的保险费,按照本保险单承保险别和背面所载条款与下列特殊条款承保下述货物运输保险,特立本保险单。

This policy of insurance witnesses that People's Insurance Company of China (hereinafter called "the company") at the request of _____ (hereinafter called the "Insured") and in consideration of the agreed premium being paid to the Company by the Insured, undertakes to insure the undermentioned goods in transportation subject to the conditions of this policy as per the clauses printed overleaf and other special clauses attached hereon.

标记 Marks & Nos.	包装及数量 Quantity	保险货物项目 Description of Goods	保险金额 Amount Insured

总 保 险 金 额:
Total Amount Insured_____

保费	费率	装载运输工具
Premium as Arranged	Rate as Arranged	Per Conveyance S.S. _____

开航日期　　　　　　　　　自　　　　　　　　　　至
Slg on or abt._____ From _____ To _____

承保险别:
Conditions:

所保货物,如遇出险,本公司凭第一正本保险单及其有关证件给付赔款。所保货物,如发生本保险单项下负责赔偿的损失或事故,应立即通知本公司下述代理人查勘。

Claims, if any, payable on surrender of the first original of the policy together with other relevant documents. In the event of accident whereby loss or damage may result in a claim under this policy immediate notice applying for survey must be given to the Company's agent as mentioned hereunder:

中国人民保险公司××分公司
The People's Insurance Co. of China
××Branch

赔款偿付地点

Claim Payable At _____　　　　_____

Date _____　　Authorized Signature

4. 一般原产地证书

(1) Exporter	Certificate No.
(2) Consignee	**CERTIFICATE OF ORIGIN** **OF** **THE PEOPLE'S REPUBLIC OF CHINA**
(3) Means of Transport and Route	(5) For Certifying Authority Use Only
(4) Country/Region of Destination	

(6) Marks and Numbers	(7) Number and Kind of Packages; Description of Goods	(8) H.S. Code	(9) Quantity	(10) Number and Date of Invoices

(11) Declaration by the Exporter The undersigned hereby declares that the above details and statements are correct; that all the goods were produced in China and that they comply with the Rules of Origin of the People's Republic of China.	(12) Certification It is hereby certified that the declaration by the exporter is correct.
— — — — — — — — — — — — — — — Place and Date, Signature and Stamp of Authorized Signatory	— — — — — — — — — — — — — — — Place and Date, Signature and Stamp of Certifying Authority

5. 装船前检验证书

浙江纺大贸易有限公司

ZHEJIANG FANTA TRADING CO. LTD

NO. 158 ZHONGSHAN ZHONG ROAD，HANGZHOU，CHINA

PRE-SHIPMENT INSPECTION CERTIFICATE

6. 船公司证明

7. 海运提单

Shipper		B/L NO.	
Consignee		ⓗ**HANJIN SHIPPING** Beyond the Ocean	
Notify party		**BILL OF LADING**	
Place of Receipt	Pre-carriage by	CONTAINERIZED(vessel only)	
Vessel Voy.	Port of Loading	☐ Yes ☐ No	
Port of Discharge	Place of Delivery	Final Destination	

PARTICULARS FURNISHED BY SHIPPER				
Container No. Seal NO. Marks & Nos.	Number & Kind of Packages or Container	Description of Goods	G. W. (KGS)	Meas. (CBM)

Total No. of Packages or Containers（in words）

Freight & Charges	Rate as	Rate	Per	Prepaid	Collect

RECEIVED by the Carrier from the Shipper in apparent good order and condition unless otherwise indicated herein, the Goods, or the container（s）or package(s) said to contain the cargo herein mentioned, to be carried subject to all the terms and conditions provided for on the face and back of this Bill of Lading by the Vessel named herein or any substitute at the Carrier's option and/or other means of transport, from the place of receipt or the port of loading to the port of discharge or the place of delivery shown herein and there to be delivered to Consignee or on-carrier on payment of all charges due thereon.	Total		
	At		
	Loading on Board the Vessel Date By		
If REQUIRED by the Carrier, this Bill of Lading duly endorsed must be surrendered in exchange for the Goods or delivery order None of the terms of this Bill of Lading can be waived by or for the Carrier except by written waiver signed by a duly authorized agent of the Carrier.	Place of B(s)/L Issue		
	No. of Original B(s)/L Signed		
	Date of B(s)/L Issue		
IN ACCEPTING THIS BILL OF LADING the Merchant agrees to be bound by all the stipulations, exception, terms and conditions on the face and back hereof, whether written, typed, stamped or printed, as fully as if signed by the Merchant any local custom or privilege to the contrary notwithstanding. IN WITNESS WHERE OF, the undersigned, on behalf of Hanjin Shipping Co. Ltd the master and the owner of the Vessel has signed the number of Bill(s) of Lading stated above all of the same tenor and date, one of which being accomplished, the others to stand void. （Terms of Bill of Lading Continued on Back Hereof）	HANJIN SHIPPING CO. LTD As Carrier By		

8. 装船通知

浙江纺大贸易有限公司

ZHEJIANG FANTA TRADING CO. LTD

NO. 158 ZHONGSHAN ZHONG ROAD，HANGZHOU，CHINA

SHIPPING ADVICE

TO：   DATE：

RE：L/C NO.   INVOICE NO.

COVER NOTE NO.

WE HEREBY INFORMED YOU THAT THE GOODS UNDER THE ABOVE MENTIONED CREDIT HAVE BEEN SHIPPED. THE DETAILS OF SHIPMENT ARE STATED BELOW.

COMMODITY：

QUANTITY：

INVOICE VALUE：

OCEAN VESSEL/SHIPPED PER S.S.：

DATE OF SHIPMENT：

PORT OF LOADING：

PORT OF DESTINATION：

MARKS：

Signature

9. 受益人证明（1）

浙江纺大贸易有限公司

ZHEJIANG FANTA TRADING CO. LTD

NO. 158 ZHONGSHAN ZHONG ROAD，HANGZHOU，CHINA

BENEFICIARY'S CERTIFICATE

TO：   DATE：

RE：L/C NO.   INVOICE NO.

WE HEREBY CERTIFY THAT...

———————————

10. 受益人证明（2）

浙江纺大贸易有限公司

ZHEJIANG FANTA TRADING CO. LTD

NO. 158 ZHONGSHAN ZHONG ROAD，HANGZHOU，CHINA

BENEFICIARY'S CERTIFICATE

TO：   DATE：

RE：L/C NO.   INVOICE NO.

WE HEREBY CERTIFY THAT...

———————————

11. 商业汇票

凭
Drawn under ---------------------------------
信用证或购买证第　　　号
L/C or A/P No. ---------------------------------
日期　　年　　月　　日
Dated ---------------------------------
按　　　　息　　　付　　　款
Payable with interest @ _____% per annum

号码　　　　　　汇票金额　　　　　　中国杭州　　　　　　年　　月　　日
No. -------------Exchange for ▓▓▓▓▓▓▓Hangzhou, China --------------200...
见票　　　　　　　　　　　　　日　后 （ 本 汇 票 之 副 本 未 付 ）　付
At ----------- sight of this FIRST of Exchange （ Second of exchange being unpaid ）
Pay to the order of_____或其指定人
金额
The sum of ▓▓▓▓▓▓▓▓▓▓▓▓▓▓▓▓▓▓▓▓▓▓▓▓▓▓▓
▓▓▓▓▓▓▓▓▓▓▓▓▓▓▓▓▓▓▓▓▓▓▓▓▓▓▓▓▓▓▓▓

此致
To ---------------------------------.

---------------------------------.

项目六　信用证方式下出口单据审核

实训目标

能够根据相关资料审核信用证方式下的出口单据：商业发票、装箱单、保险单、海运提单、商业汇票。

实训任务

：请根据提供的信用证审核单据，指出单据中的不符点并改正。

实训指导
项目六

（一）信用证

THE ROYAL BANK OF CANADA
BRITISH COLUMBIA INTERNATIONAL CENTRE
NO. 1055 WEST GEORGIA STREET，VANCOUVER，B.C. V6E 3P3 CANADA

CONFIRMATION OF TELEX/CABLE PER-ADVISED　　　DATE：APR. 8, 2019

TELEX NO. 4720688 CA　　　　　　　　　　　　PLACE：VANCOUVER

IRREVOCABLE DOCUMENTARY CREDIT	CREDIT NUMBER：01/1801-FCT	ADVISING BANK'S REF. NO.
ADVISING BANK： NANJING FINANCE CORPORATION 59 HONGKONG ROAD NANJING 210002，CHINA	APPLICANT： NEO GENERAL TRADING CO. #362 JALAN STREET, VANCOUVER, CANADA	
BENEFICIARY： DESUN TRADING CO. LTD ROOM 2501，JIAFA MANSTION，BEIJING WEST ROAD, NANJING 210005, P.R.CHINA	AMOUNT： USD 35,229.00 （US DOLLARS THIRTY FIVE THOUSAND TWO HUNDRED AND TWENTY NINE ONLY）	
EXPIRY DATE：MAY 15, 2019	FOR NEGOTIATION IN BENEFICIARY'S COUNTRY	

GENTLEMEN：

WE HEREBY OPEN OUR IRREVOCABLE LETTER OF CREDIT IN YOUR FAVOR WHICH IS AVAILABLE BY YOUR DRAFTS AT SIGHT FOR FULL INVOICE VALUE ON US ACCOMPANIED BY THE FOLLOWING DOCUMENTS：

+SIGNED COMMERCIAL INVOICE AND 3 COPIES.

+PACKING LIST AND 3 COPIES, SHOWING THE INDIVIDUAL WEIGHT AND MEASUREMENT OF EACH ITEM.

+ORIGINAL CERTIFICATE OF ORIGIN AND 3 COPIES ISSUED BY THE CHAMBER OF COMMERCE.

+ FULL SET CLEAN ON BOARD OCEAN BILLS OF LADING SHOWING FREIGHT PREPAID CONSIGNED TO ORDER OF THE ROYAL BANK OF CANADA INDICATING THE

ACTUAL DATE OF THE GOODS ON BOARD AND NOTIFY THE APPLICANT WITH FULL ADDRESS AND PHONE NO. 77009910.

+INSURANCE POLICY OR CERTIFICATE FOR 110 PERCENT OF INVOICE VALUE COVERING: INSURANCE CARGO CLAUSES (A) AS PER I.C.C. DATED 1/1/1982.

COVERING SHIPMENT OF: 4 ITEMS OF CHINESE CERAMIC DINNERWARE INCLUDING:

30-PIECE DINNERWARE AND TEA SET,

544 SETS, USD 17.50/SET, 1,260 KGS(G.W.), 1,010 KGS(N.W.), 19 CBM

20-PIECE DINNERWARE SET,

800 SETS, USD 15.00/SET, 1,590 KGS (G.W.), 1,320 KGS (N.W.), 27.8 CBM

45-PIECE DINNERWARE SET,

443 SETS, USD 19.00/SET, 950 KGS (G.W.), 780 KGS (N.W.), 17.8 CBM

95-PIECE DINNERWARE SET,

245 SETS, USD 21.60/SET, 920 KGS (G.W.), 790 KGS (N.W.), 17.3 CBM

N/M, PACKAGE: ONE SET PER CARTON

DETAILS IN ACCORDANCE WITH SALES CONTRACT NO. HSDS18027 DATED APR. 3, 2019[ ]FOB /[ ]CFR/[×] CIF/[ ]FAX VANCOUVER CANADA.

SHIPMENT FROM NANJING	TO VANCOUVER	LATEST DATE APR. 30, 2019	PARTIAL SHIPMENTS PROHIBITED	TRANSSHIPMENT PROHIBITED

DRAFT AT SIGHT TO BE PRESENTED FOR NEGOTIATION WITHIN 15 DAYS AFTER SHIPMENT, BUT WITHIN THE VALIDITY OF CREDIT. ALL DOCUMENTS TO BE FORWARDED IN ONE COVER, BY AIRMAIL, UNLESS OTHERWISE STATED UNDER SPECIAL INSTRUCTION.

SPECIAL INSTRUCTION:

+ALL BANKING CHARGES OUTSIDE CANADA ARE FOR ACCOUNT OF BENEFICIARY.

+ALL GOODS MUST BE SHIPPED IN ONE 20' CY TO CY CONTAINER AND B/L SHOWING THE SAME.

+THE VALUE OF FREIGHT PREPAID HAS TO BE SHOWN ON BILLS OF LADING.

+DOCUMENTS WHICH FAIL TO COMPLY WITH THE TERMS AND CONDITIONS IN THE LETTER OF CREDIT SUBJECT TO A SPECIAL DISCREPANCY HANDLING FEE OF US $ 35.00 TO BE DEDUCTED FROM ANY PROCEEDS.

DRAFT MUST BE MARKED AS BEING DRAWN UNDER THIS CREDIT AND BEAR ITS NUMBER. THE AMOUNTS ARE TO BE ENDORSED ON THE REVERSE HERE OF BY NEG. BANK. WE HEREBY AGREE WITH THE DRAWERS, ENDORSERS AND FIDE HOLDER THAT ALL DRAFTS DRAWN UNDER AND IN COMPLIANCE WITH THE TERMS OF THIS CREDIT SHALL BE DULY HONORED UPON PRESENTATION. THIS CREDIT IS SUBJECT TO THE UNIFORM CUSTOMS AND PRACTICE FOR DOCUMENTARY CREDITS (2007 REVISION) BY THE INTERNATIONAL CHAMBER OF COMMERCE PUBLICATION NO. 600.

David Jone

AUTHORIZED SIGNATURE

Yours Very Truly,

Joanne Hsan

AUTHORIZED SIGNATURE

（二）单据

1. 商业发票

DESUN TRADING CO. LTD
ROOM 2501，JIAFA MANSTION，BEIJING WEST ROAD，
NANJING 210005，P. R. CHINA
TEL：025-77009910 025-77008820 FAX：025-77009930

COMMERCIAL INVOICE

Invoice No.：2003SDT007

To：NEO GENERAL TRADING CO.

Invoice Date：20190420

#362 JALAN STREET，VANCOUVER，CANADA

S/C No.：HSDS18703

S/C Date：20190403

From：NANJING

To：VANCOUVER

Letter of Credit No.：01/1801-FCT

Date：20190408

Marks and Numbers	Number and Kind of Package; Description of Goods	Quantity	Unit Price	Amount
				CFR VANCOUVER CANADA
N/M	ABOUT 544 CARTONS OF 30-PIECE DINNERWARE AND TEA SET	544 SETS	USD 17.50	USD 9,520.00
	ABOUT 800 CARTONS OF 20-PIECE DINNERWARE SET	800 SETS	USD 15.00	USD 12,000.00
	ABOUT 443 CARTONS OF 45-PIECE DINNERWARE SET	443 SETS	USD 19.00	USD 8,417.00
	ABOUT 245 CARTONS OF 95-PIECE DINNERWARE SET	245 SETS	USD 21.60	USD 5,292.00
	TotaL：2,032 SETS			USD 35,229.00

SAY TOTAL：U.S.DOLLARS THIRTY FIVE THOUSAND TWO HUNDRED AND TWENTY NINE ONLY.

2. 装箱单

DESUN TRADING CO. LTD
ROOM 2501，JIAFA MANSTION，BEIJING WEST ROAD，
NANJING 210005，P. R. CHINA
TEL：025-77009910 025-77008820 FAX：025-77009930

PACKING LIST

Invoice No.：2003SDT009

Invoice Date：20190420

To：NEO GENERAL TRADING CO.
#362 JALAN STREET，VANCOUVER，CANADA

S/C No.：HSDS03027

S/C Date：20190403

From：NANJING

To：VANCOUVER

Letter of Credit No.：01/1801-FCT   Date of Shipment：20190426

Marks and Numbers	Number and Kind of Package; Description of Goods	Quantity	Package	G. W	N. W	Meas.
N/M	ABOUT 544 CARTONS OF 30-PIECE DINNERWARE AND TEA SET	544 SETS	544 CTNS	1260 KGS	1010 KGS	19 CBM
	ABOUT 800 CARTONS OF 20-PIECE DINNERWARE SET	800 SETS	800 CTNS	1590 KGS	1320 KGS	27.8 CBM
	ABOUT 443 CARTONS OF 45-PIECE DINNERWARE SET	443 SETS	443 CTNS	950 KGS	780 KGS	17.8 CBM
	ABOUT 245 CARTONS OF 95-PIECE DINNERWARE SET	245 SETS	245 CTNS	920 KGS	790 KGS	17.3 CBM
	TOTAL	2,032 SETS	2,032 CTNS	4,720 KGS	3,900 KGS	81.9 CBM

SAY TOTAL：TWO THOUSAND AND THIRTY TWO CARTONS ONLY.

3. 保险单

中国人民保险公司南京市分公司
The People's Insurance Company of China Nanjing Branch
总公司设于北京一九四九年创立
Head Office Beijing   Established in 1949
货物运输保险单

CARGO TRANSPORTATION INSURANCE POLICY

发票号 INVOICE NO.	2003SDT007	保单号次 POLICY NO.	PICCSH034582
合同号 CONTRACT NO.	HSDS03027		
信用证 L/C NO.	01/1801-FCT		
被保险人 INSURED	DESUN TRADING CO. LTD		

中国人民保险公司(以下简称本公司)根据被保险人的要求,由被保险人向本公司缴付约定的保险费,按照本保险单承保险别和背面所载条款与下列特殊条款承保下述货物运输保险,特立本保险单。

THIS POLICY OF INSURANCE WITNESSES THAT THE PEOPLE'S INSURANCE COMPANY OF CHINA (HEREIN AFTER CALLED "THE COMPANY") AT THE REQUEST OF THE INSURED AND IN CONSIDERATION OF THE AGREED PREMIUM BEING PAID TO THE COMPANY BY THE INSURED, UNDERTAKES TO INSURE THE UNDERMENTIONED GOODS IN TRANSPORTATION SUBJECT TO THE CONDITIONS OF THIS POLICY AS PER THE CLAUSES PRINTED OVERLEAF AND OTHER SPECIAL CLAUSES ATTACHED HEREON.

标 记 MARKS & NOS	包装及数量 QUANTITY	保险货物项目 DESCRIPTION OF GOODS	保险金额 AMOUNT INSURED
N/M	2,032 CTNS	4 ITEMS OF CHINESE CERAMIC DINNERWARE	US$ 35,229.00

总保险金额 TOTAL AMOUNT INSURED	SAY U.S. DOLLARS THIRTY EIGHT THOUSAND SEVEN HUNDRED AND FIFTY ONE POINT NINE.				
保费 PERMIUM	AS ARRANGED	启运日期 DATE OF COMMENCEMENT	AS PER B/L	装载运输工具 PER CONVEYANCE	JIN YOU
自 FROM	NANJING	经 VIA		至 TO	VANCOUVER
承保险别 CONDITIONS	INSURANCE CARGO CLAUSES (A) AS PER I.C.C. DATED 19820101 WAR RISKS				

所保货物,如发生保险单项下可能引起索赔的损失或损坏,应立即通知本公司下述代理人查勘。如有索赔,应向本公司提交保单正本(本保险单共有＿＿份正本)及有关文件。如一份正本已用于索赔,其余正本自动失效。

IN THE EVENT OF LOSS OR DAMAGE WHICH MAY RESULT IN A CLAIM UNDER THIS POLICY, IMMEDIATE NOTICE MUST BE GIVEN TO THE COMPANY'S AGENT AS MENTIONED HEREUNDER. CLAIMS, IF ANY, ONE OF THE ORIGINAL POLICY WHICH HAS BEEN ISSUED IN ORIGINAL(S) TOGETHER WITH THE RELEVANT DOCUMENTS SHALL BE SURRENDERED TO THE COMPANY. IF ONE OF THE ORIGINAL POLICY HAS BEEN ACCOMPLISHED, THE OTHERS TO BE VOID.

赔款偿付地点 CLAIM PAYABLE AT	VANCOUVER	中国人民保险公司南京市分公司 The People's Insurance Company of China Nanjing Branch
出单日期 ISSUING DATE	2019-04-25	
地址(ADD)：中国南京石鼓路 225 号 邮编(POST CODE)：210005 电话(TEL)：(025)6521049 传真(FAX)：(025)4404593		Authorized Signature

4. 海运提单

Shipper DESUN TRADING CO. LTD ROOM 2501，JIAFA MANSTION，BEIJING WEST ROAD， NANJING 210005，P. R. CHINA	B/L No.
Consignee or Order TO ORDER OF THE ROYAL BANK OF CANADA	**SINOTRANS** 中国外运江苏公司 SINOTRANS JIANGSU CO. OCEAN BILL OF LADING

SHIPPED on board in apparent good order and condition（unless otherwise indicated）the goods or packages specified herein and to be discharged at the mentioned port of discharge or as near thereto as the vessel may safely get and be always afloat.

The weight，measure，marks and numbers，quality，contents and value，being particulars furnished by the Shipper，are not checked by the Carrier on loading.

The Shipper，Consignee and the Holder of this Bill of Lading hereby expressly accept and agree to all printed，written or stamped provisions，exceptions and conditions of this Bill of Lading，including those on the back hereof.

IN WITNESS where of the number of original Bills of Lading stated below have been signed，one of which being accomplished the other(s) to be void.

Notify Address NEO GENERAL TRADING CO. #362 JALAN STREET，VANCOUVER，CANADA	

Pre-carriage by	Port of Loading NANJING
Vessel JIN YOU	Port of Transshipment HONG KONG
Port of discharge	Final destination VANCOUVER

Container. Seal. No. or Marks and Nos.	Number and Kind of Packages	Description of Goods	Gross Weight (KGS)	Measurement (CBM)
N/M	544 CTNS	30-PIECE DINNERWARE AND TEA SET	1,260	19
	800 CTNS	20-PIECE DINNERWARE SET	1,590	27.8
	443 CTNS	45-PIECE DINNERWARE SET	950	17.8
	245 CTNS	95-PIECE DINNERWARE SET	920	17.3

WE HEREBY SHOWING THAT ALL THE GOODS HAVE BEEN SHIPPED IN ONE 20' CY TO CY CONTAINER.

Freight and Charges FREIGHT PREPAID SHIPPED ON BOARD		Regarding Transhipment Information Please Contact	
Ex. Rate	Prepaid at	Freight Payable at	Place and Date of Issue 20190428
	Total Prepaid	Number of Original B(s)/L THREE	Signed for or on Behalf of the Master As Agent(s)

5.商业汇票

BILL OF EXCHANGE

No. _____52589D41_____

For _____USD 35,229.00_____   _____2019 05 05, NANJING, CHINA_____

(amount in figure)   (place and date of issue)

At _____***********************_____ sight of this   FIRST   Bill of exchange (SECOND being unpaid)

pay to _____NANJING FINANCE CORPORATION_____ or order the sum of

U.S. DOLLARS THIRTY FIVE THOUSAND TWO HUNDRED AND TWENTY ONLY

(amount in words)

Drawn under   THE ROYAL BANK OF CANADA

L/C No. _____01/1801-FTC_____ dated _____APR. 8, 2018_____

To: THE ROYAL BANK OF CANADA   For and on behalf of
BRITISH COLUMBIA INTERNATION CENTRE
1055 WEST GEORGIA STREET, VANCOUVER,   DESUN TRADING CO. LTD
B.C. V6E 3P3 CANADA

_____

(Signature)

实训目标

能够根据相关资料填制信用证方式下的有关进口单据：开证申请书、入境货物检验检疫申请单、进口货物报关单。

实训指导
项目七

实训任务

✎任务：请根据下述有关资料填制开证申请书、入境货物报检单、进口货物报关单。

（一）销售合同

<table>
<tr><td colspan="3" style="text-align:center">SALES CONTRACT</td></tr>
<tr>
<td rowspan="2">Seller：
LPG INTERNATIONAL CORPORATION
333 BARRON BLVD., OTTAWA, CANADA</td>
<td colspan="2">No.：
CONTRACT 01</td>
</tr>
<tr>
<td colspan="2">DATE：
20190819</td>
</tr>
<tr>
<td>Buyer：
EAST AGENT COMPANY ROOM 2401，WORDTRADE MANSTION，JINGZHOU ROAD 47＃，HANGZHOU, P. R. CHINA</td>
<td colspan="2">Signed in：
OTTAWA</td>
</tr>
<tr><td colspan="3">This contract is made by and agreed between the BUYER and SELLER, in accordance with the terms and conditions stipulated below.</td></tr>
</table>

1. Commodity & Specification	2. Quantity	3. Unit Price	4. Amount
			CIF SHANGHAI
CANNED SWEET CORN ARTICLE NO. 01005 3060GX6TINS/CTN	800 CARTONS	USD 14.00/CARTON	USD 11,200.00
Total：	800 CARTONS		USD 11,200.00

<table>
<tr><td colspan="2">With 5% more or less of shipment allowed at the sellers' option</td></tr>
<tr><td>Total Value</td><td>SAY U. S. DOLLARS ELEVEN THOUSAND TOW HUNDRED ONLY</td></tr>
<tr><td>6. Packing</td><td>3060G X 6 TINS/CTN
EACH OF THE CARTON SHOULD BE INDICATED WITH ITEM NO., NAME OF THE TABLE, G. W., AND C/NO.</td></tr>
<tr><td>7. Shipping Marks</td><td>E.A.C.
SHANGHAI
C/NO.1-800</td></tr>
<tr><td>8. Time of Shipment & Means. of Transportation</td><td>ALL OF THE GOODS WILL BE SHIPPED ON OR BEFORE SEP. 20,2018，SUBJECT TO L/C REACHING THE SELLERS BY THE END OF AUGUST, 2018. PARTIAL SHIPMENT AND TRANSHIPMENT ARE NOT ALLOWED</td></tr>
<tr><td>9. Port of Loading & Destination</td><td>FROM TORONTO TO SHANGHAI</td></tr>
<tr><td>10. Insurance</td><td>THE SELLER SHALL ARRANGED MARINE INSURANCE COVERING ICC(A) PLUS INSTITUTE WAR RISKS FOR 110% OF CIF VALUE AND PROVIDE OF CLAIM, IF ANY, PAYABLE IN CHINA, WITH U.S. CURRENCY.</td></tr>
<tr><td>11. Terms of Payment</td><td>BY 100% IRREVOCABLE SIGHT LETTER OF CREDIT IN OUR FAVOR</td></tr>
<tr><td>12. Remarks</td><td></td></tr>
<tr><td style="text-align:center">The Buyer(signature)</td><td style="text-align:center">The Seller LPG INTERNATION CORPORATION(signature)</td></tr>
</table>

（二）补充资料

1. 吴淞海关进口

2. 卖方：东方代理公司（代码3122240320）

3. 船名及航次：ZAANDAM　V.203

4. B/L DATE：SEP.2，2019

5. B/L NO.：STBLN000001

6. 集装箱号码：TBXU3605231

7. 集装箱规格：20英尺

8. 集装箱自重：1,760千克

9. 商品编号：20058000

10. 船舶进口申报日：20190920

11. 进口货物申报日：20190923

12. 委托报关单位：浙江外贸报关有限公司

13. 报关人员：张三 31222800060014

14. 海关编号：×××20191000000123

(三) 单据

1. 开证申请书

IRREVOCABLE DOCUMENTATRY CREDIT APPLICATION

TO：   DATE：

Beneficiary (full name and address)	Applicant (full name and address)	

Partial Shipments ☐not allowed ☐allowed	Transshipment ☐not allowed ☐allowed	Issued by ☐airmail ☐express delivery ☐brief advice by teletransmission ☐teletransmission(operative)

Loading on board/despatch/taking in charge at/from For transportation to Not later than	Amount

Date and Place of Expiry ☐FOB ☐CFR ☐CIF ☐or other terms	Credit Available With ☐by sight payment ☐by deferred payment ☐by acceptance ☐by negotiation against the documents detailed herein ☐and beneficiary's draft for % of invoice value at on

Documents Required：(Marked with ×)
1. ( )Signed commercial invoice in__copies indicating L/C NO. and Contract No.
2. ( )Full set of clean on board ocean bills of lading made out to order and blank endorsed, marked "freight to 〔 〕collect/〔 〕prepaid 〔 〕showing freight amount" notifying 〔 〕the applicant/〔 〕_____.
3. ( )Air waybills/cargo receipt/copy of railway bills issued by _____ showing "freight 〔 〕to collect /〔 〕prepaid 〔 〕indicating freight amount" and consigned to.
4. ( )Insurance policy/certificate in__copies for ____% of the invoice value showing claims payable in _____ in currency of the draft, blank endorsed, covering 〔 〕ocean marine transportation/〔 〕air transportation/〔 〕overland transportation All Risks/〔 〕war risks/〔 〕_____.
5. ( )Packing list /weight memo in__copies indicating quantity, gross and net weights of each package and packing conditions.
6. ( )Certificate of quantity/ weight in__ copies issued by_____.
7. ( )Certificate of quality in____ copies issued by 〔 〕manufacture/〔 〕public recognized surveyor/〔 〕_____ _____.
8. ( )Beneficiary's certified copy of fax/telex despatched to applicant within___hours after shipment advising 〔 〕name of vessel/〔 〕flight NO. /〔 〕wagon NO., date, quantity wight and value of shipment.
9. ( )Certificate of origin in__copies issued by____.
10. ( )Other documents if any：

Description of Goods：

Additional Instructions：
1. ( )All banking charges outside the opening bank are for beneficiary's account.
2. ( )Documents must be presented within days after the date of shipment but within the validity of this credit.
3. ( )Third party as shipper is not acceptable. Short form B/L is not acceptable.
4. ( )Both quantity and amount   % more or less are allowed.
5. ( )Prepaid freight drawn in excess of L/C amount is acceptable against presentation of original charges voucher issued by shipping Co. /or its agent.
6. ( )All documents to be forwarded in one cover unless otherwise stated above.
7. ( )Other terms, if any：

2. 入境货物检验检疫申请单

中华人民共和国海关

入境货物检验检疫申请

申请单位(加盖公章):　　　　　　　　　　　　　　* 编号:＿＿＿＿＿＿＿＿

申请单位登记号:　　　联系人:　　电话:　　　　　　申请日期:　年　月　日

收货人	(中文)		企业性质(画"√")		□合资 □合作 □外资
	(外文)				
发货人	(中文)				
	(外文)				

货物名称(中/外文)	H.S.编码	原产国(地区)	数/重量	货物总值	包装种类及数量

运输工具名称号码		合同号	
贸易方式		贸易国别(地区)	提单/运单号
到货日期		启运国家(地区)	许可证/审批号
卸毕日期		启运口岸	入境口岸
索赔有效期至		经停口岸	目的地

集装箱规格、数量及号码	

合同订立的特殊条款 以及其他要求		货物存放地点	
		用　　途	

随附单据(画"√"或补填)	标记及号码	* 外商投资财产(画"√")	□是 □否
□合同　□到货通知 □发票　□装箱单 □提/运单　□质保书 □兽医卫生证书　□理货清单 □植物检疫证书　□磅码单 □动物检疫证书　□验收报告 □卫生证书　□ □原产地证　□ □许可/审批文件　□		* 检验检疫费	
		总金额 (人民币元)	
		计费人	
		收费人	

申请人郑重声明: 1. 本人被授权申请检验检疫。 2. 上列填写内容正确属实。 　　　　　　　　　　　签名:	领取证单	
	日期	
	签名	

注:有"*"号栏由海关填写

3. 进口货物报关单

中华人民共和国海关进口货物报关单

（××海关）

预录入编号：　　　　海关编号：　　　　　　　　　　　　　　　　　　　页码/页数：

境内收货人	进境关别	进口日期	申报日期	备案号
境外发货人	运输方式	运输工具名称及航次号	提运单号	货物存放地点
消费使用单位	监管方式	征免性质	许可证号	启运港
合同协议号	贸易国（地区）	启运国（地区）	经停港	入境口岸
包装种类	件数	毛重（千克）	净重（千克）	成交方式	运费	保费	杂费
随附单证及编号				
标记唛码及备注				

项号	商品编号	商品名称及规格型号	数量及单位	单价/总价/币制	原产国（地区）	最终目的国（地区）	境内目的地	征免

报关人员	报关人员证号	电话	兹申明对以上内容承担如实申报、依法纳税之法律责任。	海关批注及签章
申报单位			申报单位（签章）	

226